P9-CNC-279

WITHDRAWN

Bloom's Modern Critical Interpretations

Bloom's Modern Critical Interpretations

Bloom's Modern Critical Interpretations

Carlos Fuentes'
The Death of Artemio Cruz

Edited and with an introduction by
Harold Bloom
Sterling Professor of the Humanities
Yale University

CHELSEA HOUSE
PUBLISHERS
An imprint of Infobase Publishing

Bloom's Modern Critical Interpretations: The Death of Artemio Cruz

©2006 Infobase Publishing

Introduction © 2006 by Harold Bloom

All rights reserved. No part of this publication may be reproduced or utilized in any form or by any means, electronic or mechanical, including photocopying, recording, or by any information storage or retrieval systems, without permission in writing from the publisher. For more information contact:

Chelsea House
An imprint of Infobase Publishing
132 West 31st Street
New York NY 10001

Library of Congress Cataloging-in-Publication Data
Carlos Fuentes' The death of Artemio Cruz / Harold Bloom, editor.
    p. cm. — (Bloom's modern critical interpretations)
  Includes bibliographical references and index.
  ISBN 0-7910-8587-2 (hardcover)
  1. Fuentes, Carlos. Muerte de Artemio Cruz. I. Bloom, Harold.
II. Series.
  PQ7297.F793M833 2006
  863'.64—dc22   2006002320

Chelsea House books are available at special discounts when purchased in bulk quantities for businesses, associations, institutions, or sales promotions. Please call our Special Sales Department in New York at (212) 967-8800 or (800) 322-8755.

You can find Chelsea House on the World Wide Web at http://www.chelseahouse.com

Contributing Editor: Amy Sickels
Cover design by Keith Trego
Cover photo Church of San Antonio de Padua / © Angelo Cavalli/zefa/Corbis

Printed in the United States of America
Bang EJB 10 9 8 7 6 5 4 3 2 1

This book is printed on acid-free paper.

All links and web addresses were checked and verified to be correct at the time of publication. Because of the dynamic nature of the web, some addresses and links may have changed since publication and may no longer be valid.

Contents

Editor's Note

My Introduction relates Fuentes' allegorical novel to its principal literary sources: Octavio Paz, Carpentier, Faulkner; and to a prime visual source in *Citizen Kane*.

Lanin A. Gyurko begins this volume with two critical essays, on the thematic structure of *The Death of Artemio Cruz*, and the novel's relation to the cinematic masterpiece of Orson Welles, *Citizen Kane*.

The shuttle between the Mexican Revolution (1910 and onwards) and the fragmented self of Cruz is explored by Wendy B. Faris, while Steven Boldy interprets the novel as an allegory not just of the divided Mexican self and the Mexican Revolution, but of all family divisions as well.

Britt-Marie Schiller decides to view time and memory as social history in *The Death of Artemio Cruz*, after which Richard Walter contrasts the relation of literature to history in Fuentes, Vargas Llosa, and García Márquez.

You can argue that Henry Jamesian "point of view" perspectivism is always crucial in Fuentes, though Santiago Tejerina-Canal judges *Artemio Cruz* to be simple enough beneath its surface complexities, while Robin Fiddian salutes the novel for its supposed "iconoclasm" in regard to Latin American linguistic evasions of social reality.

Currie Thompson surveys symbolic architecture in *Artemio Cruz*, after which Cynthia Girgen asserts that *la chingada*, "the violated woman," is the novel's "magic word."

I can detect no persuasive vision of redemption anywhere in Carlos Fuentes, but Maarten van Delden suggests that *Artemio Cruz* intimates that the sorrows of history can be overcome, while Marco Polo Hernández Cuevas finds the black African heritage of Mexico slighted in this novel.

HAROLD BLOOM

Introduction

Carlos Fuentes, praising *Distant Neighbors: A Portrait of the Mexicans* by Alan Riding (1984), said of Mexico that it was "a country far more intricate and challenging to the North American mind than anything in Europe, at times more foreign than anything in Asia."

The Western Hemisphere is the Evening Land; it is the world where Europe died, though we are slow to see this. Europe's death in the New World takes many forms, and there is little in common between the United States and Mexico. Carlos Fuentes, who for political and cultural reasons has lived much less in Mexico than in Europe and the United States, is probably the most famous of his nation's writers, but certainly not the best. The poet-essayist Octavio Paz (1914–1998) clearly remains Mexico's most eminent literary mind, while the novelist Juan Rulfo, though not very prolific, seems to me more impressive than Fuentes. Nevertheless, more American readers know Fuentes than Paz or Rulfo, and *The Death of Artemio Cruz* (1962) seems to have become the archetypal Mexican novel for us, particularly since its translation appeared in 1991.

The social and political history of Mexico, particularly since the Revolution of 1910–1920, is allegorized in *Artemio Cruz*. Briefly summarized (itself an absurd phrase in this context), that history is an all-but-endless disaster. Since I am writing this Introduction in the closing days of December 2005, I am unhappily heading into a Time of Troubles that hardly will encourage us to shake our heads at Mexico's political corruption, economic injustices, and social turbulence. We enjoy all of that, and with much more to come. We too are a plutocracy and an oligarchy, and we are becoming much more of a theocracy than Mexico has been since its early twentieth-century Revolution. Mexico at least is not conducting a Crusade in Iraq, and is not in danger of yielding to an ideological militarism.

But most Mexicans are desperate enough, as are the underclass in George W. Bush's America. Our current political corruption scarcely begins to be unveiled, and our Iraqi Crusade has its principal beneficiaries in Big Oil, Haliburton, and Bechtel. No week passes without fresh socio-economic scandals both in the United States and in Mexico. Our relation to Mexico has the ongoing irony of "illegal immigration;" I hardly can turn on the news without confronting what transcends mere irony. Since Texas, California, and our entire Southwest all were stolen from Mexico, the "illegals" in mere actuality seek to return to the lands of their ancestors.

Our politics are dreadful enough; the Democrats soon will be as obsolete as the Whigs. Yet Mexican politics are apocalyptic, in comparison. The Mexicans betrayed their Revolution of 1910–1920. From 1920–2000, Mexico was a one-party state. The self-perpetuating Party of the Mexican Revolution ruled in the interests of the landowners, the bankers, the industrialists, with each President-for-six-years selecting his replacement. In 2000, this was allowed to change. It is unclear what will happen in 2006.

One sees why *The Death of Artemio Cruz* is so popular in our multimedia-university age of Political Correctness. Fuentes laments Mexico's self-betrayal, personifying this perfidy in the dying Artemio Cruz, whose consciousness is split three ways, so that he speaks with three voices. Since time also is fragmented in this novel, a reader needs only a little patience to disentangle self and sequence. Beneath its sophisticated surface, *Artemio Cruz* is not at all a difficult novel.

I regret observing that the book is excessively derivative: Faulkner's *As I Lay Dying* and *Absalom, Absalom!* are relied on throughout, as are the major fictions of the Cuban novelist, Alejo Carpentier. Orson Welles's *Citizen Kane* is also an obtrusive presence. It is not as though Faulkner, Carpentier, and Welles are transmuted into something rich and strange that is Fuentes' own. The echoes are disturbing because they betray an anxiety of influence that Fuentes lacks the strength to surmount.

A more serious flaw, in my judgment, is the extent to which Fuentes borrows his analysis of Mexican male character from Octavio Paz's *The Labyrinth of Solitude* (1950), a remarkable portrait of Mexico's personality. The identity of Artemio Cruz is more Paz's creation than Fuentes'. Paz emphasizes that Mexican men consider all Mexican women as the *Chingada*, the violated mother. Passive and victimized, the *Chingada* is both reviled and desired. She is associated with the Spanish Conquest of Mexico, notorious for the violation of Mexican Indian women by the Conquistadores. La Malinche, the Indian mistress of Cortez, renews herself in every Mexican woman who bears the stigma of betrayal. Though this vision of Paz's is now much disputed, it certainly is the ambivalent mode in which Artemio Cruz regards all of his women.

The Death of Artemio Cruz is a Period Piece, and will suffer the destiny of all literary Period Pieces. This is not to deny the social value of the novel at this interestingly bad moment in both American and Mexican history.

LANIN A. GYURKO

Structure and Theme in
Fuentes' La muerte de Artemio Cruz

In every one of his works, from the epic *La región más transparente* to the highly problematic *Cambio de piel* and from the mythopoetic *Zona sagrada* to the heretical *Cumpleaños* and the mammoth *summa* that is *Terra Nostra*, Fuentes sets for himself new, ambitious, and many times audacious goals. In almost all of his novels, the Mexican author experiments with language and structure, and develops innovative and challenging techniques of characterization. The *cambio de piel* motif constituting the thematic and structural basis of the novel with that title can be seen as a creative principle governing his entire work, which, more than the production of any other modern Latin American novelist, demonstrates a capacity for artistic self-renewal. In his first major work, *La región más transparente*, Fuentes strives for nothing less than a complete portrayal of twentieth-century Mexican society—of all classes and racial groups, from the remnants of the Porfirian aristocracy to the eternally downtrodden *macehualli* and encompassing the intelligentsia, the *nouveaux riches*, and the *bourgeoisie*. The structure of this five-hundred-page novel is loose, disjointed, fragmentary, and kaleidoscopic—a structure that mirrors the post-Revolutionary society of Mexico as a world in constant tension and flux. In its incessant movement and accumulation of images, *La región más transparente* is a reflection of a nation born anew after the Revolution of 1910 and thus, centuries after the

From *Symposium* 34, no 1 (Spring 1980): 29–41. © 1980 by the Helen Dwight Reid Educational Foundation.

Spanish Conquest, still in the process of painful self-confrontation and self-definition.

We cannot comprehend the structuring of Fuentes' third novel, *La muerte de Artemio Cruz*, without contrasting it with that of *La región más transparente*. Thematically these works are very similar. The protagonists of both novels are swept up into the Revolution of 1910 without really understanding why they are fighting. After the military phase of the Revolution is over, both men, who have managed to find themselves on the winning side, exploit their privileged positions to build financial empires. Instead of acknowledging his responsibility to his own people—the *pueblo* for whom the Revolution was fought—the Indian Robles, protagonist of *La región más transparente*, emulates the very dictator he had fought to overthrow. The *mestizo* Cruz also denies his origins by marrying the daughter of a Porfirian aristocrat, oppressing and exploiting the *campesinos*, and abasing himself before new dictators who seek to stifle the Revolutionary program. Structurally, however, in contrast to *La región*, *La muerte* is a tightly organized, perhaps even over-structured work. It consists of an invariable *yo-tú-él* patterning that proceeds throughout the whole of the work. The triadic structure is a favorite one with Fuentes, utilized in both *Zona sagrada* and *Terra Nostra*, where there is a whole section devoted to the phenomenon of triality. While *La región más transparente* really has no unifying factor and all the characters and incidents are but loosely connected through the elusive and enigmatic figure of Ixca Cienfuegos, in *La muerte de Artemio Cruz* every fragment of narrative, every incident, every motif is related either directly or indirectly to the life or death of the protagonist.

One of Fuentes' prime goals in this novel is to create a single character powerful and complex enough to be convincing, not only as an individual but also as a national symbol. In *La región más transparente*, he creates a series of characters who are developed not merely as individuals but as negative symbols of post-Revolutionary Mexico—the irresolute and finally stultified intellectual Zamacona, the arrogant and materialistic Robles, the sensitive but self-deluded artist Rodrigo Pola, the *arriviste* Norma Larragoiti, and the mother of death (symbolic of the Mexican nation devouring its children) Rosenda Pola. In *La muerte de Artemio Cruz*, which represents a tremendous labor of synthesis, the diverse, contradictory aspects of the Mexican national character are compressed into the personality of but one man, who appears as both Spanish *conquistador* and as Aztec god, as Revolutionary idealist and as exploitative *latifundista*. The life of Artemio Cruz is carefully structured to include key episodes in twentieth-century Mexican history—from the Revolution through the aftermath of power struggles and the military conspiracies that characterized the Calles' epoch to the labor agitation of the 1950s.

Structure is all-important in *La muerte de Artemio Cruz*. Most of Fuentes' novels are put together in a far more open fashion, but here the structure is visible on the surface, like a literary exoskeleton, at times even like a straitjacket over the narrative. Structure is not merely the vehicle for portraying Cruz's character, it is the character of the protagonist. All three narrative voices reflect various aspects of Cruz's mind and symbolize his rapidly disintegrating self. At the outset, Cruz, prostrate on his bed, is forced to see himself mirrored in the facets of his daughter's purse, which reflects back to him a weird, misshapen self. The facets of the purse capturing the physical and, symbolically, the moral distortion of Cruz, adumbrate the structuring of the novel, in which Cruz's self appears only in bits and pieces. Narrative structure strikingly symbolizes Cruz's inability to ever transcend the narrow boundaries of selfhood. It is significant that neither the third-person plural, *ustedes* nor the first-person plural *nosotros* is utilized as a major structural unit. The *nosotros* form is used in the narrative, but sparingly. In fact, the *we* form is reduced to but a single phrase that is nonetheless a key phrase, reiterated in twelve of the first-person segments: "Cruzamos el río a caballo." This phrase, which remains ambiguous throughout much of the narrative, is finally developed and clarified as one of the few moments of self-transcendence and spiritual communion in Cruz's entire life.

Fuentes' novel is plotless. Temporally, the limits of Cruz's existence have been determined; he will not survive the day. His physical life-space has also become fixed, as he lies immobile on his deathbed. Instead of a traditional narrative of rising action, climax, and resolution, there is only the unfolding of the past, not as chronological exposition but as filtered through Cruz's psyche, to dramatize the significance that life has for the protagonist at the hour when he is about to lose it forever. Layer by layer, Cruz's inner being is revealed, and through triadic structure the complexity of his character is reflected. The narrative captures and projects the flux of consciousness, which does not proceed linearly and logically but associationally and with a multiple time sense. Constant shifting among narrative persons that represent, respectively, the present, the past-as-imagined future, and the historical past, is an attempt to represent, through the medium of language, the simultaneity of psychic flux, proceeding on many levels concurrently and superimposing sensation, perception, memory, and imagination.

The formal design of the narrative, its rigid triadic progression, constitutes an attempt to impose narrative form upon the disorder of consciousness. Although the reader is forced to follow a life-history that is not presented chronologically, in a straightforward biographical manner, but instead proceeds in fits and starts, doubling back into the remote past only to leap suddenly into the immediate present, the steady, invariable first-second-third-person rhythm enables the reader to chart and measure narrative flow. Internal, psychic chaos is thus made meaningful for the reader.

Fuentes' language is descriptive in the development of external character, analytic and conceptual in the evocation of Cruz's subconsciousness, disintegrative and dramatic in the presentation of his moribund consciousness. The lengthy, intricate, convoluted sentences of the second-person narrative contrast with the truncated, obsessively repetitive, atomistic welter of images characterizing the first-person monologue, in which language is disintegrated to convey the chaos and, finally, the paralysis of Cruz's stricken consciousness. The elaborate, abstract language of the second-person narrative is counterpointed with the concrete, emotive, noncausal flow of impression and sensation. The language of individual experience is combined with the language of philosophical and moral evaluation, and with the narrative of eternal action, to provide an in-depth portrayal of a character and a country. And, through the narrative of inwardness, Artemio Cruz's life is linked not only with the social and moral development of twentieth-century Mexico but with the existential anguish of mortal man.

La muerte de Artemio Cruz is a novel of the psyche; the external world is important only so far as an outer event serves to illuminate the central charter. Therefore, external occurrences are evoked only as they are relevant to this moribund protagonist. The past is vividly incorporated into the present, as Artemio seeks to transcend the mortal limitations of existence by extending his life back into time. In *La muerte de Artemio Cruz*, experiencing death is not intellectualized but stunningly dramatized, through the segments of first-person, direct interior monologue, that grant both an immediacy and a great intensity to the narrative. Narrative structure projects Cruz's character not only as a multiplicity of selves but also as a series of incompatible selves, never able to coalesce to achieve a self-transcendent or redemptive unity. Instead, there is continual antagonism between the first-person narrative—the self-exalting *yo*—and the second-person monologue relentlessly probing the protagonist's shortcomings as well as the unfulfilled aspects of his nature. It subjects his physical and psychological self to remorseless scrutiny and reproaches Cruz for his moral failings. The *you*-monologue is the most complex narrative form, one which serves several functions: *alter ego*, voice of conscience (both individual and national), subconsciousness, and superego.

It is important to note that this second-person voice of critical appraisal, finally stinging by rebuking Cruz, is a part of the protagonist himself. Cruz's condemnation thus becomes self-condemnation. On the national level, this is an indication that Fuentes, unlike many other Latin American authors who inveigh against external imperialistic forces seeking to dominate their respective countries, holds the Mexicans themselves responsible for betraying their own nation to outside influences. *La muerte de Artemio Cruz* posits the responsibility of both the individual and the nation for their own destinies, and the second-person narrative, with its personalized reproach, underscores self-culpability.

Trough utilization of the second-person narrative, Cruz's plight is elevated from pathos to tragedy. If Cruz had been presented via a traditionally structured narrative, he might have emerged as a one-dimensional figure, perhaps as a caricature of a robber baron, such as is found in many of the Latin American novels written in the first half of the twentieth century, that in a Manichean way contrast the greedy oppressors with the eternally oppressed. Without extensive, at times exhaustive, exploration of his contradictory motivations from several points of view, and without dramatization of the many selves within the protagonist and his tremendous capacity for a *cambio de piel*, the reader might have experienced pity for the villainous Cruz as a dying man—but little else. This is Cruz's tragedy—and symbolically, that of the country he represents. He does have an inherent idealism. Cruz is a man elevated by the Revolution to a position of great power that he could have wielded to actualize the goals of the Revolution in which he has fought. The trifurcation of self underscores the chasm between his latent idealism and his obsessive rapacity, and provides a means of dissecting failings within Cruz and of uncovering the reasons for his inability to actualize the other selves within him.

Throughout his life Cruz is incapable of integrating ego and conscience, self-serving ambition, and sense of social responsibility. Instead, he is constantly torn between preservation of his ego—of the façade of his virility—and attainment of spiritual union and communion with others that would require demolishing that ego. In the *I*-narrative, Cruz asserts that his only love has always been the material. Yet the third-person segments reveal his deep love for both Regina and Laura, who represent the spiritual side of his character. But when called upon by Laura to commit himself totally to the relationship that would involve divorcing his wife, Cruz abandons Laura, not out of love for Catalina but because he fears the scandal that would ensue and the consequent loss of social and political power. On a deeper level, commitment to Laura would involve sacrifice of self, and Cruz fears to surrender any of his precious selfhood. The obsession with self that characterizes him on his deathbed is but the final, pathetic moment of a whole lifetime of self-absorption and self-aggrandizement.

Although Cruz constantly searches for love throughout his life, it is significant, and very ironic, that one of the central themes of the narrative is not love but *violation*. This theme is exemplified in the very structure of the novel. The theme of conquering suffuses all three narrative voices, and is perhaps the one aspect they all have in common. The third-person segments depict Cruz's life as an incessant dominator—conqueror of the land, subduer of the *hacendados* (one of whom, significantly, is named Pizarro), conqueror even of his own wife, dutifully surrendered to him as a prize of war by her own father, Don Gamaliel, who quickly allies himself with Cruz in order to preserve at least part of his domains. Even the Christian doctrine of the Virgin birth is twisted by Cruz to conform to his perception of the world in terms of the violator and the violated—Mary is evoked as the trembling virgin who is ravished by Joseph. Ironically, although Cruz has participated in the Revolution and throughout his subsequent rise to power masks himself as a Revolutionary hero, the second-person voice of conscience rips off the mask of hypocrisy to reveal his true nature as a continuation not merely of a Porfirista but as a twentieth-century version of Hernán Cortés. Early in the narrative, in one of the sections of the *you*-monologue exploring Cruz's unconscious mind, a dream is revealed that depicts the protagonist as a New World conqueror, striding down the nave of a Spanish cathedral. The irony of the dream, however, is that it shows the conqueror conquered, by emphasizing that behind the Christian images in the cathedral lurks the presence of the Aztec gods, built into the church by the Indian artesans. Structurally, the *tú*-narrative itself becomes another latent conqueror: hidden for years behind the flamboyant and supercilious mask that characterizes the *I*-narrative, and now finally unleashed.

In *La muerte de Artemio Cruz*, images and scenes initially presented in the first- or second-person voices are subsequently developed on a realistic plane in the third-person segments. The third-person equivalent to the dream of Cruz as *conquistador* is found in the third-person segment of December 31, 1955 which depicts Cruz as the wizened Emperor of Coyoacán. It is no accident that Cruz chooses to restore an ancient monastery in Coyoacán—the very same section of Mexico City where Hernán Cortés had his headquarters after the collapse of Mexico-Tenochtitlán. It is also noteworthy that Cruz's wife has the same name as the ill-fated wife of Cortés: Catalina. But although on the surface Cruz wields awesome power over the hundred guests he annually summons to pay homage to him, the inner monologue—the dialogue with self that in this segment becomes a part of the third-person narrative—depicts Cruz as wistful and frozen into memory, reliving his past with his son Lorenzo. The conqueror is secretly mocked by his guests, and is humiliated by the very mastiffs he has selected to be the symbols of his power but instead drag him from his throne.

Defeat of Artemio Cruz by an external force could perhaps be most effectively portrayed by use of the third-person action narrative throughout the novel. But Cruz remains undefeated in the outside world. This is one of the main differences between him and the revolutionary fighter turned banker/industrialist, Federico Robles in *La región más transparente*—the plutocrat who is brought down at the very pinnacle of his career. In contrast with Robles, Cruz has killed, subdued, bribed or intimidated all of his enemies except one—the enemy within himself. It is highly significant that the second-person monologue is not only a voice of conscience, but represents his physiological self as well—the biological self, now broken down permanently. The second-person voice, with its words to Cruz's egotistical self, "te venzo," mark the affirmation of the final conqueror in the life of Cruz.

Yet, in a sense, Cruz's death represents a rebirth of self. Previously, the *I* dominated Cruz and, throughout his life, suppressed the second-person voice. But now, when he lies in agony, the *I*-narrative withers. Structurally, this disintegration is expressed through the drastic shortening of the *I*-sections, as Cruz loses control over both his body and his conscious mind. In contrast, the second-person voice retains its strength and its authoritativeness throughout the narrative. Although the severely debilitated *I* seeks desperately to recompose itself, to recreate the masterful and aggressive Cruz of the past, it is the second-person, the powerful, self-composed, assertive *you* voice, that intervenes between *I* and *he*, controlling the course of Cruz's mental reconstruction. This *you* voice takes its vengeance on the *I* by suppressing from his conscious self precious images like that of his son Lorenzo which Cruz would like to conjure up and cling to and, on the other hand, compels him to relive certain key episodes in his life, forcing him to confront his cowardice, treachery, and guilt. Many of the incidents developed in the third-person section are not memories the egotistical Cruz would voluntarily recall—for example abandonment of his own men on the battlefield, betrayal of Gonzalo Bernal and the Yaqui while he bargained for his own life, being jilted by the very woman, Lilia, whom he has paid to be his weekend mistress, foolishly playing a diabolical form of Russian roulette with "el hombre gordo" in which he could have lost his life. But now Cruz's whole being is violated by the second-person self which also represents his physiological self, the self Cruz's ego has preferred to ignore as it nurtures the delusion that it is impregnable against time. The emphasis placed on the verb *chingar* by the second-person monologue is ironic. Cruz is literally an *hijo de la chingada*. Violation gave him life—rape of a slave woman by his father Atanasio Menchaca; violation pervades his life, and violation (mental and physical) characterizes his death.

Even the details of structure of *La muerte de Artemio Cruz* have been carefully worked out to mirror the basic themes of the novel. It is important, for example, that the last third-person segment (that of April 9, 1889), provides a flashback to the moment of Cruz's birth. This third-person segment is followed immediately by a section of first-person narrative relating the exact moment of the protagonist's death. Structurally, therefore, there is but an instant between birth and death—an ironic juxtaposition severely undercutting Cruz's vaunted pretensions to be an all-powerful ruler who can rival even God. So great is Cruz's pride, even on his deathbed, that he attempts to bargain with God by offering to acknowledge belief in Him in return for terrestrial salvation. The trinity of selves in Cruz refers ironically to the divine trinity, alluded to in one of the epigraphs of the novel, a quotation from Gorostiza's *muerte sin fin*: "de mí y de Él y de nosotros tres ¡siempre tres! ..."

The juxtaposition of birthday and deathday is not a mere aesthetic *tour de force* on Fuentes' part. Rather, it transmits through the very structure of the work one of its central themes—the abnormal closeness of life and death throughout the whole of Cruz's existence, and the corresponding importance placed on mere survival.[1] From the very moment of his birth, death hovers close to Cruz, in the form of his own father, who approaches the hut in order to kill his illegitimate son. A lifetime later, on the very day prior to his fatal attack, the plane on which Cruz is traveling experiences engine difficulties and almost crashes. Ironically, death prolongs Cruz's life. Only because his father himself is killed is the life of Cruz possible, and over and over again in this narrative Cruz's existence is extended only because someone else dies in his place—the unknown soldier on the battlefield whom Cruz responds to as a twin, Gonzalo Bernal, even the sacrifice of his own son. Thus Cruz on his deathbed attempts to summon up the images of those who have sacrificed themselves for him, in order to demand that they renew that sacrifice. But Cruz's trinity of selves constitutes a false god, one who becomes more like an Aztec deity, parasitically demanding blood sacrifice in order to perpetuate himself. Memory is thus not merely nostalgic for Cruz, it is a fundamental means of preserving and extending his life. More excruciating than the pain of his physical illness is his inability to recall the episodes of his life most meaningful to him.

The structural juxtaposition of birth and death also underscores the cyclic time structure of Fuentes' novel. This fatalistic time is also emphasized through the circular movement of the *yo-tú-él* shifts in perspective. Within the second-person monologue, Cruz's life span is reduced to an instant between life and death, as he is situated within the inexorable and infinite flow of cosmic time, which, like his existence, is a circular span from nothingness to nothingness, from the dawn of creation to dissolution of the universe. The effect is to reduce the significance of Cruz's existence by showing the protagonist as a mere fleck of life caught up in an eternal process of creation and destruction. This cosmic cycle is given an historical parallel in the endless circle of revolution and counterrevolution, of destruction of an old order of tyranny and oppression only to raise a new order of corruption in its place. The aging Don Gamaliel, himself a participant and a victim of the process, comments on the pernicious cycle of historical parricide that afflicts Mexico: "Desventurado país—se dijo el viejo mientras caminaba, otra vez pausado, hacia la biblioteca y esa presencia indeseada pero fascinante— desventurado país que a cada generación tiene que destruir a los antiguous poseedores y sustituirlos por nuevos amos, tan rapaces y ambiciosos como anteriores."[2]

The basic structure of *La muerte de Artemio Cruz* is a paradoxical one, in several aspects. The second-person narrative evinces this paradox in a most striking manner—fusion of the future and the past—"Pero insistirás en recordar lo que pasará" (p. 15). Fusion of contradictory times is a formal means of signifying a paradoxical fusion between freedom and fate. Although the second-person voice seems to posit a future for Cruz, that future is not an open one but rather an illusory one consisting only in reliving the past as if it were a new time. Cruz's whole life has been characterized by paradoxical fusion of freedom and fate. Although he has the ability to choose, every choice is a fatalistic one because, instead of asserting his freedom, choosing only restricts his future options. Another paradox is found in the narrative progression. The structural movement, constant alternation among *yo-tú-el*, seems, on the surface at least, to be a dynamic one. But the fact that the sequencing is invariable and that the same images are incessantly repeated in the *I*-narratives indicates that this movement too leads not to progress—or to salvation for Cruz—but only to stasis, paralysis, and death. Although some critics have responded negatively to the rote quality of the *yo-tú-él* sequencing, this rigid structure is most effective in conveying to readers the quality of Cruz's mind, which has become locked in a sterile, repetitious patterning.

All these structural paradoxes coincide with and serve to reinforce a thematic one—Cruz's paradoxical character. The second-person voice articulates this ambivalence: "Nunca has podido pensar en blanco y negro, en buenos y malos, en Dios y Diablo; admite que siempre, aun cuando parecía lo contrario, has encontrado en to negro el germen, el reflejo de su opuesto: tu propia crueldad, cuando has sido cruel, ¿no estaba teñida de cierta ternura? Sabes que todo extremo contiene su propia oposición: la crueldad la ternura, la cobardía el valor, la vida la muerte" (p. 33). It is ironic that while the tone of the first-person monologue becomes increasingly anguished and despairing, and Cruz's life-space in the first-person monologue becomes more and more constricted, the tone of the second-person monologue reaches a pitch of exaltation and wonder and its space expands to encompass the entire universe:

> Girará la tierra en su carrera uniforme sobre un ojo propio y un sol maestro.... Se moverá toda la corte del sol dentro de su cinturón blanco y el reguero de pólvora líquida se moverá frente a los conglomerados externos.... Desde todos su manantiales, toda la luz del universo iniciará su carrera veloz y curva, doblándose sobre la presencia fugaz de los cuerpos dormidos del propio universo.... (pp. 309–10)

An extension of the paradox is the ambivalent way in which readers respond to Cruz—their ambivalence is thoroughly conditioned by the continual structural variations. The first-person segments plunge us directly into Cruz's turbulent mind, and we are thus compelled to perceive the world from his severely distorted perspective. The pain, anguish, and delirium Cruz experiences are conveyed through various stylistic devices: ellipses, irrational thought association, jumbled fragments, endless reiteration. In direct contrast with the *I*-sections, which tend almost automatically to increase our empathy with Cruz, in the second-person segments we are drawn away from him, and attain a much broader and more balanced perspective.

Thus far I have been emphasizing the use of the extremely fragmented structure to convey Cruz's negative states, his permanent isolation, alienation, and disintegration. The trajectory of his personal life is toward increasing rigidity, total lack of communication with others, and incarceration within the walls of self. But, in Fuentes' highly contradictory narrative, there is also a positive side to the trifurcation of self. The creation of multiple selves constitutes an attempt by the failing Cruz to revivify himself and thereby to score a victory over death. Survival has always been an obsession for him, and, and at the hour of his death, his mind struggles for a way to transcend it by a force of will. Through the first-person monologue, Cruz valiantly attempts to deny the severity of his attack and to thwart death by struggling to separate his commanding and powerful self of the past from his helpless, moribund self of the present. In the opening section of the novel, he begins his soliloquy in the first person, but later addresses himself in the second, and then makes another transition to refer to himself in the third person. Thus, within the initial first-person monologue is contained the encapsulation of the structure that will be developed, of the three selves the narrative will subsequently separate and animate: "Aaay, yo sobreviví, ¿qué hice ayer?: si pienso en lo que hice ayer no pensaré más en lo que está pasando. Ese es un pensamiento claro. Muy claro. Piensa ayer. No estás tan loco; no sufres tanto; pudiste pensar eso. Ayer. Ayer Artemio Cruz voló de Hermosillo a México. Sí. Ayer Artemio Cruz. Antes de enfermarse, ayer Artemio Cruz.... No, no se enfermó" (p. 12).

Grammatical shifts correspond to Cruz's attempt to create an alternate self to be held up as a shield against death. Cruz struggles to convince himself that it is not his true self who is dying but the false, putrefying double that must be exorcized: "Ayer Artemio Cruz estaba en su despacho y se sintió muy enfermo. Ayer no. Esta mañana. Artemio Cruz no enfermo no. No Artemio Cruz no. Otro. En un espejo colocado frente a la cama del enfermo. El otro Artemio Cruz. Su gemelo. Artemio Cruz está enfermo; no vive; no, vive. Artemio Cruz vivió. Vivió durante algunos años ..." (p. 12). Both the first-person monologue depicting Cruz as sujbect to the will and whim of others and the third-person segments are fated narratives projecting the image of Cruz as a helpless giant, as a once powerful magnate now reduced to a babbling imppotency. The first-person monologue goes nowhere; careful analysis of all of the *yo*-segments reveals that the same images flicker across the stage of Cruz's anguished psyche without being developed. The third-person segments demonstrate only a reiterated patterning of *cainismo*, extending back even to Cruz's ancestors and thus acting as a predetermined curse on the life of the protagonist, doomed to continue the cycle of treachery and oppression that his father both exemplifies and falls victim to. But the second-person monologue captures, stylistically, the paradox in Cruz as both blasphemer and believer, coward and *macho*, idealist and cynic. It posits not only the horde of proto-Cruces, created by Cruz, who will, like Jaime Ceballos, perpetuate his corruption and oppression, but also the successors of the idealistic self that Cruz has both betrayed and feared. Pessimistic with regard to Cruz the individual, the subversive second-person voice at the end acquires a visionary role and prophesies a future revolution that will ultimately attain the goals of unity and of social justice for which the Revolution of 1910 was fought. Here, countervailing the determinism that rules both the first- and the third-person segments, is an optimistic portrayal of the redemptive future:

> No verás otra vez esos rostros que conociste en Sonora y en Chihuahua, que un día viste dormidos, aguantándose, y al

siguiente encolerizados, arrojados a esa lucha sin razones ni paliativos, a ese abrazo de los hombres a los que otros hombres separaron, a ese decir aquí estoy y existo contigo y contigo y contigo también, con todas las manos y todos los rostros vedados: amor, extraño amor común que se agotará en sí mismo: te lo dirás a ti mismo, porque lo viviste y no lo entendiste, al vivirlo: sólo al morir lo aceptarás y dirás abiertamente que aun sin comprenderlo lo temiste durante cada uno de tus días de poder: temerás que ese encuentro amoroso vuelva a estallar. (p. 276)

The second-person segments also provide the structural exemplification of one of the five epigraphs to this novel—a quotation from Stendhal's *Le rouge et le noir*: "Moi seul, je sais ce que j'aurais pu faire.... Pour les autres, je ne suis tout au plus qu'un peut-être." Here, at the very beginning of the work is posited the dichotomy between the self-in-self and the self-in-others, the self-serving Cruz vs. the potential, altruistic *alter ego*. Although the self-deluded first-person narrative fanatically asserts the plenitude of Cruz's existence and the immense satisfaction he has derived from his career of exploitation and usurpation, the *tú*-monologue incessantly undercuts Cruz's *I* and shows how much of his existence is false, consisting in merely aping foreign models and spiritually vacuous. And, on the symbolic level, the narrative is an indictment of the Mexican nation, which from Fuentes' pessimistic perspective is caught in the Frozen Revolution, and like Cruz, slavishly imitates the value systems of European and North American nations.

It is ironic that although a whole series of alternate existences are posited for Cruz—some of which, if he had the opportunity to relive his life, he might have chosen—these alternatives are not articulated until the very day of his death, when there is no longer any chance of their ever being actualized. All of the soul-searching in which Cruz engages leads nowhere; the moment of death brings him no illumination, no reconciliation with his wife and child, no conviction that he has misspent his life.

A hallmark of the contemporary novel is the elevation of the status of the reader from a mere passive recipient of the vision of an omniscient author, such as occurs in the nineteenth-century novel, to the role of co-creator of the narrative. As with so many contemporary novels, such as Rulfo's *Pedro Páramo*, Cortázar's *Rayuela* and *62: Modelo para armar*, and Fuentes' own works like *Cambio de piel* and *Terra Nostra*, the reader of *La muerte de Artemio Cruz* is required to become an active participant in the novel and to re-construct the life of the protagonist from mere fragments of narrative thought and action. What significance does the Mexican

Revolution have for contemporary Mexico? Is Cruz to be condemned or exonerated for his actions? And, on the universal level, what is the meaning of a man's life on the day of his death? How is death to be confronted, with calm resignation and a detailed rehearsal of his own luxurious funeral (the way Don Gamaliel does) or with staunch affirmation of life and refusal to succumb, the way Cruz responds? Fuentes' vision of post-Revolutionary society examines these problems from many distinct perspectives—and instead of imposing a single value judgment, allows the reader to arrive at his own conclusions concerning both Cruz and modern Mexico. It is significant that, throughout his life, Cruz is denied the redemptive unity he seeks. The relationships with Lunero, his boyhood protector and mentor, and with Regina, the person he most deeply loved, are severed by death. The opportunities for self-renewal and self-transcendence found at the beginning of his relationships with both Catalina and Laura are negated, this time by Cruz's own false pride and cowardice, that impel him above all to preserve his ego intact. This is the culminating irony of the narrative. Cruz can actualize himself—the heroic self he had betrayed but he still cherishes—but only through the death, the blood sacrifice of the one remaining person who could grant spiritual wholeness to his emotionally and morally shattered existence: his son Lorenzo. The only unity Cruz finally does attain is an ironic one—the negative unity of all of his three selves, as all are compressed into one bewildered and chaotic self as a prelude to his extinction: "Yo no sé ... no sé... si él soy yo ... si tú fue él ... sí yo soy los tres ... Tú ... te traigo dentro de mí y vas a morir conmigo ... Dios ... El ... lo traje adentro y va a morir conmigo ... los tres ... que hablaron ... Yo ... lo traeré adentro y morirá conmigo ... solo ..." (p. 315).

La muerte de Artemio Cruz functions on the individual, the national, and on the universal levels. Cruz's self-incarceration becomes symbolic of the self-imposed isolation of Mexico, which Fuentes in *La región más transparente* has depicted as a conglomeration of classes permanently divided. The gigantic chasm separating the Indian Mexico from the middle and upper classes seemed to have been bridged as a result of the Mexican Revolution. Yet, following the anti-Revolutionary stance of authors like Azuela, Romero, and Rulfo, Fuentes interprets the Revolution of 1910 not as a continuing process, as it is represented by the official state propaganda, but as only a single, brief moment of national unity and transcendence before the nation once again sinks back into dispersion and alienation among its extremely diverse components. If we see Cruz as a symbol of modern Mexico, then the permanent splintering in his identity mounts the stinging attack that Fuentes makes in both this novel and in *La región más transparente*—an indictment of a country whose idealists—Madero, Zapata, the students in the Plaza of

Nonoalco Tlatelolco—are continually sacrificed, just as is the idealistic center of Cruz himself.

Structurally, this single moment of national unity that quickly disintegrates into conflicting idealogies, goals, and political forces, is symbolized by that single phrase, the one that remains enigmatic and haunting for the reader until the end of the narrative: "Cruzamos el río a caballo." This is an allusion to one of the most precious moments in Cruz's life, the moment when he and his son were united in their courage and idealism, the moment when Cruz genuinely experienced a *cambio de piel*, a redemptive self-renewal that neither he nor Mexico could sustain. Literally, the river to which Cruz refers is one on the estate of the Menchaca family at Cocuya, where, in a quest for his origins and in an attempt to relive his youth, Cruz has had the old, burned-out mansion restored. Crossing the river, a memory that obsesses Cruz, also acquires a symbolic meaning. It adumbrates Lorenzo's crossing the ocean alone, and his subsequent fighting and dying in Spain. It is significant that although Cruz carefully nurtures his son's idealism and desire for adventure by removing him from the overly protective care of Catalina and bringing him to the shores of the sea, Cruz proves too cowardly to accompany his son on this fateful crossing, other than in his imagination.

NOTES

1. For a detailed examination of this theme, see my "Self-Renewal and Death in Fuentes' *La muerte de Artemio Cruz*," *Revista de letras* (São Paulo) 15 (1973), 59–80.

2. Carlos Fuentes, *La muerte de Artemio Cruz* (México: Fondo de Cultura Economica, 1962), p. 50. Subsequent parenthetical page references are to this edition.

LANIN A. GYURKO

La muerte de Artemio Cruz *and* Citizen Kane: *A Comparative Analysis*

In several interviews, Fuentes has commented on the enormous impact exerted on him by *Citizen Kane*—a film that he first saw at the age of ten and most certainly has viewed many times since. According to Fuentes: "When I came with my father to the World's Fair in 1940, *Citizen Kane* was being shown in New York. I saw it and that was the beginning of the world for me. It is probably the single most influential aesthetic thrill I've had in my life.... That movie left a very, very profound mark on my spirit."[1] The question that this essay addresses is, "what specific influence has Orson Welles' brilliant film had on Fuentes' art?" One novel in particular demonstrates how Carlos Fuentes, who throughout his work is a very visual writer, who has collaborated in the making of several films, and who originally wrote one of his major novels, *Zona sagrada*, as a filmscript, has been inspired by Welles— *La muerte de Artemio Cruz*. The protagonist of this novel is a composite figure, one whose role as revolutionary fighter turned opportunist and plutocrat corresponds to actual historical figures, to the careers of many of the revolutionary generals who later exploited their privileged positions to construct lavish mansions for themselves, aping the Porfirian aristocrats whom they had overthrown and betraying the ideals of land, labor, and educational reform for which the Revolution had been fought. Yet a significant part of the genesis of Artemio Cruz, as we shall see, is found in

From *Carlos Fuentes: A Critical View*. © 1982 by the University of Texas Press.

fantasy, namely in Welles' Charles Foster Kane—like Cruz a poor boy suddenly wrenched away from a childhood realm of innocence, launched on a career of social idealism that finally degenerates into demagoguery and self-aggrandizement. Both men amass huge fortunes and control vast conglomerate empires but fail to achieve what they most desire. And the influence of *Citizen Kane* on *La muerte de Artemio Cruz* does not stop with character creation; it is found in the structure of Fuentes' novel, with its multiple and constantly shifting points of view on the protagonist, its evocation of Cruz's life not as a chronological progression from birth to death but as a series of fragments that shift rapidly in time, from Cruz's early career to his old age and back to his childhood in response to the associational flux of his stricken consciousness, and in its style—its dramatic intensity, its mannered delivery, and its baroque pyramiding of images. This is not to detract from the uniqueness and the profundity of Fuentes' creation, a novel that has already become a modern classic of Latin American literature, but rather to demonstrate how the influences on Fuentes by leading artists such as Welles have brought about the opening up of Mexican literature, resulting in its emergence as a truly universal art form.

The fact that Fuentes chose to create a symbol of modern Mexico in the form of a dying plutocrat itself owes much to Welles' film, which begins at the end—by focusing on its protagonist as he lies on his deathbed. Both novel and film concentrate on the development of a single, titanic individual who is given the awesomeness and the complexity necessary to stand as a symbol of an entire nation. The bold, brash, irreverent spirit of Kane is symbolic of a young country rapidly moving away from its nineteenth-century rural traditions toward massive industrialization, resulting in the consolidation of gigantic trusts that Kane both invests in and fights to break up. Kane's vitality—his enormous enthusiasm, his boundless energy, his obsessive emphasis on bigness ("If the headlines are big enough, it makes the news big"), his single-handed transformation of a small, staid newspaper into a far-flung journalistic empire—is symbolic of a young nation flexing its economic and military might and for the first time in its history assuming a commanding role in world affairs. Kane defines himself first and foremost as an American, and it is significant that the script for the film was originally entitled *The American*. Naremore, in his extensive analysis of *Citizen Kane*, interprets the protagonist as "a man designed to embody all the strengths and failings of capitalist democracy" and comments on the relationship between the development of the individual and that of the nation: "America moves from the age of the Tycoon, through the period of populist muckraking, and into the era of 'mass communications,' with turn-of-the-century types like Kane being destroyed by the very process they have set into motion."[2] Several of the characters in *Citizen Kane* are both individuals and national symbols. Significantly, Susan Alexander, Kane's second wife, is referred to as "a cross-section of the American public." Kane's brutal manipulation of her and his virtual imprisonment of her at Xanadu even while professing his love and need for her are symbolic of his basic ambivalence toward the American people—his deep desire to be loved by them but his feelings of superiority and his marked contempt for the masses and his incessant exploitation of them in order to rise to power.

Like Welles, Fuentes is a master at creating characters who function not only as individuals but as national symbols. In *La región más transparente* and in *La muerte de Artemio Cruz*, primary and secondary characters become symbols of both ancient and modern Mexico. Artemio Cruz is developed in terms of both Hernán Cortés, to indicate the continuing influence that the archetype of the *conquistador* wields in Mexican society, and an Aztec emperor—a modern version of Moctezuma or even of the Aztec god Huitzilopochtli, as Cruz relentlessly demands blood sacrifice in order to renew himself. Cruz's self-betrayal is symbolic of Mexico's failure to actualize the ideals of the Revolution of 1910; Cruz's desperate struggle for rebirth and for self-transcendence symbolizes the nation that time and again throughout its sanguinary history has struggled to re-create itself—after the conquest, after its independence from Spain, after the liberal reforms of the Juárez era, after the Revolution of 1910, after the nationalization of its petroleum resources under Cárdenas. Yet Cruz's final and irrevocable incarceration in self, his inability to reconstitute the shattered remnants of both his moral and his physical self, constitutes Fuentes' warning to his countrymen about the extreme dangers to the national integrity and autonomy that could result from Mexico's failure to unify the fragments of the national self—its diverse social classes, the poverty and disease-stricken masses on the one side and its economic and social elite on the other, its Indian and its *criollo* identities, its pre-Columbian heritage and its commercial and technological present.

The paradoxical nature of Cruz and Kane is evident from the very beginning of both works. At the outset of the film, in the *March of Time* newsreel, headlines from newspapers across the world convey the markedly ambivalent nature of Kane, and serve to adumbrate the entire structure of the film—the multiple and contradictory points of view concerning the protagonist: "Entire Nation Mourns Great Publisher as Outstanding American"; "Death of Publisher Finds Few Who Will Mourn for Him"; "Stormy Career Ends for 'U.S. Fascist No. 1'"; "Kane, Sponsor of Democracy, Dies."[3] Kane's guardian, the financial tycoon Thatcher, denounces the iconoclastic trust-buster as a communist, yet one of the workers whose devotion Kane has attempted to gain excoriates him as a fascist. Welles himself has commented on the deliberate inconsistencies in Kane's nature. The result of these paradoxes is to leave the viewer with an unsolvable mystery concerning Kane's true identity—as unsolvable as that of Howard Hughes, another multimillionaire who, like Kane, died in seclusion, and, ironically, who also had an island retreat, aptly called the *Hotel Xanadu*: "Kane, we are told, loved only his mother—only his newspaper—only his second wife—only himself. Maybe he loved all of these, or none. It is for the audience to judge. Kane was selfish and selfless, an idealist, a scoundrel, a very big man and a very little one. It depends on who's talking about him. He is never judged with the objectivity of an author, and the point of the picture is not so much the solution of the problem as its presentation."[4]

Ambivalence toward the protagonist is found not only among the various people—the once idealistic and now cynical Leland, the embittered Susan Alexander, the servile Bernstein, the greedy and sinister Raymond—but even within the same account. For example, from the perspective of Susan Alexander Kane, the person whose career and whose life Kane has almost destroyed, the protagonist is evoked as both ruthless and pitiable.

A similar ambivalence characterizes Artemio Cruz, who not only on his deathbed but throughout his life is portrayed as a congeries of warring selves that are given bold structural form through the use of a triadic perspective—first, second, and third person accounts of the life of Cruz, each person widely varying in its assessment of the protagonist. The self-exalting *I*-narrative of Cruz the potentate contrasts markedly with the self-evaluating and self-condemning second-person voice of conscience. Just as the problematic Kane represents a significant departure from the unidimensional protagonists of so many Hollywood films made before and after *Citizen Kane*, so too does Artemio Cruz break through the Manichean mold into which so many characters in Latin American literature are cast—either ruthless, despotic *cacique* or submissive *peón*, corrupt foreign exploiter or self-sacrificing, heroic *criollo*. The multiverse of Cruz's self, his dual nature as both national defender and *malinchista*, as both unscrupulous *hacendado* and extremely sensitive and guilt-ridden victim desperately reaching out for love—and fearing rejection—is conveyed through the *tú* narrative. This second-person narrative in itself is an awesome paradox, both superego and representative of Cruz's physiological self, both individual and collective, both condemning Cruz and yet seeking to penetrate his motives. Obsessed with the recapitulation of Cruz's past and scrutiny of his moral failings, this voice addresses him in the future tense: "Ayer volarás," as if self-renewal and salvation were still possible for him: "Confess that always, even when it has seemed otherwise, you have found in black the germ of its opposite; your own cruelty, when you have been cruel, has it not been tinged with a certain tenderness? ... Your bravery will be the brother of your cowardice and even its twin; your hatred will be born of your love.... You will not have been either good or evil, generous or selfish, faithful or traitorous" (pp. 28–29). Both Kane and Cruz are extraordinarily complex characters. According to Fowler, "The Welles film ... gave the most searching and complete analysis ever made on film of an individual, imaginary or real."[5] And certainly Artemio Cruz is one of the most three-dimensional characters in all of Latin American fiction.

The theme of the fall from paradise—and the desperate, often pathetic attempts by both protagonists throughout their lives to regain that lost paradise—is a key one in both film and novel. The following remark by Welles applies equally to both works: "Almost all serious stories in the world are stories of a failure with a death in it.... But there is more lost paradise in them than defeat. To me that's the central theme in Western culture, the lost paradise."[6]

Early in his life Cruz suffers the warping of his idealism and of his capacity to love. He is expelled from the natural paradise that is the world of his youth at Cocuya, Veracruz, from the romantic paradise within the hellworld of war that he shares but briefly with Regina before her brutal death, and from the illusion of redemptive unity that he seeks with Catalina. His primary response in protecting his fragile, inner self against the threat of further frustration and hurt is to retreat into a self-made and self-sustained world in which he can feel secure. For the spiritual paradise of love that he has been denied, Cruz substitutes a material paradise that seems to proclaim his invincibility—the old monastery at Coyoacán that he transforms into a palace. His actions parallel the retreat by Kane from the external world into a self-made and self-contained universe—the world of Xanadu. Both protagonists fashion themselves to be demigods, creating the universe anew. Kane transforms marshland into mountain; he imports his own scenery— entire forests; he constructs Xanadu as a world in which he can reign supreme. Both protagonists rise up as satanic figures. Artemio Cruz, exulting in his power as a terrestrial god, even attempts to bargain with God for his salvation, promising to believe in Him in exchange for being granted perpetual life on earth: "And the heaven that is power over uncounted men with hidden faces and forgotten names, named by the thousand on the payrolls of my mines, my factories, my newspaper.... This is to be God, eh? [To be feared and hated and all the rest, this is to be God, truly, eh?] (p. 155).[7]

An essential part of the structuring of both film and novel is the incorporation of leitmotivs. In works that shift so rapidly and often abruptly in point of view, that reverse so often the temporal sequence, the use of these leitmotivs accomplishes two goals: it grants continuity to the many truncated scenes and episodes and infects a deep sense of mystery and suspense that in a more traditional novel or film would be provided by the development of the plot. In *Citizen Kane* there are two major leitmotivs, one explicit and the other more subtly developed but just as significant: Rosebud and the glass ball. Similarly, in *La muerte de Artemio Cruz* there are two major leitmotivs—the *convolvulus* or moonflower, and the enigmatic phrase that appears in twelve of the thirteen sections of Cruz's first-person monologue: "Cruzamos el rio a caballo." The leitmotivs in both film and novel represent the remote past of the protagonists; they also symbolize the spiritual center that is lacking in their lives.

Like almost every aspect of *Citizen Kane*, the motif of Rosebud is complex and ambiguous. The reporter Thompson is instructed to solve the mystery of this single word, uttered by Kane at the moment of his death. Yet, although Thompson delves methodically into Kane's past, his investigation is ultimately futile. Although the viewer of *Citizen Kane* is seemingly privileged by being allowed to witness what Thompson will never discover— the word "Rosebud" emblazoned on the sled that is tossed like a piece of rubbish into the furnace at Xanadu—the revelation of "Rosebud" only heightens the mystery of Kane. The sled has a multiple significance. First of all, it is a symbol of Kane's past—of past innocence and also of past trauma, because it represents the childhood of which he was deprived. It symbolizes the exuberance and joy of Kane's childhood in Colorado and it also becomes the weapon—an ineffectual one—that Kane utilizes to defend his childhood world against the intruder Thatcher. Similarly, the boy Cruz with equal bewilderment and desperation will take a rifle blindly to keep his world from being shattered by the agent of the new *hacendado*, who has come to take Cruz's guardian and surrogate father Lunero away.

The second major visual leitmotiv—one that appears briefly at the beginning of the film, is later reduced almost to inconspicuousness as it is glimpsed among Susan's possessions in her apartment, and then reemerges to the explicit level at the climax of the film, as the demented Kane rampages through Susan's room at Xanadu and is halted in his destructive fury only by the encountering of the object—is the glass ball, which contains a snow scene. In a sense, this glass ball, a dimestore object of trivial material value, constitutes a spiritual response to the vast and treasure-laden but mausoleum-like Xanadu. As Naremore states, "It symbolizes an ideal—a self-enclosed realm, immune from change, where Kane can feel he has control over his life."[8] And, like Rosebud, it symbolizes the irrecoverable past—the halcyon boyhood in the snow, the family home in Colorado, the maternal love from which Kane was permanently severed by his mother's decision to send him away.

Welles expertly uses the technique of suspended coherence, as he keeps returning to the theme of Rosebud without clarifying it until the very end. Fuentes too utilizes the device of suspended coherence in the sense that Humphrey defines the term, as a "method of suspending sense impressions and ideas in the memory for so long that they reappear at unexpected and seemingly unreasonable places."[9] Through his use of this technique, Fuentes, like Welles, underscores the enigmatic nature of the protagonist. The deaths of the protagonists, evident from the outset of both film and novel, remove all possible suspense concerning the outcome. Suspense comes instead as a result of the layer by layer revelation of the extraordinary characters of both protagonists.

Fuentes interpolates into the sections of Cruz's subjective, anguished, first-person monologue two leitmotivs that are clarified—and then only partially—only at the very end. The first mystery is that of the *convolvulus* flower, symbolic of immortality. It is startling that this very delicate, poetic image should appear in the monologue of Artemio Cruz, replete with images of brutality and obscenity, with memories of power plays and acts of oppression of those attempting to claim the rights they ostensibly had won as a result of the revolution. The image of the moonflower is originally triggered involuntarily within Cruz's moribund psyche, as a response to the sudden darkening of his room—symbolic of the shadow of death. Desperately, heroically struggling to raise up barriers against death, to obtain terrestrial immortality, Cruz recalls—and identifies with—the image of the flower that comes to life in the darkness: "They closed the curtains, right? It is night, right? And there are plants that must have the light of darkness in order to flower, they wait until darkness comes out, the moonflower, it opens its petals in the evening. The moonflower. There was a moon-flower vine on that but near the river. It opened its flowers in the evening" (p. 135). It is significant that this image is the only one now left to Cruz of his boyhood realm at Cocuya, an idyllic life that he once believed to be eternal—a childhood paradise that he had returned to over and over again, even to the extent of restoring the burned-out mansion of his ancestors. The thrust toward the past that is characteristic of much of Cruz's life is very similar to the absorption into the past of Kane, who first encounters Susan Alexander as he is on his way to the Western Manhattan Warehouse to inspect the family belongings that he has had shipped East from Colorado. It is ironic that Kane, who for much of his life has traveled incessantly, should finally prefer to remain a recluse at Xanadu, which thus becomes an enormous protective womb. Similarly, Cruz toward the end of his life retreats into Coyoacán in a futile attempt to conquer time and death. The observation that Leland makes concerning Kane, "He was disappointed in the world, so he built one of his own," applies equally well to Artemio Cruz, who like the arrogant but essentially childish Kane, attempts to live life totally on his own terms:

> He preferred these old walls with their two centuries of sandstone and tezontle. In a strange way they took him back into their own past and reflected a land that did not want everything to be transient. Yes, he was quite aware that there had been a process of substitution, the waving of a magic wand. And there was also no doubt that the old timbers and stone, the ironwork and mouldings, the refectory tables, the cabinets, the grainwork, the inlays, that these conspired to bring back to him, with a faint perfume of nostalgia, the scenes, the smells, the tactile sensations of his own youth. (p. 244)

Both protagonists, who publicly appear so dedicated to the future, to the building of new worlds, are privately obsessed with recovering the security, comfort, and love that the past represents.

The theme of idealism—and of the repeated betrayal of those ideals—is an important one in both of these works. Kane's very name constitutes an allusion to the biblical Cain; the slaying of Abel is paralleled by Kane's destruction of the career of his soulmate, Jed Leland, and his impelling of Susan Kane, whom he purportedly loves, to an attempt to commit suicide. First the rustication then the firing of Leland represent Kane's gradual suppression of the idealistic part of himself. An ominous revelation of Kane's unprincipled nature behind his idealistic façade is evident from the start of his journalistic career. The impetuous Kane takes over a staid and musty but highly reputable newspaper, the *Inquirer*, and although mouthing reformist phrases on the one hand, immediately concocts a story that blows up a routine missing person case into a murder mystery—viciously accusing an innocent man of the merely purported crime. Both Kane and Cruz ceaselessly inflate, distort, and sensationalize the news, slandering their enemies while at the same time pandering to the lowest denominator of public taste—the demand for the lurid—Kane in order to gain power and fame, Cruz in order to destroy his enemies and to divert the attention of the public away from his own acts of brutal oppression.

Initially Kane is a crusader—he attacks monopolies, rails against the corruption of machine politics, and becomes an impassioned advocate of the common man. Yet although professing his unstinting dedication to the public service and the public good, the reckless Kane really has little understanding and no genuine concern for the needs of the people. At best

Kane's paternalism is a type of *noblesse oblige*, at worst it is rampant opportunism. The demagoguery of Kane is matched by that of Cruz. Like Kane, Cruz is extremely skillful at manipulating the media, at creating an elaborate public façade as champion of the people. It is significant that Cruz too owns his own newspaper, one that even after his death will promulgate the false image of him as revolutionary hero and national architect, just as the *Inquirer* trumpets the monumental deeds of Charles Foster Kane. Kane and Cruz have accrued tremendous wealth and power that they could utilize to actualize their ideals and to construct new, progressive societies. As the head of a publishing empire, Kane has an unparalleled opportunity to enlighten public opinion, to unify a vast nation in its development of a collective conscience and in its pursuit of a common good. Instead Kane squanders his immense talent and energy, dedicating much of his career to the stirring up of jingoistic fever, even manufacturing a war through his headlines. At the close of the military phase of the Mexican Revolution, Cruz too has the opportunity—even greater, relatively speaking, than that of Kane—to reshape the whole of his society to benefit his countrymen, all of *los de abajo* who had fought for social equality. Cruz has the position and the authority to break the stranglehold of cyclic time that throughout the centuries—from the epoch of the Aztec conquerors—has acted as a curse on his country, repeatedly demolishing an old set of exploiters and oppressors only to raise up a new set in their place. Yet the insecure and exceedingly ambitious Cruz, like Kane, forfeits his initial idealism and plunges into a career of self-aggrandizement. Both become transfixed, and, finally, enslaved by their drive for power.

Shortly after assuming control of the *Inquirer*, Kane feels compelled to make a public declaration of his idealism, as he prints on the front page his *Declaration of Principles*:

> I. I will provide the people of this city with a daily newspaper that will tell all the news honestly.
> II. I will also provide them with a fighting and tireless champion of their rights as human beings.

But Kane's principles are undercut, right from the start, by the mocking words of Leland, who acts as Kane's conscience. Leland ends his assessment of Kane's intentions on a note of ironic deflation: "I'd like to keep that particular piece of paper myself. I have a hunch it might turn out to be something pretty important, a document ... like the Declaration of Independence, or the Constitution ... and my first report card at school" (CC, p. 352). The plummeting from the mentioning of historical documents of universal significance to the mundane level of elementary school achievement is an indication that Leland from the very start suspects the worthlessness of Kane's declaration. Kane will betray the people's trust and betray too his best friend, as he fires Leland for daring to write a negative review of Susan's singing performance. But most of all Kane will betray himself, as he becomes obsessively dedicated to a massive and futile campaign to prove to the voting public that they were wrong in rejecting him.

Kane's pseudoidealism is also mocked by the very structure of the film. An example of visual undercutting, accomplished through a rapid alteration in point of view, is analyzed by McBride: "Welles undercuts the spirit of Kane's high-minded speech by cutting to the dandyish Leland on the words 'the workingman and the slum child' and to Bernstein and his unsavory associates applauding after the words 'the underprivileged, the underpaid and the underfed.'"[10]

The spectre of Cain pollutes the lives of both Kane and Cruz. In Fuentes' novel, *cainismo* falls as a generational curse over the Menchaca line, from which Cruz descends, and, symbolically, as a seemingly indelible curse over the whole of Mexican history, which is evoked by Fuentes in this and other works as a series of betrayals, beginning with that of Moctezuma and ending with those of Porfirio Díaz, Victoriano Huerta, and the revolutionaries themselves. On the individual level, Cruz's father is ambushed and killed after he is betrayed by his own brother, Pedro, who carries a loaded gun and who could have defended him. Pedro's desertion of his brother adumbrates a whole series of betrayals by Artemio. The double who functions as a conscience figure is important in both *Citizen Kane* and *La muerte de Artemio Cruz*. Paralleling Kane's many encounters with Leland are the episodes in which Cruz is forced to confront a figure who both resembles him physically and who incarnates the moral qualities—courage, strength of convictions, honor, capacity to love—that Cruz has betrayed. The unknown soldier on the battlefield who strangely resembles him and who dies in his place, Gonzalo Bernal, Laura, Lorenzo, all are spiritual doubles of Cruz, and all are sacrificed by the protagonist just as Kane sacrifices Leland for daring to challenge him and for tearing down the carefully elaborated façade of social benefactor that Kane has erected. The death of these idealists symbolizes Cruz's lifelong suppression of his own idealistic potential, which he replaces by a rhetorical façade of revolutionary commitment merely to curry the favor of the *campesinos*, while secretly selling their land to purchase building lots for himself in Mexico City. Cruz's behavior becomes a perfect example of what Mariano Azuela has referred to as *el complejo de la Malinche*—the surrendering of his identity by the Mexican to foreigners before whom he remains awed—repeating the pattern of La Malinche and the other Indian women who voluntarily gave themselves to the Spaniards, whom they perceived as gods. The constant undermining of the idealistic pretentiousness of Cruz is done both thematically—through key confrontations between Cruz with the genuine idealists, and structurally, through the continual antagonism between the first-person and the second-person narratives, as the second person voice challenges and probes and squelches the vaunted ego. The second person voice of conscience castigates Cruz for his sellout of his *mexicanidad*, as he apes the values and lifestyle and even the dress of those who have exploited his country: "You will not be Artemio Cruz ... you will not ... wear Italian silk shirts, collect cufflinks, order your neckties from New York, wear three-button blue suits, prefer Irish cashmere, drink gin and tonic, own a Volvo, a Cadillac, and a Rambler Wagon" (pp. 238–239).

Yet both men have the capacity for self-awareness and for self-criticism. When Jed Leland writes an honest review of Susan's disastrous performance at the Chicago Opera House, Kane's markedly ambivalent nature is manifested by his first completing the review for Leland—in exactly the same negative manner as it had begun—and then summarily firing the drama critic for failing to perform the self-abasing role that Kane expects all of those around him to play. Cruz too finally achieves self-awareness and even rejects that aspect of himself affirmed in the first-person narrative—Cruz the power broker, demagogue, and robber baron. Yet, ironically, Cruz's self-critique and self-rejection occur when it is too late for him to alter his life. Suddenly forced into confrontation with the Cruz of the past, the aggressive, rapacious Cruz projected by the voice on the tape recorder, the dying Cruz is brought to an admission of the hollowness of the role that he has so thoroughly mastered. On his deathbed, he seeks first sensual then spiritual consolation—and, in what appears to be the operating of poetic justice, finds neither:

> *Tell him to establish a clear contrast between an anarchic, bloody movement that is destructive of private property and human rights alike, and an ordered revolution, peaceful and legal, such as the Mexican Revolution, which was directed by a middle class inspired by Jefferson. The people have short memories....*
>
> Oh, what a barrage of meanings, implications, words. Oh, what fatigue. They won't understand my gesture, my fingers can hardly move: but let it be shut off now, I'm bored with it, it means nothing, just crap, crap.... (p. 197). Italics in English edition.

Kane has been described as a kind of "Barnum who conceals his private self behind a dazzling set of public images."[11] Similarly, Artemio Cruz is a master of masquerade, hiding his fragile, sensitive inner self behind an assortment of masks. The inner world of Cruz and his other selves that will remain mere potentialities are penetratingly revealed and explored in the second-person narrative that breaks through the elaborate façade of *machista* and *conquistador* that Cruz has constructed. Similarly, Kane alludes to the other self, the truly great self that will never be actualized:

KANE: Well, I always gagged on that silver spoon. You know, Mr. Bernstein, if I hadn't been very rich, I might have been a really great man.
THATCHER: What would you like to have been?
KANE: Everything you hate. (CC, p. 340)

In addition to leitmotivs, mirror imagery is utilized extensively in both film and novel. In *Citizen Kane* there is an eery incident in which the aging Kane, immediately after Susan walks out on him, is seen reflected endlessly in a hall of mirrors at Xanadu. This incessant duplication suggests several aspects of Kane's character—his multiplicity of selves and also his failure to integrate them. The myriad reflections symbolize Kane's enormous ego but also the futility of his actions—his permanent entrapment in the self. It is ironic that the newspaper magnate, who has dedicated his career to the creation of images, should now himself be reduced to but a series of images. Bernstein too is evoked as both self and image as he is shown reflected in a glass desk top. Dominated by the portrait of Kane above his desk just as he was dominated by Kane while the magnate was alive, Bernstein's reflected image—the image of Kane's will—seems to acquire more life than the man himself.

As in *Citizen Kane*, mirror imagery is utilized throughout *La muerte de Artemio Cruz*—to emphasize the disjointed nature of Cruz, the permanent split in his identity, as his conscience is suppressed, isolated into a form, the *tú* narrative, that always remains structurally independent of the first-person monologue. Mirrors emphasize the tremendous discrepancy between the actual and the potential Cruz. At the very beginning of the narrative, the dying Cruz is forced to see himself reflected grotesquely in the facets of Teresa's purse, which present him with a cubist portrait of himself. The subsequent structuring of the novel into mere fragments of identity that will never be recomposed is adumbrated by this bizarre mirroring.

It is ironic that the socially responsible self, the true revolutionary that Cruz could have been, appears to him as but a reflected image, as he enters a revolving glass door. This simulacrum that seems to act independently of Cruz is a projection of his conscience that is struggling to assert itself. Cruz the corporate magnate has remained oblivious to the poverty and suffering all around him—the adverse social conditions that men like himself, *los de abajo*, had fought and died in an attempt to eradicate:

> Vendors of lottery tickets, bootblacks, women in rebozos, children with their upper lips smeared with mucous swarmed around him as he moved toward the revolving door and passed into the vestibule and adjusted his necktie in front of the glass and through it, in the second glass, which looked out on Madero, saw a man identical to himself, wearing the same double-breasted suit, but colorless, tightening the knot of the same tie with the same nicotine fingers, a man surrounded by beggars, who let his hand drop at the same instant he in the vestibule did, and turned and walked down the block, while he, for the moment a little disoriented, looked for the elevator. (p. 17)

Time and again when Cruz confronts his mirrored image, he refuses to acknowledge it. The last of these reflections is that of the aged and decrepit Cruz as he falls against his glass desktop, shattering it, and ironically merging his two selves. Only on his deathbed does the *alter ego*, the second-person voice, claim its victory—"te venzo"—by forcing Cruz to confront his past and his past failings.

Both Fuentes and Welles expertly fuse theme and structure. The severe alienation that characterizes the lives of their protagonists—estrangement not only from those around them but also from self, from their origins, from the selves they had the potential to become—is not merely described, it is given structural form, and its impact is thus intensified. In *The Magic World of Orson Welles*, Naremore shows how carefully constructed the scenes are to emphasize visually the extreme social alienation of the characters:

> ... the actors often took unnatural positions, their figures arranged in a slanting line that ran out in front of the camera, so that characters in the extreme foreground or in the distance became subjects for the director's visual commentary. Actors seldom confronted one another face to face, as they do in the shot/reverse shot editing of the ordinary film. The communications scientists would say that the positions of figures on the screen were "sociofugal," or not conducive to direct human interaction, and this slight physical suggestion of an

inability to communicate is fully appropriate to the theme of social alienation which is implicit in the film.[12]

The increasing estrangement between Kane and Emily is brilliantly telescoped—and intensified—by a montage in which the same scene— husband and wife at the breakfast table—is shown repeatedly as the years pass. The first time the scene is shot, the newlyweds are seated close together at one end of a small table, but each time the scene is repeated, they are farther and farther apart, until finally each is seen at the opposite end of a huge table, each engrossed in a different newspaper. Like Welles, Fuentes uses many techniques to depict the crippling isolation of his characters, many of whom—Cruz, Catalina, Ludivinia, Pedro, Don Gamaliel—remained locked within their pride, delusions of grandeur, guilt, or fear. At several points in the narrative, in particular in episodes that depict confrontations between Cruz and Catalina, Ludivinia and Pedro, Fuentes shows two people who are desperately seeking to reach out toward one another but cannot find any basis of communication. Fuentes develops these scenes in terms of a dialogue—to indicate the need to communicate— but significantly, remits that dialogue to the level of soliloquy. Thus the intense, conflictive drama of the encounter is emphasized and also, by the technique of recording words that are never uttered, the unbridgeable chasm between mother and son, or husband and wife, is stressed. The disdain that Ludivinia evinces toward her pusillanimous son Pedro, the one who could not uphold the *macho* code of the Menchaca line, and the withdrawing of her affection from one of her children while she glorifies the stronger, adumbrates the social relationships in the next generation. Within this closed, fatalistic familial structuring, the exclusivity demonstrated by Ludivinia will be repeated by Cruz's contempt for his daughter Teresa and his favoring of the *macho* figure Lorenzo:

> They looked at each other, mother and son, with a wall of a resurrection between them.
> *Are you here*, she said to him silently, *to tell me that we no longer have land or greatness? That others have taken from us what we took from others? Have you come to tell me what I have always known since my first night as a wife?*
> *I came with a pretext*, he replied with his eyes. *I didn't want to be alone anymore.*
> *I would like to remember what you were like as a child*, she went on. *I loved you then. When a mother is young, she loves all her children. As old women, we know better. No one has a right to be loved without a*

reason. Blood ties are not reason enough. The right reason is blood loved without reason.

I have wanted to be strong like my brother. For example, I have treated that mulatto and the boy with an iron hand. I have forbidden them ever to set foot in the house. (pp. 287–288)

Both Cruz and Kane suffer from an inability to love. Cruz loves genuinely only once—in his relationship with Regina, which is severed by death. So great is the loss of Regina that Cruz will never again risk exposing his inner self to even the possibility of hurt, humiliation or defeat in love. Thus, although he wants to love Catalina, he will never confess to her his guilt over her brother's death, fearing that his wife will interpret any show of humility on his part as a sign of weakness that will arouse only her contempt. Similarly, Cruz refuses to sever his relationship with Catalina in order to marry Laura, again because he fears that by giving himself totally to her as he had to Regina, he will once more expose himself to the possibility of losing that love. Thus, at the end of his life, Cruz prefers the loveless relationship with Lilia to the genuine love he could have shared with Laura—because he need only command and Lilia, although resentful, will obey him.

Love and the irremediable loss of love plays an important part in Kane's life as well. The lifelong effect that the loss of Regina has upon Artemio Cruz is paralleled by the indelible mark that Kane's separation from his mother leaves upon him. Much of his life is spent in a futile attempt symbolically to regain that love. It is significant that the voting public is perceived by him as a source of love that is greater than that offered to him by his wife and child. When Emily attempts to convince Kane to withdraw from the election in order to save their marriage, Kane is stung by her words and demonstrates the extent to which he is emotionally committed to the electorate:

EMILY: … if you don't listen to reason, it may be too late….

KANE: Too late for what? For you and this public thief to take the love of the people of this state away from me? (CC, P. 384)

The stunning loss at the polls is perceived by Kane as a rejection by this "lover"—and as a repetition on the public scale of his abandonment by his mother. Just as Kane attempts to reconstruct the physical fragments of the past, so also does he desperately strive to regain the devotion of the public through his fanatic promotion of Susan Alexander. Susan's walking out on Kane represents but another repetition of his original, childhood trauma.

Kane desperately clutches the glass ball that becomes his pacifier and that reminds him of "Rosebud," a word he utters plaintively, and which perhaps gives him some insight into his actions.

It is significant that Kane purchases countless statues of Venus, the love goddess. He thereby attempts to compensate in marble—in objects that he can possess one hundred percent—for the loss of maternal love and the security of his childhood. Kane reduces human beings to collectibles, just as the wizened Cruz annually summons one hundred guests to his mansion at Coyoacán—ostensibly to celebrate the New Year but in reality to pay homage to him—to perform at his command. Kane marries a woman whom he does not love—Emily Monroe Norton, the niece of the president, as a means of ascending to national political power. The whole future course of the relationship between Kane and Emily—their basic incompatibility, Kane's ruthless exploitation of her, and finally his abandonment of both her and his son—are summed up in Bernstein's flippant remark concerning Kane's behavior prior to his marriage:

LELAND: World's biggest diamond. I didn't know Charlie was collecting diamonds.
BERNSTEIN: He ain't. He's collecting somebody that's collecting diamonds. Anyway, he ain't only collecting statues. (CC, p. 361)

Kane's insensitivity, his regarding Emily as just one more prize to be added to his collection, is paralleled by Cruz's claiming of Catalina from her father as a prize of war. Like Emily with Kane, Catalina, the sheltered daughter of a Porfirian aristocrat, grants Cruz the social respectability necessary for his political advancement—even in a post-revolutionary society.

There is a distinct neogothic quality to both *Citizen Kane* and *La muerte de Artemio Cruz*. In the film, this is particularly evident in the opening and closing scenes in which the huge, disintegrating Xanadu, evoked at night, emerges from the mists as a phantasmagoric structure, mysterious and foreboding. As Naremore states: "In *Kane*, space becomes demonic, oppressive; ceilings are unnaturally low, as if they were about to squash the character—or, conversely, at Xanadu rooms become so large that people shrink, comically yet terrifyingly dwarfed by their possessions."[13] An air of demonism suffuses both the palatial estate of Xanadu and the opulent world of the monastery at Coyoacán. In *Citizen Kane*, the outsize material possessions seem ready to devour the inhabitants. This looming and menacing quality of the material world finds a particularly powerful image in the scene in which Susan Alexander reclines listlessly before the gargantuan fireplace, which looms above her like a huge gaping maw that is threatening to devour her. As Kane stands in front of the fireplace, the immense flames behind him attest to the infernal nature of the world that he had fashioned as a paradise realm. When Kane orders his guests to attend a picnic, the file of cars slowly and silently driving across the Florida sands seems much more like a death march than the celebration of a festive occasion. And the picnic itself is evoked in a rapid series of grotesque, nightmarish images—strange birds, roasting flesh of the animal slaughtered to provide the picnic fare, rhythmic but tormented music.

In *La muerte de Artemio Cruz* the same hallucinatory atmosphere is conveyed, although by means of a different technique. Welles creates his bizarre world by concentrating on a seemingly real but actually expressionistic exterior setting. Fuentes, with the conceptual advantage that the written word has over the visual image, penetrates directly into the warped mind of Cruz, who mentally twists what is ostensibly a celebration of life into a ritual of death. Undercutting the sumptuousness of the banquet are the morbid images floating through Cruz's consciousness. Like Kane at Xanadu, the wizened Cruz is obsessed with demonstrating his power, which he longs to impose directly and sadistically over those around him. As Cruz watches the drunken revelers, he envisions a swift, violent attack on them by the enormous rats that lie in wait in the beams of the monastery. Fanatically questing for self-preservation and self-renewal, Cruz is imbued with the demonic spirit of an Aztec god, demanding the blood sacrifice of his guests in order to nourish himself:

> and in his sensitive ear heard the secret shuffle of immense rats, black fanged and sharp muzzled ... that at times scurried impudently across the corners of the room, and that waited, in the darkness, above the heads and beneath the feet of the dancers, by the hundreds and thousands waited, perhaps, for an opportunity to take them by surprise, infect them with fevers and aches, nausea and palsy ... if he raised his arm again for the servants to drop the iron door-bars, the ways of escape ...; then his retinue would find themselves obliged to remain with him, unable to abandon ship, forced to join him in sprinkling the corpses with vinegar and lighting perfumed faggots, in hanging rosaries of thyme around their necks, in brushing away the green buzz of flies, while he commanded them, to dance, dance, live, live, drink. (pp. 253–254)

In this expertly constructed work, Cruz's terrifying vision is but the phantasmagoric expression of what the protagonist has practiced throughout his life. Cruz allows others, even his own son, to die in his place, forges a new life for himself on the sacrifices of others, and even at the hour of his death calls for repeated blood sacrifices of those like the unknown soldier, Regina, and Bernal who gave up their lives once for him. In the same way, Kane relentlessly sacrifices those around him—Leland, Susan Alexander, Emily, even his own son—all of those attracted by his spellbinding presence. The bitter words of Cruz's daughter Teresa, cast aside by her father because she could not fulfill his egomaniacal purpose: "Even what he loved, he destroyed" (p. 196) find their equivalent in the life of Kane.

As we have seen, fragmentation is both a basic theme and an important structural technique in both of these works. In *Citizen Kane*, dialogue is continually interrupted, and much of the movie seems to be like the *March of Time* newsreel, affording us mere glimpses into the life—and into the soul—of Kane. Throughout *La muerte de Artemio Cruz*, the fragments of first-, second-, and third-person narrative symbolize not only Cruz's multiplicity of selves but also the incompatibility of those selves and the inability of Cruz—on his deathbed as throughout his life—to integrate self-serving ego and self-negating conscience, *yo* and *tú*, opportunism and idealism. Similarly, the splintered, at times highly compartmentalized selves of Kane—his brutality and his tenderness, his shyness and his aggressiveness, his vaunted idealism and his rapacious opportunism, his imaginative exuberance and his rigidity, his love of country and his monstrous *amour propre*—are all strikingly conveyed through the technique of fragmentation of dialogue, scene, and point of view.

Cruz leads a split life, maintaining a mere façade of a marriage with Catalina while living openly with his mistress Lilia at Coyoacán. He also is a split personality, outwardly maintaining a supreme aloofness, not even allowing his guests to approach him, but inwardly yearning for reunion with his son. As the dancing couples summoned by Cruz to his New Year's Eve celebration whirl about before him, their conversations are not recorded objectively by the omniscient author but are instead filtered through the consciousness of the protagonist. Instead of coherent dialogue, only free-floating fragments of conversations are perceived, as the dancers approach, withdraw, and approach again. The partial, confused, kaleidoscopic patterning of the conversation is similar to the random, illogical movements of a consciousness at the prespeech level. Taken as a whole, the montage produced by concatenation of the fragments constitutes an exteriorization of Cruz's own misshapen identity, a mocking echo of his own life, and a microcosm of the narrative structure as a whole:

"... lovers, about twenty years ago ..."
"... how can he give suffrage to that gang of Indians ..."
"... and his wife alone at home, never ..."
"... questions of high politics; we received the ..."
....
"... they're investing a hundred million ..."
"... it's a heavenly Dali ..."
"... and we'll get it back in a couple of years ..."
"... the people at my gallery sent it over ..."
"... in New York ..."
"... she lived several years in France; deception ... they say ..."
(p. 255)

The disintegration of Cruz's physical self and the shattering of his spiritual self attested to here are stunningly evident from the very beginning of the novel, expressed through the extreme fragmentation of language that characterizes Cruz's first-person monologue. Similarly, at the outset of *Citizen Kane*, the dropping by Kane of the glass ball—the object that, ironically, is the only one of his numerous possessions that still retains any meaning for him, and the smashing of the ball into fragments, one of which reflects and distorts the image of the nurse at his bedside—provides an adumbration of the incessant fragmentation that will characterize the entire film. It also foreshadows the distortion of Kane by others and by Kane himself.

Another example of the skillful use of fragmentation in the film is provided by the enormous jigsaw puzzles that Susan Alexander incessantly labors over in an attempt to fill the vacuum of her life at Xanadu. The actions of Susan in composing the puzzles are paralleled by the actions of the reporter Thompson as he doggedly attempts to fit together all the pieces of Kane's life—the interviews and the partial impressions that he has received concerning Kane. In one of the concluding scenes, the camera in an overhead shot pans over huge mounds of boxes, in a vision that is but the magnification of the huge crossword puzzles—fragments of Susan's own shattered existence, and pieces of the immense mystery that is Citizen Kane.

The continual emphasis on fragmentation also strikingly underscores the theme of the tragic incompleteness of both lives. It is significant that for all of its imposing splendor, Xanadu is never finished. Supposedly built for Susan Alexander but in reality another monument to Kane's ego, the incompleteness of the edifice signifies not only the truncated relationship between Kane and Susan but also the unfulfilled, the *manqué* nature of Kane himself. Another indication of Kane's stunted existence is that the major part of his treasures at Xanadu are never uncrated—they are essentially worthless to him. Similarly, Artemio Cruz is denied—throughout his lifetime and even on his deathbed—the fulfillment that he is seeking. Ironic testimony to the horrendous power of materialism that converts Cruz into a deathbed Midas is that although the anguished Cruz struggles desperately to recall the face of his dead son, he is unable to summon that image to consciousness, and yet the memories of his possessions—even at the very moment of his death—are amazingly precise and elaborate: "... pass close touching, smelling, tasting, smelling the sumptuous robes—the rich marquetry—the gold frames—chests of bone and tortoise—shell—locks and hasps—cutters with iron corners and key escutcheons—fragrant benches of ayacahuite wood—choir benches—baroque robes and miters" (p. 298). Unable to break down the wall of his fierce pride in order to respond to Catalina's attempts to achieve a reconciliation with him, Cruz fails to attain even the resignation and contentment of his paternal surrogate, Don Gamaliel, who derives a perverted satisfaction from rehearsing his own funeral. The calculating and cold-blooded Gamaliel dies secure in the knowledge that in the opportunistic Cruz he has found a successor—a true son, one that the introspective and romantically idealistic Gonzalo never could have been—a successor in ruthlessness. But neither Kane nor Cruz have a successor—both indirectly destroy their sons, and Teresa has no reality for Cruz, who fails to attend her wedding. When the audacious, conniving Jaime Ceballos dares to approach the aged Cruz, in what is another example of the cyclical time patterning that characterizes the work—a repetition of the boldness of the young Cruz in confronting Don Gamaliel—the monarch of Coyoacán summarily rejects his own double in opportunism. Instead, like the withered Kane, Cruz remains trapped in an idealistic past, absorbed in an inner dialogue, a dialogue with his dead son—the only one whom Cruz judges worthy enough to be his successor. Ironically, Cruz now must become his son's successor by keeping alive his memory:

> "You accepted things as they are; you became realistic...." "Yes, that's it. Like you, Don Artemio...." He asked him if he had never wondered what lies on the other side of the sea; for to him it seemed that all land was much the same, only the sea was different. "Like me ...!" He said that there are islands.... "... did you fight in the Revolution, risk your hide, to the point that you were about to be executed ...?" Sea that tasted like bitter beer, smelled of melon, quince, strawberry...... Eh ...?" "No, I ...." A ship sails in ten days. I have booked passage.... "Come to the banquet before it's over, eh? You hurry to gather up the

crumbs...." You would do the same, Papi.... "... on top for forty years because we were baptized with the glory of that...." "Yes..." "... but you, young man? Do you think that that can be inherited? How are you going to continue...?" Now there is a front and I think it is the only front left. (p. 260)

Kane's grasping of the glass ball—after Susan leaves him and again at the hour of his death—is a striking manifestation of his deep desire to unify present and past in order to gain spiritual wholeness. Similarly, in *La muerte de Artemio Cruz*, the dying protagonist struggles determinedly to effect a *cambio de piel* in order to reconstruct and renew himself. Completely alienated from those around him—Catalina, Teresa, the priest who has come to administer the last rites—rejecting all their attempts to console him because he recognizes the hypocrisy of these comforters, who are interested only in the whereabouts of his will, Cruz is forced to take refuge in self. The once mighty Cruz now comes to envy the lowly sponge for possessing a power that he is denied—the marvellous capacity to regenerate a complete self from a mere fragment.

It is significant that the only time when the unifying form, the first-person plural *nosotros*, is employed in Cruz's monologue is to depict his adventures at Cocuya with Lorenzo. Yet these brief moments of unity, of spiritual transcendence between father and son, are but a prelude to their inevitable and permanent separation. Kane's attempts to unify self and Other also are thwarted. It is ironic that the young Kane, playing exuberantly in the snow, should shout "the Union forever!" as part of the mock Civil War battle that he is fighting—at the exact moment when his mother is signing the document which will dissolve her family forever. Both Kane and Cruz die in spiritual isolation. The only unity ever attained among Cruz's three antagonistic selves is an extremely ironic one, as, at the end, all three voices merge as a prelude to Cruz's death.

In both works there is a constant interplay between free will and fate. Despite the tremendous wills of both of these protagonists, despite the immense power that they wield over thousands of persons, both Kane and Cruz are reduced to puppets. The fatalism of both works is emphasized by the fact that the lives of the flamboyant protagonists are explored as pasts, or, in the case of Artemio Cruz, as a past relived as only an illusory future. The dying Cruz cannot modify the past except in his febrile imagination; the possibilities for self-recreation and self-transcendence are presented when it is really too late for Cruz to choose again, even if he decided to:

you will break the silence that night and will speak to Catalina asking her to forgive you; you will tell of those who have died for you to live and will ask her to accept you as you are ...

you will stay on with Lunero at the hacienda, you will never leave your place

you will stay with your teacher Sebastián, as he was, as he was, and will not go to join the revolution in the north. (p. 238)

Citizen Kane is also a fatalistic work, one that creates a false future similar to the one operating in *La muerte de Artemio Cruz*. As McBride points out, referring to the manner in which the life of Kane has been structured: "A system has been created in which all of Kane's actions are now in the past tense—and hence no longer of any effect. Welles' use of time counterpoints Kane's apparently powerful actions with the audience's foreknowledge that those actions will fail and that he will remain as he was shown at the beginning of the two hours: destroyed. The events of his life as we will see them exist in a limbo of moral futility."[14]

Film and novel evoke their respective protagonists from ironic perspectives—both as exalted potentates and as towering examples of self-destruction, they are finally brought down because of their intransigence and egomania. Kane is photographed in the company of the leaders of Europe; Kane is shown as the master of Xanadu, like the biblical Noah commanding that two of every kind of animal be brought to populate his island empire, his private universe. Yet each time that the self-deified Kane is presented, there occurs a change in point of view, that radically alters our impression of Kane by reducing him from puppetmaster to puppet. Many times the dynamic and exuberant Kane is presented as the apparent victor only to be mocked—by a remark of Leland, by an ironic juxtaposition, by a clumsy action, as when at a dedication ceremony he accidentally drops wet cement over his expensive coat or, most strikingly, by an abrupt change in perspective, as the camera angle changes in order suddenly to deflate Kane's image as conqueror. When Kane first appears at an election rally, he is already savoring his imminent victory as governor, with the path to the presidency seeming to open up before him. Yet Kane the man himself is dominated by a huge poster of himself, symbolizing the triumph of the mere hollow image over the man, the image that can be shattered just as quickly as it was inflated. As Kane pompously and self-righteously continues his speech, the camera pulls back to focus on the target of Kane's attacks—his opponent, Boss Jim Gettys, who, as Naremore points out, "stands high above the action, the stage viewed over his shoulder, so that he dominates the frame like a sinister power. It is Gettys who is truly in control of this campaign...."[15] Thus Welles provides a visual adumbration of the downfall of Kane even while the central action depicts him at the height of his power and glory.

Another swift undercutting of the imperious Kane comes when he arrogantly states to Susan as he stands in front of the monstrous fireplace at Xanadu, "This is our home, Susan." Yet the camera depicts a Kane who is just the opposite of the grandiose baron of Xanadu role that Kane wants to play. He is shown as a miniature, dwarfed by the immense logs in the fireplace, and his words seem to refer not only to Xanadu but to the mammoth flames of the fireplace—the hellworld that his own will has constructed for both Susan and himself.

A similar undercutting—both thematic and structural—of the imperiousness of Cruz appears repeatedly in Fuentes' novel. The prime mechanism through which the vaunted *I* is deflated is the second-person consciousness, which becomes stronger as the *I*-narrative becomes increasingly atomistic and incoherent, to indicate the disappearance of Cruz the rapacious *conquistador*. The power of the second-person voice over Cruz is indicated stylistically, by the lengthy, convoluted sentence structure, the phrases that pyramid over one another and seem to acquire a life of their own, while the *I*-narrative, which through Cruz's life has been the dominant voice, now lapses into incessant and sterile repetition. Cruz's subconsciousness at first links him, through a weird dream, with the *conquistador* Cortés. Like the arrogant Spanish *marqués* in the sixteenth century, Cruz emerges as the twentieth-century master of the New World. Yet this dream of Cruz's is a paradoxical one; it raises the vision of his grandeur and of his victory over men and over time, only to undercut the allusion by showing the conqueror conquered. The self-assurance of Cruz, who like the original *conquistadores* founds a personal empire on the blood of his victims, is emphasized through the use of an imperative future: "for you will have created night by closing your eyes, and from the bottom of that inky ocean there will sail toward you a stone ship that the noon sun, hot and drowsy, will comfort in vain: ship of thick blackened walls raised to defend the church against the attacks of pagan Indians and to unite the military and religious conquests.... You will advance down the nave to the conquest of your own New World" (p. 31).

Testimony to the careful way in which *La muerte de Artemio Cruz* has been structured is that this dream of conquest is given a chilling actualization within the third-person narrative of December 31, 1955, in which the omniscient author depicts Cruz's self-styled role of emperor of Coyoacán. Like the gods, Cruz attempts to score a victory over time, to gain immortality—but his victory is shown to be a spurious one. Cruz succeeds in preserving only a misshapen, soulless husk of a self, and is mocked by his guests as "la momia de Coyoacán." This final defeat has been adumbrated by Cruz's dream, in which the Conqueror, striding through the nave, seemingly invincible, is mocked by the idols that the Indian sculptors have placed within the church—hidden presences that they endow with Christian masks. Like the Spanish *conquistadores*, the arrogant Cruz too will be conquered from within. The impassive stone idols symbolize all-conquering death: "angels and saints with faces of the sun and moon, with harvest-protecting hands, with the index fingers of guide dogs, with the cruel, empty, useless eyes of idols and the rigorous lineaments of the cycles. Faces of stone behind kindly rose masks, ingenuous and impassive—dead, dead, dead" (p. 32).

Like Welles, Fuentes also uses structural devices to provide an ironic perspective on his protagonist. The Mexican author adroitly utilizes the cinematic technique of foreground and background action as he juxtaposes the silent figure of Cruz's wife Catalina, who is struggling with her conscience and against her temptation to submit physically to Cruz, with a backdrop that depicts the conqueror Cruz. The narration of June 23, 1924, skillfully interweaves the passivity of Catalina, mired in indecision and anguish, with the activity of Cruz, portrayed in the process of relentlessly destroying the power of the *hacendados*—not to establish a revolutionary system, as he pretends, but instead to build his own empire. This scene provides another example of the excellent fusing of theme and structure. The omniscient author time and again interrupts Catalina's brooding monologue and, through the use of flashbacks and spatial montage, records Cruz's rapid rise to provincial hegemony. Catalina's thoughts are repeatedly cut off by the action narrative depicting Cruz, just as her life has been suddenly and brutally interrupted by the bold and forceful Cruz. Yet the juxtaposition of Catalina and Cruz is an ironic one, for although Cruz masterfully dominates the old aristocratic order and eliminates all his enemies, this solitary and seemingly fragile woman who nevertheless possesses an intense will successfully resists him, allowing only her body to be surrendered. The ending of the scene shows the conqueror once again conquered—forced to take an Indian girl as mistress.

The great and lasting appeal of *Citizen Kane* and *La muerte de Artemio Cruz* is that both film and novel are total creations, traditional and experimental, historical and mythic, epic in that they capture the spirit of whole countries, lyric in their sensitive portrayal of the inner worlds of the protagonists. Both works are highly structured, perhaps even over-structured, and yet both are open creations in their central ambiguity and in the unresolved problems that they pose. Both combine action and conquest with philosophical concerns, as each probes the metaphysical problems of time, memory, death, and immortality. Both represent a dramatic break with the previous history of their respective genres. As Cowie states, referring to the expert craftsmanship of *Citizen Kane*: "... *Citizen Kane* marked much more than the bright spark of a new decade, and it is tempting and justifiable to divide cinema history into the pre-1940 and post-1940 periods. The gangster films, comedies and Westerns of the Thirties had all established an elaborate iconography of their own. But dialogue and situation took precedence over style and expression."[16]

La muerte de Artemio Cruz is an eclectic work of art, expertly combining the novel of character, plot, and action with the narrative of innerness, as it deftly explores the consciousness and even the subconscious mind—and the collective unconsciousness—of its protagonist. *La muerte de Artemio Cruz* pays homage to the novel of the Mexican Revolution—to Azuela's *Los de abajo* and *Andrés Pérez, maderista*, to Guzmán's *La sombra del caudillo*, while at the same time going beyond these classic works of Mexican literature to explore psychological and metaphysical dimensions, and to experiment with language and style, particularly in the second-person narrative.

These two masterful creations are epic in scope, tracing the destinies of both a character and a country. Both are striking examples of a stylistic *tour de force* and yet neither is dated; both are open creations that are as relevant to the 1980s as they were to the times when they were created. The variations in mood, tone, and style found in *Citizen Kane* are emphasized by Gottesman: "How, for instance, do the mysterious, impressionistic, dreamlike qualities of the opening sequence relate to the factual, objective, realistic characteristics of the newsreel? What are the functions of the magical invocation and the documentary capsule?"[17] Similarly, *La muerte de Artemio Cruz* encompasses a tremendous range of styles, tempos, and tones: eloquent and halting, declamatory and implorative, denunciatory and exalting. The crisp, factual, historical narrative containing description and dialogue that characterizes the third-person segments contrasts markedly with the associational, highly emotionalized welter of images in Cruz's first-person monologue, and also with the dense, overwrought, at times surrealistic vision presented by the second-person voice: "Chorus, sepulcher, voices, pyre: and you will imagine in the forgotten region of consciousness the rites, the ceremonies, the endings: burial, cremation, embalming: exposed upon the height of a tower, so that it be not the earth, but the air itself will rot you; sealed in the tomb with your dead slaves; wailed by hired mourners; buried with your most valuable possessions, your company, your black jewels: death watch, vigil" (p. 240).

Another significant parallel between *Citizen Kane* and *La muerte de Artemio Cruz* is their extreme intensity. In both film and novel, every scene, every character, every incident serves to reflect, to illuminate—or to problematize—the life of the protagonist. Fuentes has characterized himself as "a putter-inner, not a taker-outer."[18] The reader of this highly intricate, baroque narrative is at times overpowered by the dazzling display of images. The supercharged quality of Welles' style and the techniques used to achieve that intensity are analyzed by Naremore:

> The short focal-length of the lens enables him to express the psychology of his characters, to comment on the relationship between character and environment, and also to create a sense of barely contained, almost manic energy, as if the camera, like one of his heroes, were overreaching.
>
> This highly charged, nervous dynamism of imagery and action can be found everywhere in *Kane*, and is produced by other techniques besides photography. Fairly often Welles will stage important moments of his story against some counterpointing piece of business, as if he were trying to energize the plot by throwing as much material as possible onto the screen.[19]

Both novel and film are expansive in their sweep of time and history and intensive in their probing into the hidden lives of their respective protagonists. *Citizen Kane* has been characterized by Higham as "a work of confidence and excess, as bold as a fresco, and it reminds one again that the cinema has continued a nineteenth century fiction tradition of size and grandeur when the novel (in English at least) has largely shrunk to the trivial."[20] There is little doubt that *La muerte de Artemio Cruz* is also a work "of confidence and excess" and that Carlos Fuentes has done more than any other Latin American novelist and perhaps even any other novelist in the world writing today to restore the novel to the prodigious stature that it maintained in the nineteenth century, when its scope encompassed generations of families and the portrayal of entire societies.

Another aspect that both works have in common is the significant role that is given to the viewer/reader, who can no longer remain a mere passive recipient of verbal and visual images, but is given the freedom to put together the fragments of the protagonists' lives and to render his or her own value judgment. The reader/viewer is compelled to be active, to bring order to chaos, to synthesize the myriad perspectives and to come to grips with the problematic nature of the two protagonists. In attempting to discover unifying factors to the works, the reader/viewer duplicates the attempts of the dying Cruz to find a transcendental meaning to his life and those of the reporter Thompson to discover the true meaning of the paradox that is Charles Foster Kane. Does *Citizen Kane* condemn or ultimately vindicate its protagonist? Critics are divided in their opinions. Although some see in the film a strong indictment of American materialism and of the power of the

media, others see it as lauding Kane. As Crowther states unequivocally: "...
at no point in the picture is a black mark actually checked against Kane. Not
a shred of evidence is presented to indicate absolutely that he is a social
scoundrel. As a matter of fact, there is no reason to assume from what is
shown on the screen that he is anything but an honest publisher with a
consistently conscientious attitude toward society."[21] In his final evaluation
of Kane, Higham is reluctant to assume the role of what Julio Cortázar
would describe as the *lector cómplice* collaborating with the artist in
completing the creative endeavor: "One is left only with the wish that Welles
had drawn his own conclusions about this friend of the working man, the
Jeffersonian, the fascist, the master of empires, instead of leaving us with an
enigma as baffling as a great stone Easter Island face."[22]

We might ask as well, is the paradoxical hero of Fuentes' novel to be
condemned or exonerated? Although both Fuentes and Welles are moralists,
and both subject the lives of their protagonists to relentless scrutiny, neither
is didactic. Cruz and Kane are evoked with a mixture of damnation and
reverence. The lives of both protagonists confound easy moral judgment,
particularly when the persons surrounding them—the lackey Bernstein, the
dissipated and senile Leland, the shrill and shrewish Susan Alexander in
Citizen Kane; and the sycophantic Padilla, the acidulous Teresa, the grasping
Catalina, and the cold-blooded Don Gamaliel in *La muerte de Artemio
Cruz*—are portrayed as far less sympathetic characters than either Kane or
Cruz. Although in one episode Cruz appears as the coward and traitor,
deserting his men, leaving them to die on the battlefield, in another scene he
is a bold and courageous hero, riding straight into the enemy and scoring a
victory over them. In one encounter a crude and blatant opportunist, in the
next he is evoked as cultured and sensitive, questing for an ideal and a
genuine love with Laura. Unlike the fawning, hypocritical Catalina and
Teresa, who sanctimoniously attend to him and whose feeble attempts at
reconciliation serve only as a shabby mask of their avarice, Cruz remains
defiant, unapologetic, and brazenly impenitent. His greed is coupled with a
bold lust for life that the dour, crabbed women in their petty miserliness can
never understand. They will reap the material benefits of his wealth but are
deprived of Cruz's capacity to enjoy it—the sensualism that even in his final
hours he continues to exult in.

Like the release of *Citizen Kane*, the publication of *La muerte de Artemio
Cruz* at first confounded many tradition-minded critics, who praised the
third-person action segments of the narrative because they could readily
understand them and who even wished that Fuentes had written the entire
novel from this orthodox perspective, so characteristic of the novels of the
Mexican Revolution. Ironically, the intricate second-person narrative, a

paradoxical form that contributes so much toward making Cruz a three-dimensional person, initially received a markedly negative response from several critics who were confounded by its excesses. Yet with its breathtakingly expansive scope that incorporates not only the conscience of a character and a nation but a universal consciousness, from genesis to the apocalypse, a theme that Fuentes later developed masterfully in *Terra Nostra*, the second-person narrative is the most original—and the most profound—aspect of the novel.

No comparison between *La muerte de Artemio Cruz* and *Citizen Kane* would be complete without consideration of the respective geniuses behind each of these creations. The similarities between Welles and Fuentes are striking: both are intense, explosive talents; both tackle projects that other creative artists shy away from. Actor, writer, director, Welles has done movie versions of Shakespeare's *Macbeth* and *Henry IV*, Kafka's *The Trial*, and Tarkington's *The Magnificent Ambersons*. Novelist, essayist, dramatist, film reviewer and script writer, diplomat, and teacher, Fuentes too demonstrates a remarkable range of talents. Tightly condensed short stories of the fantastic and the macabre like Aura are followed by mammoth displays of history, philosophy, visual art, and theology such as are found in Cambio de pie] and in Fuentes' eight-hundred page work *Terra Nostra*. Hermetic, metaphysical works like *Cumpleaños* are succeeded by dazzling spy thrillers like *La cabeza de la hidra*. In works such as *La región más transparente*, Fuentes boldly attempts to portray not only the totality of modern Mexico—all social classes, from *los de abajo* to the remnants of the Porfirian elite, but also to encapsulate the whole of Mexican history, from the Aztec epoch to the present, in a display of imaginative power that has no equal in Mexican letters. And in *Terra Nostra* Fuentes' imaginative constructions are even more dazzling—whole civilizations, the Rome of Tiberius, the Spain of the Hapsburgs, the New World from its cosmogony to its apocalypse. The *cambio de piel* motif, a central one in Fuentes' works, characterizes the artist himself. Like Welles, Fuentes has an extraordinary capacity for self-transformation and self-renewal.

In addition to being consummate artists, both Fuentes and Welles are masterful showmen as well. Both love to dazzle and to *confound* their audiences, as Welles did in his electrifying radio broadcast on the Martian invasion of America. Both are bold experimenters. Both artists display eclectic tastes; both are fond of dialectic, of constant thesis and antithesis that result in a compelling tension and a marked ambiguity in their works. The remark of Johnson, commenting on the use of opposites in Welles' work, can also apply to that of Fuentes: "The struggle between tradition and progress, old and new, order and disorder, is one of the most powerful forces behind

Welles' work. It is reflected in his American background and his love of Europe, and in his filmmaking that embraces both Shakespeare and modern American thrillers."[23]

There is no more fitting way to conclude our presentation than to quote a director who, like Orson Welles, is a master of the cinema: François Truffaut. Like Fuentes, Truffaut was also greatly influenced by *Citizen Kane*, and the French director's eloquent summation of the film can be applied almost verbatim to *La muerte de Artemio Cruz*:

> We loved this film because it was complete: psychological, social, poetic, dramatic, comic, baroque, strict, and dramatic. It is a demonstration of the force of power and an attack on the force of power, it is a hymn to youth and a meditation on old age, an essay on the vanity of all material ambition and at the same time a poem on old age and the solitude of exceptional human beings, genius or monster or monstrous genius.[21]

NOTES

1. Alfred MacAdam and Alexander Coleman, "An Interview with Carlos Fuentes," *Book Forum*, 4, no. 4 (1979): 680–681.

2. James Naremore, *The Magic World of Orson Welles* (New York: Oxford University Press, 1978), p. 83.

3. "RKO Cutting Continuity of the Orson Welles Production, *Citizen Kane*," in *The Citizen Kane Book* (Boston: Little, Brown and Company, 1971), p. 312. Subsequent references are included in the text, preceded by CC.

4. Orson Welles, "Citizen Kane Is Not about Louella Parsons' Boss," in *Focus on Citizen Kane*, ed. Ronald Gottesman (Englewood Cliffs, N.J.: Prentice Hall, 1971), p. 68. This article was originally published in *Friday 2*, February 14, 1941, p. 9.

5. Roy A. Fowler, "*Citizen Kane*: Background and a Critique," in *Focus on Citizen Kane*, p. 88.

6. Interview with Welles conducted by Juan Cobos and Miguel Rubio, "Welles and Falstaff," *Sight and Sound*, 35 (Autumn 1966): 158–163. For an extensive examination of the theme of lost paradise in Fuentes' novel, see Lanin A. Gyurko, "Self-Renewal and Death in Fuentes' *La muerte de Artemio Cruz*," *Revista de Letras* (São Paulo), 15 (1973): 59–80.

7. Although citations are to the Sam Hileman translation, *The Death of Artemio Cruz*, occasional additions by the author are enclosed in brackets.

8. Naremore, *Magic World*, p. 94.

9. Robert Humphrey, *Stream of Consciousness in the Modern Novel* (Berkeley: University of California Press, 1965), p. 67.

10. Joseph McBride, *Orson Welles* (London: Secker and Warburg, 1972, p. 50.

11. William Johnson, "Orson Welles: Of Time and Loss," in *Focus on Citizen Kane*, p. 26.

12. Naremore, *Magic World*, p. 43.

13. Ibid., p. 50.

14. McBride, *Orson Welles*, p. 37.

15. Naremore, *Magic World*, p. 86.

16. Peter Cowie, *A Ribbon of Dreams: The Cinema of Orson Welles* (New York: A. S. Barnes and Company, 1973), p. 20.

17. Ronald Gottesman, "*Citizen Kane*: Past, Present, and Future," Introduction to *Focus on Citizen Kane*, p. 6.

18. Interview with Fuentes conducted by Emir Rodríguez Monegal, in *Homenaje a Carlos Fuentes*, ed. Helmy F. Giacomán (New York: Las Américas, 1971), p. 43.

19. Naremore, *Magic World*, p. 50.

20. Charles Higham, *The Films of Orson Welles* (Berkeley: University of California Press, 1974 p. 46.

21. Bosley Crowther, review of *Citizen Kane*, *New York Times*, May 4, 1941, in *Focus on Citizen Kane*, p. 50.

22. Higham, *Films of Orson Welles*, p. 24.

23. Johnson, "Orson Welles," p. 32.

24. François Truffaut, "Citizen Kane," trans. Mark Bernheim and Ronald Gottesman, in *Focus on Citizen Kane*, p. 130. The original article was published in *L'Express* (November 26, 1959).

WENDY B. FARIS

Fragmenting Forces in the Revolution and the Self: The Death of Artemio Cruz

The Death of Artemio Cruz (1962) is Fuentes's best-known novel, an acknowledged masterpiece in the boom of recent Latin American fiction. The book focuses on the experiences of one man, but through them it portrays the dynamics of the Mexican Revolution of 1910–1920 and of Mexican society in succeeding years. The memories of Artemio Cruz on his deathbed form a meditation on his past life and his accomplishments. In parallel fashion, the novel as a whole reflects back on the Revolution and its aftermath. Cruz uses his memory to fight against death; the book might be said to fight for memory of the original ideals of the Mexican Revolution, forgotten and betrayed in later years. The novel is a successful portrait of both the man and Mexican society because it reveals the progressive fragmentation of both.[1] Artemio Cruz has become splintered; he is now several different selves. He speaks in multiple voices which appear on the pages as separate sections of text. These voices correspond, on the personal level, to the conflicting factions in the Revolution and in contemporary Mexico.

The book reveals a continual interplay of historical and individual forces. The brutality of the Revolution mirrors Cruz's brutality in business and personal affairs. Sometimes it seems as if the cruelty Cruz experienced as a boy and during the fighting in the Revolution explains his later ruthless

From *Carlos Fuentes*. © 1983 by Frederick Ungar Publishing Co.

behavior. At other times we wonder whether the Revolution might have achieved more lasting success if it had brought to power better men than Artemio Cruz. In short, is Cruz brutalized by society and the Revolution, or does he corrupt them?[2] Contemplating Cruz, the reader remains suspended between sympathy and condemnation.

The Death of Artemio Cruz, published four years after Where the Air is Clear, condenses and intensifies the panorama of Mexican society in the earlier novel. The past pervades both texts. Progressive discovery of Artemio Cruz's personal past structures his story, and the Revolution provides the dominant historical presence in the novel. Memories of the Revolution are thus joined to the ancient—the "prehistorical"—Aztec traditions that show through the portrait of modern Mexico City in Where the Air is Clear. The three voices within Artemio Cruz correspond structurally to the many separate voices of the city in Where the Air is Clear. Whereas in the earlier novel, Fuentes weaves elaborate and often surprising connections between inhabitants of Mexico City, in The Death of Artemio Cruz and in The Good Conscience he stresses the divisions within one character. Where the Air is Clear constitutes a more polemical and explicit investigation of the Mexican national character than does The Death of Artemio Cruz, which represents a stocktaking, a confirmation of existing traits. Many of the central figures in Where the Air is Clear are quite young; we see them in the process of becoming. Artemio Cruz, on the other hand, approaches the end of his life, and we see what he has become.

CENTRAL EVENTS AND IMAGES

Just before the novel opens, Artemio Cruz has made a trip to keep intact a vast chain of graft. On his return to Mexico City, he collapses. From the beginning of the novel, he languishes in bed, surrounded by his family, thinking and remembering. In occasional counterpoint to Cruz's thoughts, a tape recorder plays back conversations with officials of American firms for which Cruz has served as a Mexican "front man." We hear of bribes, the suppression of riots, intimidation of the press, plans for American intervention in Mexico's commercial and political affairs. This background suggests what Cruz's life has become by 1959. Memories of his earlier life unfold against this setting in twelve sections. Cruz narrates these twelve sections in the third person, referring to himself as Artemio Cruz. Each of these sections is accompanied by a monologue in the first person and another monologue in the second person. The sections range backward and forward in time; if we straighten out the chronology, Cruz's story unfolds in the following manner.

Artemio Cruz is the illegitimate son of a plantation owner and a mulatto servant. He grows up in the country and joins the Mexican Revolution on the side of the rebels. In 1913, Federal troops kill all the Indians in one village, including Regina, Artemio's first love. One day in 1915, he is captured by a revolutionary force opposed to his own. That day he witnesses the execution of a fellow prisoner, Gonzalo Bernal. Sometime before Bernal is shot, Cruz left their common cell to bargain for his own safety. It is unclear whether or not he could have helped Bernal by remaining with him. Perhaps he would only have died as well. But Cruz will later feel guilty about having abandoned Bernal.

Cruz escapes, and in 1919, when the fighting is over, he gains entrance into the Bernal household by claiming that he was at Gonzalo's side when he died and that Gonzalo asked him to go see his family. His plan is to woo Bernal's sister Catalina, ingratiate himself with their father, and take over the hacienda. Old Bernal, deeply in debt, can no longer run the hacienda and tells Catalina she should marry Cruz so that he will save them from ruin. Catalina resists at first. She loves someone else, she resents Artemio's opportunism, and she does not believe his story about her brother. But she succumbs in the end to her father's wishes and to her own sensual attraction to Cruz, an attraction she herself does not fully understand.

Cruz steadily gains control of more and more land and wealth. Elected a federal deputy, he consolidates his financial empire through corrupt deals with American businesses. Catalina Cruz bears two children, Lorenzo and Teresa, and the family moves to Mexico City. Catalina's father dies. In 1939, Lorenzo is killed fighting with the international brigades for the Republican side in the Spanish Civil War. All this time, Catalina continues to resent Artemio and he turns to a series of mistresses.

This sequence of events is punctuated by a complementary structure of images that accents central moments and ideas. Mirrors, for example, appear throughout Cruz's story. He looks in one as he enters his office building, as he shaves in a hotel room in Acapulco, as he comes downstairs in his house. This succession of mirrors provides an emblem for the narrative that contains them. Cruz is doubled in mirrors as he is multiplied by the various voices of memory which record his past.[3] Mirrors also provide moments of reflection in a life of action. Generally, Cruz dislikes seeing his reflection, but is drawn to study it just the same. We sense a simultaneous desire and reluctance to know himself. Or perhaps Cruz dislikes the mirror's reflection of a single, aged, physical self—not the numerous possible selves of the imagination. This defeat of the imagination characterizes Cruz's memory of the moment before he lapses into his mortal illness. He sees himself reflected in the glass top of his desk, and he thinks: The "twin in the glass will join the other, who is yourself, join the seventy-one-year-old old man."[4] Mirrors stifle him and remind him of his age: "I am not old although once in a mirror I was old" (136). He is attracted to his image when he can concentrate on the "green eyes and energetic mouth"—both youthful and, strong. But he is repelled by the sight of his own false teeth and turns away from the mirror to insert them (142).

His green eyes are another recurring image. They recall Artemio's Spanish heritage, suggesting aristocratic pride, power, dominance over others. They also reveal inherent force, liveliness, charisma, and sensuality. Catalina gasps when she first sees him: "Dear God, how can I help but respond to such strength, to the force in those green eyes?" (96). Moreover, Artemio's father had green eyes, as did his son Lorenzo. They suggest, then, the importance of personal heritage, just as Artemio's long meditation on Mexico will stress the significance of a national heritage.

THE REVOLUTION—AND AFTER: HISTORY AND THE LAND

From the novel's central focus on the conflicts within Cruz, the reader moves outward to the conflicts that divide Mexican society as a whole, and particularly to the problems posed by the Mexican Revolution. Fuentes has compressed about one hundred fifty years of Mexican history into the novel. As in Cruz's personal story, so in this historical panorama of Mexico the narrative digs back and back in search of origins. Throughout the book, the presentation of historical events follows two principles: the repetition of important moments of conflict and the revelation of persistent social patterns, though the people who embody those patterns may change. What's more, Cruz's individual life fits into an ancient mythic pattern as well as into these historical events, for he gives a New Year's party, symbolically closing his life, 52 years after he sets out on his own from Cocuya. (Aztec time was divided into cycles of 52 years each.) Here, as in the rest of Fuentes's work, mythic structures persist, but their contents are significantly modified by history.

Through the figure of Artemio Cruz's paternal grandmother, old Ludivinia Menchaca, the historical narrative may be said to begin in 1810, for she was "born in the year of the first Revolution, brought into the world behind doors battered by terror" (264). The first Revolution, the war of independence from Spain, begins a process that will lead to the next one, a hundred years after. Ludivinia Menchaca represents the old order, the landed aristocracy, which resisted reform movements even back in the middle of the nineteenth century. Artemio Cruz is born on her family's land, but denied its heritage. He goes off to fight in the Revolution against the order upheld by families like the Menchacas and finally ends up in virtually the same position as his grandmother, denying a voice to later revolutionaries.[5]

The figure of Miss Rosa in Faulkner's *Absalom, Absalom!*, who walls herself up in her house after the destruction of the Civil War, would seem to be a precursor of Ludivinia Menchaca, who does just the same after the mid-nineteenth-century struggles in Mexico. Ludivinia's room "was hot and musty and smelled of the tropics," a "nest of closed-in smells" (281); Miss Rosa's room was "a dim hot airless room all closed and fastened for forty-three summers." The two women even speak in much the same way: a sharp "yes" or "no" at the start of a paragraph, a list of rhetorical questions, a repetitive style.

Ludivinia's vision of "the green-eyed child," Artemio Cruz, outside her window, forms the link between the tumultuous period she lived through and the later Revolution. In between came the years of the dictator Porfirio Díaz. Díaz originally rose to power when he opposed the reelection of the former president, Benito Juárez, in 1870. In order to strengthen Mexico financially, the Díaz regime allowed many foreign concessions to enter Mexico, gave away huge properties made up of land taken from the Indians, denied freedom to the press.

The second Revolution began in 1910 when Francisco Madero opposed the reelection of Díaz. His sympathy for land reform gained him the support of the *campesinos* and their leaders, Pancho Villa and Emiliano Zapata. Madero became president in 1911, but his government was weakened by continued fighting and agitation for land reforms it failed to carry out. As a result of the general confusion, Victoriano Huerta took over in 1913 and Madero was killed by Huerta's forces. These acts provoked Venustiano Carranza and Alvaro Obregón to rise against Huerta and to uphold the original constitution against Huerta's politics of personal power. Carranza and Obregón were supported intermittently by the forces under Villa and Zapata.

In 1913, when we first see Artemio Cruz in the Revolution, he is fighting with the forces of Carranza against Huerta. By the day in 1915 when Gonzalo Bernal is shot, Villa and Carranza have quarreled, Villa has been defeated by Carranza's ally Obregón, and Villa's forces are in retreat. These Villistas capture Bernal and Cruz just before Carranza's forces catch up with them. When they are still in their cell, Bernal says that "as soon as Zapata and Villa are eliminated, only two caudillos [chiefs] will remain, your present leaders" (Carranza and Obregón). He asks Cruz, "Which one will you follow?" Cruz replies that "my leader is General Obregón" (188). This is the first of Cruz's fortunate alliances, for in 1920 Obregón overthrows Carranza, who is killed, and becomes president.

Fuentes suggests that early in the Revolution, leaders concentrated too much on ideas and ignored practical concerns: "the general found the best policy was to take immediately what money there was from the wealthy ... and to leave to the final triumph of the Revolution the details of the land and workaday reforms. Now they had to get to Mexico City and chase the drunkard Huerta, the murderer of Don Panchito Madero, out of the presidency" (65). But as the story of the Bernal hacienda will reveal, these "details of the land and workaday reforms" are essential to the common people. Later on in the Revolution, the power struggle between different leaders and their factions diffused the earlier strength of revolutionary reform. In the beginning, the Revolution passed through the pueblos cancelling the peasants' debts and releasing political prisoners. But "the purpose today is to glorify leaders" now that "the men who believed the Revolution's purpose was to liberate the people have been eliminated" (186).

In addition to a survey of Mexican history, Fuentes provides vignettes which evoke the natural scenery and the artistic traditions of Mexico. Though Cruz is confined to his room in Mexico City, his mind covers the country in reverie. One section of narration constitutes a kind of hymn to Mexico, the land and its traditions. This is the really valuable inheritance Artemio Cruz's family will receive, not the money they are so eagerly waiting for. It is also Cruz's own heritage:

> Remember this country? You remember it. It is not one; there are a thousand countries, with a single name. You know that. You will carry with you the red deserts, the hills of prickly pear and maguey, the world of dry cactus, the lava belt of frozen craters, the walls of golden domes and rock thrones, the limestone and sandstone cities, the texontle-stone cities, the adobe pueblos ... the Veracruz combs, the Mixtec braids, Tzotil belts ... you will inherit the land.... (266–68)

But Artemio Cruz knows that he has not added to this heritage. He curses himself. "You will bequeath the futile dead names ... men despoiled of their names that you might possess yours...." (269). In an attempt to create a personal setting appropriate for this national heritage, a kind of return to the cultural past, Cruz has decorated his mansion with Mexican antiques. He clings to the memory of these possessions as he lies dying. The novel's description of the mansion (pp. 242–43, 249) forms an ironic parallel to the earlier description of an elaborate church from the colonial period (p. 31). That church represents the real artistic heritage of

Mexico. It endures in spite of men like Artemio Cruz and their pseudo-antique house's.

SOCIAL CRITICISM

The betrayal of the Revolution by Artemio Cruz calls forth Fuentes's own revolutionary perspective. Four specific failings of post-revolutionary Mexican society recur throughout *The Death of Artemio Cruz*: class domination, Americanization, financial corruption, and the failure of land reform.[6]

A cluster of details at the start of the novel sets the critical tone. Here Cruz rides to his office in his limousine as his wife and daughter enter a shop:

> The chauffeur was sweating in the heat of the sun and could not turn on the radio. He [Cruz], in back, reflected that he had not done badly in associating himself with the Colombian coffee-growers when the war in Africa began, and the two women entered the shop and the shop-girl asked them please to be seated while she advised the proprietress (for she knew who they were, this mother and daughter, and her instructions were to inform the proprietress the moment they entered). (13–14)

As in *Where the Air is Clear*, here the comfort of the rich who work in skyscrapers and ride in cars contrasts with the discomfort of the poor who either drive them or walk. Furthermore, there are parallels between this scene and the next one. As we switch scenes, we do not hear about Cruz's feelings for his wife or daughter or any conversation between the two women, but instead the detail about the proprietress hurrying to greet them. As Catalina and Teresa enter the shop, Teresa registers a feeling of despair as she is indoctrinated into this hierarchy of dominance by her mother, who motions to her not to make room on the sofa for the saleswoman to sit down with them.

A little farther on, another transition between Artemio Cruz's activities and those of his wife and daughter again provides a socially critical detail (and another mirror image):

> Cruz moved toward the revolving door ... he saw a man identical to himself, wearing the same double-breasted suit, but colorless, ... a man surrounded by beggars, who let his hand drop at the same instant he in the vestibule did.

> Again the outstretched hands of beggars disheartened her, and
> she squeezed her daughter's shoulder to hurry her into the
> artificial coolness and the scent of soaps and cosmetics ... she
> asked for a jar of "theatrical" cold cream and two lipsticks.... (17)

The beggars are noticed in passing—a flash in a revolving door, a glimpse of
hands outside a drugstore/restaurant. The images form only small intrusions
in the story. That is part of the problem: the rich and powerful Cruz family,
and even we readers who follow their thoughts and actions, pass by people
suffering social oppression—chauffeurs, saleswomen, beggars. We are all on
the way to something more "important." For Cruz, it is a meeting with
American geologists and financiers; for the women it is the buying of
cosmetics and the eating of nut waffles and orange juice.

The counterpoint of these two scenes also underlines the second point
of social criticism in the novel. This is the domination of Mexican finances
and natural resources by North American business, and the concomitant
aping of American culture in Mexico.[7] As Catalina and Teresa eat their
North American raisin bread and waffles with syrup, they carry on a long
dispute about how to pronounce the last name of Joan Crawford. They get
it wrong of course, and to pile irony on irony, their food is served during the
discussion by a waitress in a Mexican folkloric costume. This costume is
designed to appeal primarily to the American tourists who eat at the exclusive
Sanborn's and to Mexicans who imitate them. For Fuentes, "The great
cultural farce has consisted in disguising the past and presenting it clad in the
bright colors of folklore."[8] Meanwhile, back at his office, Cruz is extracting
a two-million-peso bribe from the Americans so that he will be their
"figurehead" for the exploitation of Mexican sulphur domes. Waffles served
by a waitress in a Mexican costume parallel American interests filtered
through a Mexican front man. Neither activity represents a true appreciation
of Mexican culture or economics. Artemio Cruz is actually a denial of the
popular idea that the Revolution has made Mexicans proud to be Mexican.
After remembering the scene where he obtained a larger bribe than the
Americans would like to have given him, he reflects that he is particularly
satisfied to have imposed his will on them because he regrets "the
geographical error that has prevented [him] from being one of them." Cruz
admires the efficiency and comfort of the United States and finds
"intolerable the incompetence, misery, dirt, the weakness and nakedness of
this impoverished country that has nothing" (28).

The third point of criticism, financial corruption, is well illustrated by
the example of Cruz receiving his bribe. That is only one of many such
frauds. The fourth problem, the lack of meaningful land reform, appears as

Artemio Cruz takes over the hacienda of his father-in-law, old Gamaliel Bernal. He does not give the peasants land, as they had been promised. Instead, Cruz drives off the smaller landowners, consolidating the surrounding land into an even larger unit than before. He then sells it off to farmers in exchange for urban lots he knows will increase in value. The farmers will not operate large enough haciendas to support the peasants in the area, who will then be forced to leave the land, since they own none themselves. Ironically, after all of this, Artemio Cruz is nominated for Federal Deputy in recognition of his efforts on behalf of agrarian reform.

PRIVATE POWER

We shall soon see how Fuentes represents memory as power, how Cruz's memory triumphs (temporarily at least) over his surroundings. The text that he narrates is perhaps his final attempt to dominate before he is definitively conquered by death. But besides this, struggles for power pervade the individual and social relations within the novel.[9] To move beyond Cruz himself is to notice that the hunger for power everywhere disrupts both public and private domains, both society and marriage. The original impetus of the Revolution was fragmented, its spirit weakened by the power struggles of its generals. In the political life that has followed the Revolution, this disruptive desire for power persists.

Private power struggles, fragmenting and disintegrating intimate relationships, are most fully developed in the "war between the sexes" that rages between Artemio and Catalina Cruz. Here again, Cruz's origins are significant. Ludivinia recalls that the boy's mother had been chased away by his natural father, Atanasio (296). Cruz continues this pattern of dominance in his own marriage. When he first meets Catalina, he wonders, "Did she feel the assertion of possession that he scarcely disguised?" (36–37). Catalina herself is divided between nights of passion and days of hatred. She, too, sees the relationship as strife: "At night you conquer me, but I defeat you during the day" (97). And she reflects that they have both lost "the dream, the innocence" of their lives (107). But Catalina says this to herself, not to Artemio. Her understanding of the situation remains inside her; it does not begin to bridge the gap between them. Similarly, Artemio does not dare to say the words that he believes might enable them "to forget and begin anew": "Don't hate me. Have compassion for me, beloved Catalina. For I love you. Weigh my guilt against my love and you will see that my love is the greater" (107). If this appeal were to fail—as well it might, given Catalina's attitude— he would have shown weakness, lost ground in the power struggle.

This tension between Artemio and Catalina is only one manifestation of the continual play of opposite forces in the novel. Like Artemio Cruz, who is divided between past and present, body and mind, lover and dominator, husband and father, brutality and tenderness, Mexico is divided between "sons of bitches and poor bastards," rich and poor, Spanish and Indian heritages, modern buildings and ancient rituals, women and men, revolutionary ideals and everyday problems. Compressed into the mind of one man, as he lies dying, these divisions take on urgency and universal significance.

The Self: "Memory Is Desire Satisfied"

The situation which the reader confronts on the first page of the novel, when he learns that Artemio Cruz is on his deathbed, shapes the story that follows. The title is also a directive: before we open the book, we know that Cruz will die. From this the events draw psychological urgency, since we sense that the narrator does not have "all the time in the world." Much of what we hear is a kind of "return of the repressed" before it is too late. Though Cruz is not a practicing Catholic, he has grown up in a country where final confessions are traditional. We might regard this book, then, as a final confession in a nontraditional mode, where the reader, not the priest, will condemn or absolve Cruz.

This certain approach of death at the end of the novel permits memory freedom of action within a closed form. Emotional recollection, not logical chronology, orders the events. We go back and forth in time, searching with Cruz for some kind of truth about him.[10] This process is highlighted by the fact that we see his origins, his birth, only near the end of the book.[11] The element of suspense is projected toward the past, rather than toward the future. The consequent closeness of birth and death warns us about the shortness of all human life and the necessity of choosing our actions well.

The very fact that he can recall the events of his past is a satisfaction to Artemio Cruz. For Cruz has divided himself in order to survive; he has cut out of his everyday existence most of his emotion for Catalina, his despair at Regina's and Lorenzo's deaths, his disappointment at losing Laura—a woman with whom he had a serious love affair, perhaps even his own fear of death. But, as he says, keeping up a proud exterior forever is killing: "Pride. Pride saves us. Pride kills us" (195). So that, now, he is glad that memory can revive these emotional experiences. They help him "survive" spiritually his own coldness and postpone the literal coldness of death. This is the sense in which "memory is desire satisfied: / and with memory you will survive, before it becomes too late / before chaos prevents memory" (58). Duplicating the self in memory's narrative thus conquers, for a time, the reflections of the body, in mirrors. But the triumph of memory is not eternal; the chaos that threatens it is death.

NARRATIVE TECHNIQUE

This confrontation between memory and death continues throughout the novel. It motivates the most striking aspect of *The Death of Artemio Cruz*— the division of the text into three different modes of narration, and three different verb tenses. The interest of the novel depends to a large extent on the carefully orchestrated interplay between the different voices of Cruz. Fuentes's formal innovation succeeds particularly well here because narrative strategies correspond to psychological configurations.

Except for occasional intrusions from Catalina's thoughts, and a chapter recounting Lorenzo's experiences in Spain, Artemio Cruz narrates the entire book. His sickness and imminent death are recounted in the first person and the present tense, his meditations and desires in the second person and the future tense, and the events of his past life in the third person and the past tense. While the persons and tenses of the voices are clear, the perspectives of the voices elude exact description, for they share many images and ideas. They are often categorized as three distinct parts of the mind: consciousness, the subconscious, and memory.[12] Fuentes has explained that in addition to Cruz's first and third person voices,

> there is a third element, the subconscious, a kind of Virgil that guides [Cruz] through the twelve circles of his hell, and that is the other face of his minor, the other face of Artemio Cruz: the You that speaks in the future tense. It is the subconscious that clings to a future that the I—the dying old man—will never know. The old I is the present while the He digs up the past of Artemio Cruz. It's a question of a dialogue of mirrors between the three people, the three times that constitute the life of this hard and alienated character. In his agony, Artemio tries to regain through memory his twelve definitive days, days which are really twelve options.[13]

The use of these three different voices permits the juxtaposition of different scenes, figures, and images. They demonstrate the coexistence of Cruz's separate selves immediately, from the inside. For instance, in a first person sequence—in Cruz's room—Cruz sees Catalina and Teresa rummage first through his suits, and then through his shoes, in search of his will. Cruz greatly enjoys their ridiculous physical—and moral—position. "To see those two women on all fours among the scattered suits, their wide buttocks elevated, their cheeks fluttering with an obscene panting, fumbling through my shoes. Bitter sweetness closes my eyes. I raise my hand to my heart and close my eyes. 'Regina ...'" (157). The contrast between Regina's disinterested love, narrated earlier in the past tense and evoked later in the future tense and the present greed of Cruz's wife and daughter is clear and forceful.

The first voice the reader meets is the *I* of Artemio Cruz dying; it concentrates on the unpleasant physical sensations he experiences: "My stomach ... ah! ... and my chest continues sleeping with the same dull tick-tick-tick that taps in my wrists ... I—am—body, I" (5). These unpleasant sensations provide the impetus to escape the physical present and take flight through his other voices. Memory is power for him now. The motivation is made explicit early on. At one point, for example, Cruz's eyes feel like, lead, and after "another injection," he asks himself, "But why?" and continues, "No, no, let me think of something else, quick, something else, for that hurts, it hurts, it" (end of section). After this painful present, Cruz switches to another self—in the future: "You will close your eyes and you will see again, but you will see only what your brain wants you to see: more than the world, yet less.... Desire will send you back into memory and you will remember" (55–58). The episode in the past tense that directly follows this meditation contains the love scenes with Regina during the Revolution. Just before the injection that provokes the reverie, he has said, "I have forgotten your face, who loved. Oh, God, I have forgotten that face. No, I don't have to forget it. Where is it? ... how can I summon you up to be with me here?" (55). The memory that follows accomplishes that desire.

In these first person sections, particularly near the end, the reader participates in a moving battle. Cruz's voice fights for the right to define him against other voices which threaten to take over the description of him—Catalina, Teresa, the priest, the doctor. His secretary Padilla is his ally in this battle, for Padilla manages the tape recorder that plays Cruz's voice when it was stronger than it is now—better able to drown out the others. The use of interior monologue here, as in *Ulysses*, besides presenting a character's inner depths, is also a sign of his solitude. The second voice the reader hears is the second person, the *you*—"*tu*" in Spanish. This "*tu*" is the second person familiar, the form of intimate address. In addition to presenting a private side of Artemio Cruz, direct address draws Artemio Cruz and the reader together, and strengthens the idea that Cruz represents all Mexicans, perhaps even all men. Even after the reader has learned that Cruz is speaking to himself and not to the reader, the sensation of being implicated in the story persists.

In the first transition from an *I* section to a *you* section, Cruz reveals the reason why the *you* is addressed in the future tense: he adopts the future because it denies the presence of death. He wants to look ahead and to see something besides his presently arriving death; but the only things he has to distract him from the present pain of the dying process are memories. He therefore puts them in the future tense, the tense of hopes and plans, the only action he can manage now: "In your half-darkness your eyes would prefer to look ahead, not behind, and they do not know how to foresee the past. Yes: yesterday you will fly home from Hermosillo" (8). The "Yes" that separates the past tense from the future means yes, Cruz has found a way to satisfy his desire to believe in a future for himself.

The second person sections contain the fullest memories of Cruz's son Lorenzo, including lyrical descriptions of their ride together on the coast at Veracruz before Lorenzo leaves for Spain. This is Cruz's most persistent happy memory. In one of these memories of Lorenzo, Cruz modulates between past and future tenses. It is as if he wants to shape his hope in the future rather than accepting its end in the past: "you rode your horses; he asked you if you would ride together as far as the sea: he will ask you where you are going to eat and he said—he will say—papá, he will smile lifting his arm" (159). Once again, he succeeds; the passage continues in the future. This voice of the future that speaks of the past represents a triumph over time: "You will invent a time that does not exist, and measure it ... and you will end by thinking that there is no other reality than that created by your mind" (198).[14]

The futurity of these sections represents, as I have noted above, a potential Artemio Cruz, who is possible only in thought and who is soon to be extinguished by death. Such passages constitute Artemio's attempt to pardon himself by holding out the idea of the better person he might have been.[15] Cruz includes in them an alternate set of events—what this secret self wishes he had, done:

> you will choose to leave him [Lorenzo] in Catalina's hands, ...
> you won't push him to ... that fatal destiny which could have been yours ...
> you will tell Laura: yes
> you will tell the fat man in the blue room: no you will elect to stay in the cell with Bernal and Tobías, to share their fate ...
> you will be a peon
> you will be a blacksmith ...
> you will not be Artemio Cruz, you will not be seventy-one....
> (237–38)

But it is clear that Cruz's effort to revise the past cannot succeed; he has done what he has done, and he knows it. His failure to redeem himself in his own eyes makes the story of his death all the more moving. Cruz's judgment of himself is ultimately more important—and more condemning—than our external judgment of his business deals, his cowardice, his coldness, his infidelity.[16]

The third voice we encounter, the *he*, constitutes another example of memory as escape from death. These memories present the finished past and lack the sense of potential change included in the you sections. But they still provide Artemio Cruz with an alternate—and an extended—time frame. As I've mentioned earlier, these twelve sections are dated, and they recount Cruz's story through the events of twelve key days that span his life. The hard facts they contain lead us to judge him more harshly than the events he longs for and imagines or the emotional needs he reveals.

So far I have emphasized the *different* functions of these three voices. But at the end, as Artemio Cruz dies, they are necessarily compressed into one: "Artemio Cruz ... Name ... heart massage ... hopeless ... I carry you inside and with you I die. The three, we ... will die. You ... die, have died ... I will die" (306). The future tense is the last one to go—always the greenest, the most hopeful. But its last expression is joined to the *I* of the present, to inescapable death. The technique of alternating the three voices in small sections rather than presenting three long narratives foreshadows this final compression. It heightens the tension the reader experiences between sympathy for, Artemio Cruz and judgment of him, between allowing him to live as he wishes in the past of his potential goodness or to die as he must in the present of his accomplished harm. As Fuentes has said of Artemio Cruz, "Good or bad, the reader must choose."[17] The shifting perspectives make the choice engaging, but difficult.

STYLE AND LANGUAGE

The different voices that represent Artemio Cruz speak in a variety of styles. Although the entire novel theoretically takes place in Cruz's mind, only the first and second person sections are rendered, in a stream-of-consciousness form of narration, where the reader follows directly the pattern of Cruz's thought. The third person sections do contain thoughts, but these thoughts are filtered through a voice that also narrates exterior events. These events, in contrast to Cruz's more lyrical reveries in the second person sections, are recounted in spare prose. This is the language of the practical Artemio Cruz, the language of action: "He stood and lightly touched his wounded forehead. He ought to go back to the wooded thicket, there he would be safe. He staggered" (71).

Even the description of Artemio's farewell to his first love, Regina, though it contains a foreboding contrast between a violently killed coyote and beautiful flowers, reveals the same simple sentence structure: "It was early. They went out on the street, she in her starched skirt, he in his felt sombrero and white tunic. They lived near the barranca: bell flowers hung over its void, and a rabbit killed by the fangs of a coyote was rotting in the foliage.... Their hands joined" (65). Compare this style with the baroque images and sentences in Cruz's reveries about the cathedral (p. 31) or the rich produce of Cocuya (p. 136).

In the second person sections, Cruz's thoughts often resemble incantations, ritual songs of praise or lament, to Mexico (pp. 266–67; see above, 54), to Cruz's former self (in the "you will choose" section, 237–38; see above, 64), to the body (when he remembers how all his organs used to function properly, pp. 83–84). The words of such sections may even be arranged as in a poem. One such "mini-poem" plays on a slang obscenity that has particular significance in Mexican culture. The section begins:

> You will say it, it is your word and your word is my word: ...
> imprecation, snapping greeting, life word, brother word, memory
> ... resumé of our history....
>   Fuck your mother
>   Fuckin' bastard
>   We fuck 'em all
>   Quit fucking around (137)

There are twenty more lines in the same vein. The thematic importance of this chant merits a small digression here. First, the obscenity is an affront, a challenge to the polite reader, a gauntlet of language thrown down. It also constitutes a poetic recognition of a brutal aspect of Mexico's heritage. And beyond this, it is a recognizable act c age to Octavio Paz.

The Spanish word here translated as "fuck" is the verb "chingar." In *The Labyrinth of Solitude*, Octavio Paz explains that: "in Mexico the word has innumerable meanings.... But ... the ultimate meaning always contains the idea of aggression ... an emergence from oneself to penetrate another by force.... The person who suffers this action is passive, inert and open, in contrast to the active and aggressive and closed person who inflicts it. The *chingón* is the *macho*, the male; he rips open the *chingada*, the female."[18] However schematic this formulation, Paz uses these terms to suggest that in a metaphorical sense, all Mexicans are *"hijos de la chingada"*—sons of a violated mother. This is because the Spanish conquistadores violated the native women, just as Spain invaded the new world, and from that violation came the mestizo race, the dominant population of Mexico.

The relevance of the expression to Artemio Cruz should be immediately clear. He is literally an "*hijo de la chingada*"—born from the violation of a native servant by the descendant of a Spaniard—and he returns to the expression throughout his story. For him, "You are what you are because you knew how to fuck 'em without letting them fuck you" (138). Mexico's history begins with the violation of her "mother" earth by foreigners, and the pattern of violence continues in men like Cruz, who have absorbed the word "*chingar*" and made it their plan of action. Dominate or be dominated. The philosophy extends to the idea of "one life for another." This is why Artemio Cruz feels pain when he repeats the words "I survived." Cruz doesn't merely survive; he survives by climbing somehow on the deaths of others—of Regina, or Gonzalo, or Lorenzo.[19]

A related habit of speech is Cruz's repetition of words, a sort of mental stutter, particularly in the *I* sections. The very first of these sections provides a good example: "Iron hammers in my ears and something, something, something ... I am this, this am I ... I am this eye, this eye I am ... and I am these cheeks, cheeks, cheekbones where the white whiskers are born. Are born. Face. Face. Face, grimace ..." (4). This repetitive style projects a sense of desperation, an effort to grasp even the physical realities of life, which are quickly slipping away.

Through these stylistic variations Fuentes integrates some of the rhythmic and sensual power of poetry into his prose. This lyricism augments the novel's emotional force. At the same time, the classical elegance of the rigorous tripartite narrative voice holds in place the often baroque richness of the text.

NOTES

1. Critical reactions to *The Death of Artemio Cruz* have generally been favorable. For a survey, see Isabel Siracusa, "Las novelas y su repercusión," *Nueva Crítica* 2 (1970), 148–55.

2. Hernán Vidal sees naturalistic determinism and moral vision meet in Fuentes's portrait of Artemio Cruz, and associates the observation with Fuentes's declaration that Marx and Nietzsche divide each man; "El modo narrativo en *La muerte de Artemio Cruz* de Carlos Fuentes," *Thesaurus: Boletín del Instituto Caro y Cuervo* 31 (1976), 322.

3. In his excellent article on "Self, Double, and Mask in Fuentes' *La muerte de Artemio Cruz*," *Texas Studies in Language and Literature* 16 (1974), 363–84, Lanin Gyurko points to a number of characters who can be identified as doubles of Artemio Cruz. These doubles serve "first of all to dramatize the complexity of Cruz's character, which is a fusion of opposites." Gyurko divides the figures into two groups. "Compensatory doubles" represent Cruz's positive potential (Regina, Bernal, Lorenzo, Laura). "Antagonistic doubles" seem at first to be the opposites of Cruz, but he finally comes to resemble them,

as the compensatory figures are sacrificed (Gamaliel Bernal, Father Paez, Catalina). This concept of character doubling resembles the tripling of Artemio Cruz's narrative voice, which I will discuss later.

4. Carlos Fuentes, *The Death of Artemio Cruz*, trans. Sam Hileman (New York: Farrar, Straus and Company, 1964), p. 11. Further references are given in the text.

5. René Jara Cuadro makes the point that Doña Ludivinia hides in her memories against old age and death just as Artemio Cruz does in his house in Coyoacán, but that the "sacred spaces" they construct enclose those very dangers; "El mito y la nueva novela hispanoamericana: A propósito de *La muerte de Artemio Cruz*," in Giacomán, p. 190.

6. Juan Loveluck considers that the ideological basis of *The Death of Artemio Cruz* is formed around three major, related concerns: Mexico and what is Mexican, Mexico and the United States, and Mexico and its revolution; "Intención y forma en *La muerte de Artemio Cruz*," *Nueva Narrativa Latinoamericana* I, i (1971), 114.

7. Fuentes dedicates the novel to the radical sociologist C. Wright Mills, "true voice of North America," because Mills has consistently criticized the economic domination of Latin America by the U.S. in cooperation with the native oligarchies. See the conversation between Mills and a number of Mexican intellectuals, including Fuentes: "Izquierda, subdesarollo y guerra fría—Un coloquio sobre cuestiones fundamentales," *Cuadernos Americanos* 19 (1960), 33–69. M. Durán imagines Artemio Cruz as a supporter of President Matte Alemán. His term, from 1946–52, saw the most concessions to North American business in Mexico; p. 63.

8. Carlos Fuentes, *El mundo de José Luis Cuevas* (Mexico City: Galería de Arte Misrachi, 1969), p. 9.

9. Fuentes speaks of his own writing as power, but a constructive sort of power: when you write, "you're there in a prodigious act of truth, of affirmation of power—of power that doesn't corrupt"; Fortson, p. 18.

10. For detailed discussions of the arrangement of Cruz's monologue, see the study by Nelson Osorio, which plots the social and moral rises and falls of Cruz's career, "Un aspecto de la estructura de *La muerte de Artemio Cruz*," in Giacomán, pp. 125–46.

11. For M. Durán, Cruz's repeated sentence about crossing the river reminds us that the river is an symbol for human life; and that the novel is thus "a journey back upstream from the point where [the river] is already spilling into the sea of death to its birth in infancy," p. 68.

12. Alberto Díaz-Lastra defines these voices in the following way: "the I is an old man in his present surroundings; the you is an authorial conscience that condemns more than it remembers; the he is a more impersonal voice"; "Carlos Fuentes y la revolución traicionada," in Giacomán, p. 349.

13. Carballo, pp. 440–41.

14. Lorenzo crosses the water. Artemio Cruz continually dreams to go fight in Spain, while Cruz remains forever on this side of the cleansing element. Boschi and Calabresi associate Lorenzo with the benevolent God Quetzalcóatl who departed by water, never to return, and Artemio Cruz with the destructive Tezcatlipoca, the smoking mirror who adopts various appearance to trick Quetzalcóatl, p. 64.

15. Boschi and Calabresi maintain that "Artemio Cruz will be able to assume unchosen options and travel freely only when death permits the enrichment of his symbolic world" and his entrance into "the temporal zone of the mythic"; p. 55. They may be correct in associating this idea with Aztec beliefs that "life and were two aspects of the same thing." But in wishing to follow Artemio Cruz through this mythic pattern, they seem to forget that the novel ends when Cruz dies. The nearness of death motivates his

mental journeys, but death itself finally annihilates them. A mythic view of Fuentes's works, while establishing many fascinating connections with ancient culture, tends to be too optimistic; it underestimates their existential elements,

16. Lanin Gyurko notes that this self-condemnation suggests that Fuentes blames Mexico itself rather than other nations for its problems; "Structure and Theme," p. 320.

17. Carballo, p. 441.

18. Octavio Paz, *The Labyrinth of Solitude: Life and Thought in Mexico*, trans. Lysander Kemp (New York: Grove Press, 1961), pp. 76–77.

19. Rodríguez Monegal argues that fratricide is central to several of Fuentes's works; with it Fuentes suggests that Mexico goes on requiring human sacrifices in modern times; *Narradores de esta américa*, II, 259.

STEVEN BOLDY

Fathers and Sons in
Fuentes' La muerte de Artemio Cruz

The dispositional chapter structure of Carlos Fuentes' *La muerte de Artemio Cruz* (the YO, TÚ and ÉL voices, the rearrangement of normal chronological structure) has attracted much critical attention.[1] It is not this aspect of structure which I wish to examine here, but a deeper structure formed by the constellations of character and their relations in three historical periods. I shall basically posit an archetypal structure of father, legitimate son and illegitimate son or symbolic heir which occurs three times in the novel. I will suggest that the two 'sons' are opposites, representing dual, alternative forces in the Mexican history and psyche. I will describe the cyclical structure of inheritance from father to heir on four main levels: the historical, the formal and literary, the mythical, and the fantastic level which involves metempsychosis and collective memory. What I hope to do in this way is to point to a more problematical and critical novel than that perceived so far, and to contribute further to breaking down the rigid classification of Fuentes' work into early sociohistorical realist novels and later fantastic *nueva novela*.[2]

A first reading of *La muerte de Artemio Cruz* immediately reveals that a major structuring factor in it is the binary opposition: the contrast, for example, between the passivity of the YO voice and the activity of the ÉL voice; the sense of freedom in the TÚ voice and the sense of predestination

From *Bulletin of Hispanic Studies* 61 (1984): 31–40. © 1984 by Liverpool University Press.

in the ÉL voice. The emotionally perceived *tierra* which Artemio inherits
with its 'extraño amor común' (276)[3] is similarly opposed to the corruption
of the legalistically denominated *país* that he bequeaths on his death, with its
'lideres ladrones, sus sindicatos sometidos, sus nuevos latifundios' (277). This
same sort of opposition is reproduced in the individual. Artemio is double: a
face and a mask, himself and his 'reflejo aprendido' or public persona, the
original promising individual and the political animal which negates it. The
traditional axis or image of such *desdoblamientos*, so common in Spanish
American literature, is the mirror. In the following passage, two panes of
glass are cleverly arranged to show Artemio a double image of himself,
walking towards Madero, synonymous with honesty and reform, and towards
the appointment which seals his destiny as traitor to the Revolution he once
stood for: 'se ajustó la corbata frente al vidrio del vestibule y atrás, en el
segundo vidrio, el que daba a la calle de Madero, un hombre idéntico a él,
pero tan lejano [...] le daba la espalda y caminaba hacia el centre de la calle,
mientras él buscaba el ascensor, desorientado per un instant,' (22). Only
when close to death, as his head falls onto the reflective surface of a glass
table, do his own face and that of his 'mellizo enfermo' (16) come together.
This double reflection is given a structural expression in the alternative
projections of the twin sons: real son and heir.

Mirrors not only duplicate a person, but create fatal barriers between
people. Pride is seen as a mirror in which Artemio and his wife Catalina
project images of themselves so petrified and fallacious as to signify the death
of their relationship, the impossibility of love and communion. Pride
becomes a Narcissus' pool in which both will drown if they try to kiss: 'ese
espejo común, ese estanque que reflejará los rostros de ambos, que los
ahogará cuando traten de besarse' (92). Artemio is not only double in
himself, but is reflected in various ways in individuals outside him. The
wounded soldier he could have saved and lets die is a twin who represents the
death of his own solidarity: 'si tuviera los ojos verdes, sería su gemelo' (75).
His son Lorenzo is an inverted and magical reflection of his betrayed
idealism. Lorenzo dies for an ideal while his lover lives; Artemio abandons
his ideal while his lover dies. Jaime Ceballos presented as his possible heir at
the end of the novel is a sadly real reflection of Cruz's cynicism.

The deep impulse behind all the works of Fuentes is the millennium,
an Arcadia in the past projected onto a utopia in the future, and often
expressed as a *unio contrariorum*. The waves of the sea to which the novel
returns so often, as in the paradisiacal scene between Lilia and Xavier *Adame*,
clearly express this unalienated fusion of opposites: 'otras las mismas—
siempre en movimiento y siempre idénticas, fuera del tiempo y espejo de sí
mismas, de las olas del origen, del milenio perdido y del milenio por venir'

(157). The equation of past and future in the text, however, takes on the travestied, alienated form of an alternation between irreconcilables or an opposition between a past of falsehood and tyranny and a similarly unacceptable future, as experienced in the tragic contrasts of Acapulco: 'Siempre los dos tiempos en esta comunidad jánica, de rostro doble, tan lejana de lo que fue y tan lejana de lo que quiere ser' (151). Fuentes sums up the agent of this alienation in Mexican reality as *la chingada*, a personal and historical curse of violation and betrayal.

The union of origin and future, which finds a natural expression in the fifty-two year cycles of the sun in Aztec cosmology, at the end of which sacrifices are made to assure the sun's rebirth, is reenacted in the San Silvestre party fifty-two years after Cruz started out on his adult life. The exaltation of the *fiesta*, however, is not followed by any sort of rebirth, but by a spiteful return to the *status quo*. The opposition between rebirth and sterile repetition expresses the ambiguity at the beginnings of the Mexican nation between Quetzalcoatl, the god of peace, culture and crops, and the Cortés who came in his place: the archetypal *chingón* bringing carnage and oppression. Cortés, like Quetzalcoatl, is dual, embodying both the 'new man' of the Renaissance and the enclosed retrogression of the Counter-Reform. Cruz, too, suffers the dual destiny of being one by day, another by night (103). In fact Artemio Cruz is basically an avatar of the phonetically similar Hernán Cortés: their Mexican careers begin in Veracruz; the violation of doña Marina is repeated in that of Regina and Cruz's own conception; don Gamaliel fulfils the role of Moctezuma.

This original ambiguity in the history of Mexico is reflected in the way many episodes in the novel are given in two versions. The two founding events in Artemio's life, his birth and his encounter with Regina, both merged with the image of the sea and projected onto the future as a paradise to be regained, manifest this dual nature. Artemio's love for Regina is one of total union, oneness with the universe and the seeds of time; making love, they are 'reducidos al encuentro del mundo, a la semilla de la razón, a las dos voces que nombran en silencio, que adentro bautizan todas las cosas' (67). They remember their meeting as poetic and idyllic: '¿Te acuerdas de aquella roca que se metía al mar como un barco de piedra? [...] Se forma una laguna entre las rocas y uno puede mirarse en el agua blanca. Allí me miraba, y un día apareció tu cara junto a la mía' (66). But their union is built on a lie, an 'hermosa mentira' (82); rather than in the sea, they are reflected in the 'smoking mirror'. The truth is that Regina was the first anonymous woman Cruz came across on entering a conquered town, she was hoisted onto the saddle of his horse and 'violada en silencio en el dormitorio común de los oficiales, lejos del mar, dando la cara a la sierra seca y espinosa' (83). This act of falsification repeats Artemio's own origins, presented through the distorting lens of nostalgia as a paradisiacal life by the river near the sea, fishing and swimming in the clear waters and working in harmony with the mulatto Lunero. Only at the end of the novel do we learn that Artemio was the fruit of another rape, that his mother Isabel was one of many casually taken by force by Atanasio. Artemio is thus an *hijo de la chingada* before confirming the self-perpetuating curse of la Malinche by taking in turn the mask of the *chingón*.

As an alienated travesty of the cyclical Aztec time, Mexican reality is seen to obey the rule that the outrage practised on one will be avenged by its imposition in turn on another: 'el ultraje que lavaste ultrajando a otros hombres' (147); that the dispossessed will in turn dispossess. This is the sense of Artemio's enigmatic refrain on his death bed: 'Regresaron no se dieron por vencidos' (271). The *villistas* whom Artemio's men thought they had defeated return to the village, murder and hang Regina in his absence. The dead whom he survived return irrepressibly to his memory, to the text of the novel. The return of the repressed does not simply mean the return of evil, but also the possibility of liberation, reposing the original dilemma or choice between Quetzalcoatl and Cortés which I shall discuss in the image of the two sons.

On the historical level of the novel, this repetitive structure is seen in the replacement of one group in power by another, each one promising freedom and progress, each one reproducing the negative features of its predecessor. The three main periods are Independence, Liberalism and Revolution. The post-Independence period, with its vast possibilities after the shaking off of the Bourbon yoke, is represented in the novel by General Santa Anna, best known for losing or selling a large proportion of Mexican territory. The second period is Liberalism, promising, after the victories of Juárez, to break the hold of theocracy, bring culture and a better land distribution. What Lerdo's disentailment did bring was the creation of a new landed oligarchy, later confirmed and institutionalized by Porfirio Díaz. The next upturn is the Revolution with its own land-reform and its own new oligarchy distinguishable only by its rhetoric from earlier ones. Minor new revolutions are posited in the novel as generations of neo-capitalists monotonously relieve each other in power, according to the pseudo-renovation of official PRI candidates.

Each one of these periods in the novel is represented by a *cacique* or patriarch figure, who fills his predecessor's position after ousting him. The first is Ireneo Menchaca, given his lands by Santa Anna at the expense of the Indians. After the liberal victories over Maximilian, his lands pass to local *juaristas*. That class is represented in the novel by Gamaliel Bernal, a minor merchant who bought his lands for a song from the church. Bernal is ousted by the Revolutionary Officer Artemio Cruz, grandson of Ireneo Menchaca, dispossessed by the movement which gave power to Bernal. As Bernal perceives, Cruz is not so much an individual as the incarnation of the new cycle: 'Artemio Cruz. Así se llamaba entonces, el nuevo mundo surgido de la guerra civil; así se llamaban quienes llegaban a sustituirlo. Desventurado país [...] que a cada generación tiene que destruir a los antiguos poseedores y sustituirlos por nuevos amos tan rapaces y ambiciosos como los anteriores' (50). Towards the end of the novel, there are indications that Cruz has a similar successor in Jaime Ceballos, the hero of *Las buenas conciencias*, and whose father-in-law dispossessed Cruz's analogue in *La región más transparente*, Federico Robles.

Each *cacique* inherits the duality of the movement which put him into power: the eternal choice between Quetzalcoatl and Cortés, between being a *pendejo* or a *chingón* (see 129). This is expressed not so much in his own person as in his two, opposite heirs: the real son who embodies his better self and a symbolic heir or usurper. On each occasion the Quetzalcoatl figure dies and his *doppelgänger* takes over the power of the father, initiating a new cycle. Textual means, which I shall explain, are used to establish the sameness of the relationships each time they occur in a cycle. The choice between twins is a constant throughout Fuentes' work. In *Zona sagrada*, for example, Guillermito and Giancarlo are the real and symbolic sons of Claudia, reactivating in their relationship a whole series of mythical twins: Telemachus and Telegonus, Castor and Pollux, Apollo and Dionysius, Romulus and Remus, etc.

Filling in the sons, the structure becomes the following: Ireneo Menchaca receives his lands in Veracruz from Santa Anna, and when the latter moved to Mexico, Menchaca followed his court there. The pattern is slightly different here in that Menchaca had two legitimate sons: Atanasio and Pedrito. Though most of the lands were lost, Atanasio returned to his origins on the land that his father had abandoned, living anachronistically and in a sense idealistically a life no longer possible. Pedrito meanwhile continued to live on frivolously in the salons of Mexico City. When Atanasio was called to pick up the remains of his dead father, he was murdered. Pedrito, who was present and had a gun, abandoned him to his fate, thus adding an element of virtual fratricide to the opposition between the authenticity of the sons. But Pedrito does not inherit the force of the father, and becomes a parasite and an alcoholic. It is Artemio, the bastard grandchild, who inherits that force.

Don Gamaliel Bernal, representing the liberals who took the Menchacas' wealth, has a legitimate son, Gonzalo, who is his opposite in that he goes off to fight in the Revolution against his father's land-owning class. He is however similar to his father in his intellectualism and vocation of martyrdom. Artemio is the usurper; he faces the possibility of a firing squad with Gonzalo, but whereas the latter opts to die idealistically, Artemio abandons Gonzalo and saves his own skin. Returning to Puebla, he takes over the position of Gonzalo as heir to the Bernal fortune. Artemio thus becomes the new *cacique*, the revolutionary oligarch. His real son Lorenzo returns to the *hacienda* by the coast which Cruz has bought and restored, while his father remains in Mexico City: following the model of Menchaca and his son Atanasio. Lorenzo goes to fight idealistically for the lost cause of the Spanish Republic, seen as a second chance for the aspirations of the Mexican Revolution, and dies where his father had opted to survive. The 'twin' of Lorenzo and the presumptive heir of Artemio is Jaime Ceballos, identical to Artemio in his cynicism, and the opposite of Lorenzo.

Though the pattern is reasonably clear as summarized here, much of the pleasure of reading the text is derived from the way in which the complex web of intratextual echoes, parallels and oppositions is created from which the pattern emerges as a half-glimpsed order from chaos in the swirling nebula in the dying Artemio's mind. The temporal chaos of the ÉL sequences and the three rival voices of the text do much to allow the loose or combinatory articulation of elements which permits different causalities to coexist, and gives the reader the aesthetic pleasure of discovery. Under the linear history as recounted in self-congratulatory official texts, the network of echoes and mirrorings in the novel through about one hundred years of Mexican history establishes better than any commentary the archetypal nature of the rival, literary structure. Within the syntax of the structure any individual in a particular slot is simply an avatar of others in a similar position, a temporal manifestation in an intemporal pattern. The impression of fantastic metempsychosis which emerges links *La muerte de Artemio Cruz* with apparently very different stories, like *Aura*, published in the same year. Here, a witch, la señora Consuelo, reincarnates her long-dead husband, a general of Maximilian, in the person of a progressive young historian.

Fuentes uses a variety of techniques in order to establish identities between individuals and situations, and set up one or more patterns. These include parallel situations, repetition of phrases, authorial comment disguised as a speech by a character, magical ceremonies, and myth. Another crucial device, which seems to me to be very important in Spanish American literature is what might be called the 'floating index'. The gun with two bullets, which is attributed to four different characters, is a good example. The gun appears in and links five scenes: Pedrito fails to use it to defend his brother Atanasio; the young Artemio takes it to kill the *enganchador* in order to allow his mulatto step-father to flee, but, firing upwards from the undergrowth, kills his uncle Pedrito by mistake; Lorenzo, in the Spanish Civil War, uses a similar gun, now rusty and useless, to shoot, again upwards, at the Nazi planes in order to facilitate the flight of the refugees. The gun also appears in the duel with the *villista* officer Zagal during the Mexican Civil War and in the parallel Russian roulette duel with the fat policeman at the time of the Cristero troubles. The index has some symbolic meaning of its own: it is an obvious phallic symbol, and its two bullets clearly suggest duality. This meaning underlines and expands the meaning of the situation where it occurs. Artemio, for example, takes over the virility and power of Pedrito who is unable to use the gun; and when Artemio in turn fails, the gun reappears in the hands of his son Lorenzo. It signals the repeated duality of the episodes: the fact that one man out of two has to die in a duel, and that another man dies in exchange, sacrificially, before or after the duel (el padre Páez after that with the *gordo*, and Gonzalo before that with Zagal). It signals the tension between choice and chance: the chance inherent in the Russian roulette and duel, against Artemio's choice in the two scenes between political allegiances; the chance of Artemio accidentally killing his uncle against the choice that he had made to act idealistically in defence of the mulatto. Being presented originally as an attribute of one person, the index becomes metonymically the whole of that person. When attributed later to another, it carries with it, by connotation, much of the meaning developed in the first situation. The identity of the first possessor is thus superimposed onto the second. This suggests how important a technique it is for works like *La muerte de Artemio Cruz* with a strong fantastic component involving metempsychosis and the idea of collective memory.

We may now see how these techniques are used to establish the identity between the individuals cast in the archetypal roles of father, son and heir, and how the structure is justified and given life by the notion of a collective memory passed from generation to generation. First, the patriarchs themselves: Ireneo, Gamaliel, and Artemio. They are linked principally by images of death. Ireneo dies 'en el verano sin letrinas, hinchado de agua putrefacta' (293), as does his grandson Artemio, whose swollen abdomen is only relieved when he vomits his own excrement. Don Gamaliel, when faced by the arrival of Cruz and the eclipse of his sun, is accompanied by a mastiff: 'El mastín saltó con alegría y lamió la mano del amo' (39). At the end of Artemio's life, when he is to face a similar interview with Jaime Ceballos, he is accompanied by not one, but two mastiffs. As a photographer takes Artemio's picture, he is almost dragged out of his seat by one of them. Most likely in Fuentes' mind the dogs are a sign of Xolotl, the dog-god which accompanies the dead to Mictlan.

I shall now concentrate on the semi-fantastic links between the real son and the heir. The real brothers Atanasio and Pedrito serve mainly to establish a pattern to be followed by others: Atanasio is sent back to the *hacienda* 'to make a man of him' in the same way that Artemio sends Lorenzo. Pedrito abandons Atanasio to his death in the same way as Artemio abandons Gonzalo. Artemio takes over from Pedrito by symbolically seizing his gun, his untried virility.

Fundamental to the whole mechanism of inheritance is Ludivinia, Artemio's grandmother. Born in 1810, the year of the 'grito de Dolores', she is contemporaneous with the birth of Mexican Independence. This first 'grito' is one hundred and twenty nine years before the second cry of Dolores, the Dolores whose scream, as Lorenzo is killed in Spain, puts an end to the hopes embodied by Artemio and the Revolution he represents. Ludivinia is a witch in the long line of such figures in Fuentes: Teódula Moctezuma in *La región más transparente*, la señora Consuelo in *Aura*, Claudia in *Zona sagrada*, Celestina in *Terra Nostra*.[4] She had lived for thirty-odd years in the *zona sagrada* of her room, where not even the fire had dared to penetrate. Like Consuelo in her decrepit old age, she makes grotesque efforts to recover her youth: 'Seguía aquí, tratando de cumplir desde el lecho revuelto los ademanes de la joven hermosa y blanca que abrió las puertas de Cocuya' (291). Ludivinia is the memory of Mexico incarnate: 'traía emplastada en el cerebro la memoria de un siglo y en los surcos del rostro capas de aire y tierra y sol desaparecidos' (291); 'Ludivinia creía ser el centro que anudaba la memoria y las presencias circundantes' (298). From this racial memory and her long isolation in her sacred enclosure, she is able to dictate the future and reincarnate the dead. The cycles of the novel, where characters repeat gestures of those long dead, are symbolically dictated by the will of this old lady. Artemio, for example, is said to have been reared by her foresight, '[criado] en el presentimiento' (306). She is not only able to love the young Artemio, with whom she has never spoken, but to live through him, survive through him with her memory: 'aún existiría un margen de vida fuera de su siglo de recuerdos: una oportunidad de vivir y querer a otro ser de su sangre' (298). It is also significantly Ludivinia who utters the curse natural to her, the 'maldición natural', which is to become the fatality of the novel. '¡Chingao!' (297, 306), she screams at her son and at the *enganchador*. From Ludivinia, then, Artemio inherits memory, to which is added the accumulated memory of all those who died for him: the hell of memory which constitutes the text of the novel.

The process of inherited memory and destiny continues as the next pair of legitimate son and usurper is formed by Artemio and Gonzalo Bernal. The two meet in a *villista* prison where they await execution together. Gonzalo is consciously a martyr to a lost cause, an idealist, and believes that 'hay deberes que es necesario cumplir aunque se sepa de antemano que se va al fracaso' (196). The opposition between Gonzalo and Artemio, who is a born pragmatist and opportunist, is thus that of thought and action, idealism and opportunism, dying and surviving. But Artemio is not impervious to the presence of Gonzalo, who thinks and shares thoughts parallel to his own, memories Artemio is desperately trying to avoid, thus becoming an enemy more formidable than the military foe: 'este nuevo enemigo armado de ideas y ternuras, que sólo estaba repitiendo el mismo pensamiento oculto del capitán, del prisionero, de él' (197). The opposition between openness and closedness is momentarily resolved in the 'abrazo violento' (198) between the two men as Artemio struggles to silence Gonzalo, i.e. to silence his own memory. This aggressive embrace characterizes doubles in Fuentes elsewhere too, as in the final fight between Franz and Javier in the pyramid at Cholula in *Cambio de piel*.

The moment clearly represents the end of a cycle: '¿Para qué ilusionar a esos pobrecitos con un nuevo sol?' (198), comments Zagal, their captor. If there is a rebirth, and the sun does rise just after Gonzalo's death, then there is a tension between the Christian and Aztec conceptions of rebirth: Gonzalo dies in solidarity with the Indian Tobías to fertilize a new cycle; Artemio survives, but seems to assume the cross of the life and sins of all Mexicans, taking them on himself like Christ.[5] Memory again is an important vehicle in the process of inheritance; Gonzalo is an invitation to remember: 'Dicen que es bueno recordar' (191). Artemio, though representing memory, refuses to remember, tries to 'disfrazar esa ansia de recuerdo' (189). 'No hay mucha vida por detrás' (191), he lies. But after the 'violento abrazo' with his 'new enemy', Artemio suddenly becomes conscious of his role as memory, and decides to live and survive so that Regina will continue to live on in him: 'Él sólo sentía ese dolor perdido de Regina, esa memoria dulce y amarga que tanto había escondido y que ahora brotaba a flote, pidiéndole que siguiera viviendo, como si una mujer muerta necesitara del recuerdo de un hombre vivo para seguir siendo algo más que un cuerpo devorado por los gusanos en un hoyo sin nombre, en un pueblo sin nombre' (198).

Artemio assumes not only the life and death of Regina, but also the unfulfilled possibilities of Gonzalo together with his material heritage. It is the fact that Artemio incorporates his double and opposite that allows him to split into two in turn when his own destiny is exhausted, and delegate the eternally unfulfilled promises of Gonzalo onto another, his son Lorenzo. In one moment of lucidity, Artemio is completely aware of the logic of his inheritance:

> La ironía de ser él quien regresaba a Puebla, y no el fusilado
> Bernal, le divertía. Era, en cierto modo, una mascarada, una
> sustitución, una broma que podía jugarse con la mayor seriedad;
> pero también era un certificado de vida, de la capacidad para
> sobrevivir y fortalecer el propio destino con los ajenos. [...] Sintió
> que entraba duplicado, con la vida de Gonzalo Bernal añadida a
> la suya, con el destino del muerto sumado al suyo: como si Bernal,
> al morir, hubiese delegado las posibilidades de su vida incumplida
> en la de él. Quizá las muertes ajenas son las que alargan nuestra
> vida, pensó. (43)

Gamaliel Bernal accepts Cruz as his heir with absolute passivity, recognizing
not only the force of historical necessity and the presence of his son, but also
bowing to fatality, assuming the role of Moctezuma in the face of Cortés.

Cruz, like Ixca Cienfuegos in *La región más transparente*, is a Wandering
Jew or Melmoth the Wanderer figure, condemned to live on earth in
different incarnations of Mexican destiny, repose time and time again the
original dilemma and contradiction, until it is finally resolved or until he
finds someone else to take over the curse. '¿Morirás?', asked the Tú voice.
'No será la primera vez' (34). As the memory of Mexico, he is condemned to
incarnate all that others say and think: 'Encarnarás lo que ella [Catalina], y
todos, pensaron entonces. No lo sabrás. Tendrás que encarnarlo. Nunca
escucharás las palabras de los otros. Tendrás que vivirlas' (34). In a dream-
like sequence in which Artemio is linked with the invading armies of Cortés,
we see how the project borne by the *conquistador*, i.e. the New World, the
Renaissance dream of Utopia, expands Cruz's memory and subconscious
back before the foundation of Mexico to Renaissance Spain: 'Avanzarás hacia
[...] la portada de la Conquista, severa y jocunda, con un pie en el mundo
viejo, muerto, y otro en el mundo nuevo que no empezaba aquí, sino del otro
lado del mar también: el mundo nuevo llegó con ellos, con un frente de
murallas austeras para proteger el corazón sensual, alegre, codicioso' (35).
The *peregrino* of *Terra Nostra*, who is also paradoxically an amnesiac and yet
who preserves the memory of the millenarian movement, is a later version of
Artemio Cruz.

We come to the final couple of twins, the final opposition between
Quetzalcoatl and Cortés in the novel: Lorenzo and Jaime Ceballos.
Lorenzo's identification with Quetzalcoatl is strongly suggested in phrases
like 'El brazo levantado del muchacho indicará hacia el oriente, por donde
salió el sol' (225). The two do not meet, and are only contrasted in their
relationships with the father figure, Artemio. Cruz forces Lorenzo to do
what he did not do, and recover his wasted life: 'lo obligarás a hacer lo que

tú no hiciste, a rescatar tu vida perdida' (246). The principal formal expression of this delegation is the episode in the Spanish Civil War (a completely mythical event for Fuentes, and also opposed to the Mexican Revolution in *La región*), where Lorenzo lives out the ideals betrayed by Artemio in the Mexican Revolution. It is related in the third person section, and the reader, initially, is cleverly led to read the ÉL which refers to Lorenzo as referring to Cruz, thus blurring their separate identities. The sequence is in fact a résumé and a reworking of many elements from Cruz's career: the *azotea* is the same one from which Artemio watched the execution of Gonzalo; both hear a baby cry; the man at the balcony who 'esperaba el regreso de alguien o aguardaba la salida del sol' (234) echoes the reference to the 'new sun' at the time of Gonzalo's execution, and foreshadows Cruz's position at the New Year's Eve party as spectator, and his seeming to await the return of his Plumed Serpent son. The rifle with two bullets is present, and Lorenzo's relation with Dolores is clearly an inverted version of Cruz's love for Regina, even in their projected reunion by the sea.

Lorenzo, of course, dies, and it is Jaime who takes his place at the party. In a complex three-page sequence (266–69), Artemio's memories of his last day with Lorenzo by the sea are brilliantly superimposed on and alternated with a dialogue between Artemio and Jaime. The disjointed phrases from the two discourses seem to answer each other, Jaime falling ambiguously and ironically into the questions and interpellations addressed mentally by Artemio to his dead son. The same sort of effect is achieved in parts of Vargas Llosa's *La Casa Verde*. Jaime's ideals, for example, of becoming part of Artemio's business empire ('Pero ya ve, yo tengo otros ideales ...') are ironically juxtaposed with the universality of Lorenzo's ideals, embodied in the immensity of the ocean ('al mar libre, al mar abierto hacia donde corrió Lorenzo'). The vision of a promised land intuited by Artemio and his son ('distinguirán en la otra ribera un espectro de tierra, un espectro, sí ...') is painfully contrasted with the superficiality of the present ceremony for Ceballos ('¿Qué le parece esta fiesta? ... vacilón, qué rico vacilón, cha cha cha'). Perhaps the most important juxtaposition is that between the leitmotiv with which Artemio always refers to his hopes in his son ('lo esperaba con alegria esa mañana') and the reality of the return of a very different figure ('¡Bah! Llegó usted tarde').

Finally, the identity between father and heir, Artemio and Jaime, is established by the repetition of a crucial phrase denoting the rebelliousness of Cruz's life. Jaime has broken the sacred rule that nobody should talk to Cruz during his parties, and when challenged, answers defiantly, 'Esas reglas fueron hechas sin consultarme, don Artemio'. This rebellion corresponds to Artemio's first lesson in life, not to be an 'esclavo de los mandamientos escritos sin consultarte' (125), and to his dictum to the pretender at the party: 'El verdadero poder nace siempre de la rebeldia.' Artemio too seems to recognize himself in the young intruder: 'Dio la cara a Jaime y el joven le miró sin pestañear ... picardía en la mirada ... juego de los labios y las quijadas ... del viejo ... del joven ... se reconoció, ah ... se desconcertó, ah ...'; 'se vieron a los ojos, sonrieron'. There is an element of ambiguity in the scene, as Jaime falls into two patterns, repeating not only the energetic rebelliousness of Cruz, but also the minor transgression of Pedrito on entering Ludivinia's sacred zone. According to which link between characters is focused, Cortés returns once again in the place of Quetzalcoatl to initiate yet another cycle, or, given the identification Jaime-Pedrito, even the cycle has lost its force. This ambiguity, however, does not affect the presence of the particular structure we have posited. The house in Coyoacán is a reproduction of the room of Ludivinia at the beginning of the first cycle, and the same oppositions are actualized: the cycle of Quetzalcoatl with its promise of a new time and the alienated repetition instituted by Cortés and the curse of the *chingada*.

We come then to the question of whether there is any way out of the cyclical curse. Is Artemio Cruz eternally to bear the dual cross of all Mexicans, to be one by day and another by night? Is the Mexican actually defined by his waiting for a definition and an identity? Is he for ever and essentially a 'set expectante' as suggested by Leopoldo Zea?[6] Is Hegel's provisional nineteenth-century definition of America as a 'todavía no'[7] to be a permanent definition? Is he a 'no-ser-siempre-todavía'[8] in the words of Mayz Vallenilla? These questions are, of course, too vast to be exhausted here.

They are posed again, exactly, by the *peregrino* in *Terra Nostra*.[9] He is told that he is permanently condemned to be defeated by the double within, to be constantly exiled and to return. His raison d'être is freedom, but freedom can only exist in opposition, as a struggle:

> Fracasarás siempre. Regresarás siempre. Volverás a fracasar. No te dejarás vencer. Conoces el orden original de la vida de los hombres, porque tú lo fundaste, con los hombres, que no nacieron para devorarse entre sí como fieras, sino para vivir de acuerdo con las enseñanzas del alba: las tuyas. [...]
>
> —Señor: me hablas de una fatalidad sin fin, circular y eterna. ¿Nunca se resolverá con el triunfo definitivo de uno de los dos: mi doble o yo?
>
> Nunca, porque lo que tú representas sólo vivirá si es negado, agredido, secuestrado en un palacio [...] Libertad es el nombre de tu tarea. Un nombre con muchos hombres. [...]

Diste la palabra a todos hermano. Y por temor ala palabra de
todos, tu enemigo se sentirá siempre amenazado. (483–85)

The answer offered by *La muerte de Artemio Cruz* is not so much a
formula or a definition as an activity, the activity of the writing of the text,
and an implicit exhortation to the reader as an individual and a Mexican. The
attribute of the *peregrino* just mentioned is vital to an understanding of the
function of the writing: 'Diste la palabra a todos, hermano, y por temor a la
palabra de todos, tu enemigo se sentirá siempre amenazado.' A plural voice
of a community of individuals is opposed to the univocal voice of authority,
of history written once and for all, of nationalist rhetoric claiming a
monopoly of reality. The writing of the novel reproduces this dialectic: the
story of Cruz's successful career can be read as a straightforward and
definitive account of the recent history of Mexico. Underneath and against
this story, however, the circularity of the text, the echoes and workings of its
intratextuality create a plurality of causalities and readings. This plurality
contests, queries and offers alternatives to the simplistic, deterministic view
of reality. The unfulfilled, censured promises of the Mexican heritage are
constantly evoked and present in Cruz's discourse. The sacrifice and
potentialities of the countless, nameless Mexicans who died futilely are
constantly surfacing, and demanding a voice and a vindication in Artemio's
memory. The text recovers their voices and possibilities from silence and
posits them once more, as living virtualities. The circular sculptures of
ancient Mexican art offer a source of inspiration for this activity of the text,
its recirculation and plurality of meaning: 'Asi nuestro arte antiguo termina
porcrearun signo de apertura: el significante no agota los significados. La
forma es más amplia y resistente que cualquiera de los sentidos que se le
atribuyan; y esta calidad formal es la que asegura, precisamente, la vigencia y
multiplicidad de los contenidos'.[10]

As in his theatre, Fuentes opposes the subverting, corrosive force of the
ritual to the falsifying epic of the realist novel: 'Por la puerta falsa de la
epopeya se cuela el autor, con la esperanza de penetrar al corazón del castillo
e instalar en él, en vez de la gesta, el ritual. Y el ritual, tanto teatral como
antropológicamente, significa la desintegración de una vieja personalidad y
su reintegración en un nuevo ser'.[11]

The second answer of the text is an ethical and existential appeal to the
reader. He is invited to become conscious of the dual nature of Artemio Cruz
in himself, and to exorcize the tyrant within, the curse of the *chingada*. The
reasons for the Mexican's separation from other Mexicans are clearly defined:
false pride, fear, insincerity, lack of humility and the courage to express love
and solidarity. Catalina's caresses on Artemio's death-bed come to tell him,

after a life of bitterness, pride and separation, that 'al final, antique sea al final, la soberbia es superflua y la humildad necesaria' (92). The myths, the writing, the complex ambiguous structures of the novel have ultimately no aim other than to create in the reader the consciousness which might encourage him to take that difficult and painful leap out of his own skin and towards others.

NOTES

1. Two interesting articles on this aspect of the structure are: D.L. Shaw, 'Narrative arrangement in *La muerte de Artemio Cruz*', *FMLS*, XV (1979), 130–43, and Nelson Osorio, 'Un aspecto de la estructura de *La muerte de Artemio Cruz*', in *Homenaje a Carlos Fuentes*, ed. H. Giacomán (New York: Las Americas Publishing Co., 1971), 125–46.

2. Liliana Befumo Boschi and Elisa Calabrese in *Nostalgia del futuro en la obra de Carlos Fuentes* (Buenos Aires: Fernando García Cambeiro, 1973) are among the few critics to treat Fuentes' works as a continuum, without an important break with *Cambio de piel* and *Zona sagrada*. They outline in that work some of the points examined here.

3. Page references in brackets refer to *La muerte de Artemio Cruz* (Mexico City: Fondo de Cultura Económica, 1970).

4. See Gloria Durán, *La magia y las brujas en la obra de Carlos Fuentes* (Mexico City: Universidad Nacional Autónoma de México, 1976).

5. There is a very similar duality between betrayal and solidarity, Christian and Aztec salvation, in the prison scene involving Gervasio Pola in *La región más transparente*.

6. Leopoldo Zea, *El pensamiento latinoamericano* (Mexico City: Pormaca, 1965), vol. I, 7.

7. José Ortega y Gasset, 'Hegel y América', in *Obras completas* (Madrid: Revista de Occidente, 1954), vol. II, 572.

8. cit. by Zea, vol. I, 7.

9. *Terra Nostra* (Barcelona: Seix Barral, 1975), 483–85.

10. C. Fuentes, prologue to *Los reinos imaginarios: teatro hispanoamericano* (Barcelona: Barral, 1971), 10.

11. *Los reinos imaginarios*, 20.

BRITT-MARIE SCHILLER

Memory and Time in
The Death of Artemio Cruz

T he thread that leads the reader through the labyrinth of Carlos Fuentes'
The Death of Artemio Cruz traces the composition and decomposition of a
morally distorted character, the seventy-one year old business magnate,
Artemio Cruz, as he lies in agony on his deathbed. Cruz has successfully
dominated and repressed any consciousness of the moral implications of the
choices and decisions that have made him into the man he now is. But on the
day when he finally can hear the voice of his other self, he is told that "when
the autonomous functions of your body will force you to be aware of them
they will dominate and master you."[1] On that day Cruz can no longer
dominate and master either those around him or the voice of his conscience.
He has lived in a separateness and silence that repeat and reflect the silence
of the mulatto Lunero, the man who raised him, the brother of Isabel Cruz,
Artemio's mother: "Lunero did not know how to explain all this. He felt the
boy would not understand. But the mulatto's real reason for silence was the
fact that if he began to trace one thread of the story, the whole story would
have to come out. He would have to explain the beginning, and he would
thereby lose the boy" (p. 278). The thread that traces the story of Artemio
Cruz finally is composed of the memories that are forced upon him by the
consciousness that his weakened will can no longer suppress. On this last day
Artemio Cruz is condemned to remember the crucial moments in his life

From *Latin American Literary Review* 15, no. 29 (January–June 1987): 93–103. © 1987 by *Latin
American Literary Review*.

when he was faced with a choice. "Each time the option he elects leaves in its wake the sacrifice of a person or of an ideal," as Walter M. Langford puts it.[2] Langford goes on to suggest that "Artemio's contemplation of the key moments in his life assumes certain aspects of a general confession."[3] But the sense of confession is, at least, partly ironic: his contemplation takes place in the presence of a priest, but has none of the outer characteristics of a confession. The priest's presence is a nuisance, an intrusion, rather than a comfort. The contemplation is not a voluntary one. Cruz is instead the victim of an erupting consciousness as he is forced or unable to avoid recognizing who or what he has made himself into. He is sentenced to remember rather than be saved or absolved by the memories that he can no longer deny or ignore. But insofar as his contemplation, as all contemplation, is his own, insofar as the consciousness imposing itself is his self-consciousness, the condemnation is also a self-condemnation.

Wendy Faris suggests that the book might be regarded "as a final confession in a nontraditional mode, where the reader, not the priest, will condemn or absolve Cruz."[4] Insofar as this is a text with a social purpose it may well be the function of the reader to make such moral judgments, but this text fills not only such a purpose. What makes *The Death of Artemio Cruz* extremely effective as a text is the way the author enters the mind of the dying man through the play of tenses and the succession of pronouns in the mirrored self or selves of a consciousness. By expressing the breakdown of a mind through the breakdown of language, Fuentes draws the reader into the text and by drawing up lists, like litanies, of regrets, smells, debts, and, above all, the multiple uses of words, he draws attention to the surface of the text.

The structure of *The Death of Artemio Cruz* is rigid; it is as Lanin A. Gyurko says, "visible on the surface, like a literary exoskeleton, at times even like a straitjacket over the narrative."[5] The formal design is, indeed, visible on the surface, but it is not really a straitjacket over the narrative. The structure is not separate from and imposed on the text; rather, it maintains the tension between order and chaos, the chaos that Cruz fears and tries to hold off through the ordering and clarifying power of his mind. The rigid order and the threat of being lost in chaos coexist, as they do in the labyrinthine design of a formal French garden where a repetitive geometric pattern denies the stroller a sense of orientation through recognition. The thread that Fuentes furnishes the reader in this stylized structure of the text is the theme of memory. We find our way in the nonprogressing narrative as our understanding of Cruz' increasingly repetitive consciousness deepens.

The structure of *The Death of Artemio Cruz* is basically triadic. The triplets of each of the twelve sections—the I, you, he point of view—return with invariable regularity in the conventional ordering of the inflective forms of the verb in the singular: I am, you are, he is. In terms of the triads, then, the structure is cyclical, while from the perspective of the whole, the structure is static. Gyurko points out that "the trifurcation of self ... provides a means of dissecting failings within Cruz and of uncovering the reasons for his inability to actualize the other selves within him: and also that "the trinity of selves in Cruz refers ironically to the divine trinity.[6] The three parts of the structure organize the literary time into the present, the past as a chosen or imagined future, and the past. The first-person sections are in the present. The experiences of the present, such as "I wake ... the touch of that cold object against my penis awakens me" (p. 3), are in the beginning fairly long and coherent, but grow shorter and more fragmented, until the final disintegration of the I, you, and he as they sink into the chaos of a final solitude: "I don't know .. don't know ... I am he or it ... you were he ... or if I am the three ... You ... I carry you inside me and you will die with me..." (p. 305).

In the second-person sections Cruz is addressed across that gap in consciousness that makes the self into a relation but not yet a self.[7] That other self tells him, or he can no longer avoid telling himself, that there are "things you want to forget by remembering something else" (p. 9). "You will detest the I, the part of your you that calls it to your attention" (p. 29). "You yourself will make forgetfulness impossible" (p. 29). "You resist yourself for you will have made a secret vow not to recognize your debts" (p. 115). "You will read and you will choose again: you will choose another life" (p. 237).

The third-person sections are dated narratives of the past and constitute, as Joseph Sommers says, "'outside' information which can be accepted as an authentic version of the circumstances surrounding the various personal decisions."[8] These exterior and public accounts balance the interior monologues, the present suffering of the I and the mirrored I—the you—struggling with time, memories, and the voice of conscience. Except for the ordering in the text, the time of the third-person sections is historical, linear, and continuous and offers an understanding of the character in terms of causality. These narrated events "explain" and fill out the fragments of memories that immediately precede them in a second-person section. The transition between the two sections is often a repetition, the echo that moves thought in associative patterns: "You will push aside the curtains so that the early breeze can enter: oh how it will empty you, and you will, ah, forget that smell of incense and the smell that follows where you lead, oh how it will cleanse you: the breeze will not let you think of any doubt, it will not lead you to the thread [1947: September 11] He pushed aside the curtains and breathed the clean air. The early breeze came in rippling the curtains" (pp. 140–141). The scene that follows shows how the aging Cruz has tried to be cleansed of the "cell of time's cancer" through "buying" a girl for his vacation (p. 147). "He observed his face in the mirror: he wanted to find it the same as always" (p. 142).

In an interview cited by Wendy Faris, Fuentes talks about the voices in Artemio Cruz in terms of mirrors: "It's a question of a dialogue of mirrors between the three people, the three times that constitute the life of this hard and alienated character."[9] The third-person sections reflect the public life and identity of Cruz. At one point he sees "an old man who was not his other he, the reflection he had made familiar, grimaced at him from the mirror" (p. 154). In the opening first-person section: "I tighten the muscles of my face and open my right eye and see it reflected in the squares of silvered glass that encrust a woman's purse. I am this, this am I: old man with this face reflected in pieces of different-sized squares of glass: I am this eye, this eye I am" (p. 4).[10] The I sees itself in the present and is a witness to its own breakdown. In the second-person sections the shaded mirrors of the I and the he are unmasked by memories that return involuntarily.

The mirror metaphor structurally connects the three sections and the three aspects of the self divided by the three pronouns. The thread that orders and unifies the parts of the person and of the text is memory, but the mirror that shatters the unified self is also constituted by the reflections imposed by memory. By splitting the I into an addressed and an addressing part, the author holds up the addressing part, the second-person sections, as a double mirror, wherein the I is unmasked on one side, while on the other, the history of the making of the character is revealed.

Artemio Cruz does not explore his memory. He is forced to return to his past through the unconscious memories that on the last day return "involuntarily to slip through the chinks in the wall of pain and repeat to you, now, words you did not hear then" (p. 85). There is nothing that Cruz wants to find by a search for lost time. His project never was one of learning but solely one of survival, and for such a purpose, awareness may only weaken the self. The exposure of the man he has become takes place not so much against his will, or in spite of his will, as it does through the breakdown of it. He is subjected, beyond his will, to a lucidity that obliges him to take note of the life he mutilated by choosing not from desire but from self-interest, from fear, and from pride. In the sections from the second-person point of view, the relentless pressure to remember is expressed in a voice that is devastatingly coherent and analytical in contrast to the fragmentary and disjointed voice of the first-person sections where the language mirrors the progressive disintegration of mind and body.

In the second-person sections Cruz is addressed as he is condemned: "No, no, this is not what you would like to remember. You would rather remember something else ..." (p. 30). The darkened part of consciousness, his suppressed conscience, returns to take its revenge: awareness and recognition. It returns on the last day to impose judgment and to pronounce sentences: "First you must remember what condemns you ... then you may remember what you will" (p. 31). The voice in these sections speaks predominantly on the level of the past as predicted future: "for you will have created night by closing your eyes" (p. 31). Fuentes' choice of the future tense in the reminders of decisions made in the past by a man who no longer has a future, underscores the culpability of Artemio Cruz. In terms of freedom and necessity, the past is fixed by the closing off of possibilities in the present. The man he could have been is progressively sacrificed as Cruz makes choices in order to survive: "You will sacrifice, you will select one path giving up all the rest: you sacrifice by choosing, you will cease to be the man you might have been" (pp. 200–201). The future, still open, holds the possibility of his being otherwise, of his image not being irrevocably reflected by only one mirror. But that which could have been otherwise is constantly stifled and betrayed by choices made from fear and self-interest. In a predetermined universe Cruz would not have been held responsible for the destiny formed by the paths he took; he would have been trapped but also saved by a fated future. In a nondetermined future, however, we are what we are not yet—our possibilities. In Sartrean terms we are a pursuit of being. So on this last day when he is pursued by the voice of a consciousness that he is too weak to suppress, on this day when there are no more choices to be made, he is condemned to recognize that the choices he made were his and that he carries full responsibility for the destiny he forged for himself, for he could have chosen differently: "You will choose from the infinite array of mirrors only one, the one that will reflect you irrevocably and will throw a black shadow over all other mirrors: you will destroy them before they offer you, once again, that infinity of possible paths to be chosen from" (p. 200).

The (apparent) temporal dislocation of the future in the fixed past thus captures a voice that delivers predictions as accusations. Gyurko suggests that "constant shifting among narrative persons that represent, respectively, the present, the past-as-imagined future, and the historical past, is an attempt to represent, through the medium of language, the simultaneity of psychic flux, preceding on many levels concurrently and superimposing sensation, perception, memory, and imagination."[11] The regularly returning second-person voice does not, however, only represent the past-as-imagined future; it also presents the past as chosen future. The voice that seems to predict what choice or decision will be made, when that choice matters, is an indicting voice that condemns Cruz for making immoral and cowardly choices. He is condemned for the past that he chose, and the choice is dramatized by a voice that revives the moment in the past when the choice was made, in the present, then, when the future that could have been otherwise was darkened by his moral failing. So Catalina's caress revives the moment when his cowardness separated them irrevocably, because, as he hears inside: "And so with pride you will deny yourself, and you will survive, Artemio Cruz ..." (p. 86). The voice he can no longer escape is, of course, no one's but his own: the condemnation is a self-condemnation, as the consciousness that reveals and revives the moments when he chose and built his character is self-consciousness.

Two memories that repeatedly return are those of Regina and Lorenzo. These repetitive fragments are not so much signs of Cruz' disintegrating mind as they are signs of love's repetition. They express the desire to remember, the desire to return to moments of desire, for "memory is desire satisfied" (p. 58). Cruz wants to revive the memory of Regina and thus keep alive his desire for her: "Maybe to think of her would be enough to have her always beside him. Maybe memory may really prolong life, lace their legs together ..." (p. 75). In a transformed way he does keep the memory of Regina alive with his displaced desire for other women: Catalina, Laura, and Lilia. The intensity of the desire is sustained in the unconscious repetitions while the energy is scattered on substituted objects of passion and affection. But as his mind is in the final stages of disintegration, Cruz tries to hold on to life, brain, mind, and reason by remembering, wondering "how shall I revive ... your memory to await your ... return Regina Regina" (p. 265). The pressure to remember here originates not in a suppressed voice of conscience, the darkened half of (his) consciousness, but in the effort to survive.

Although the memory of Lorenzo condemns him, it also comforts him, for it recaptures a time when the alienation and isolation of Artemio's life were broken and briefly suspended. "That morning I waited for him with happiness. We rode our horses across the river." The phrase appears repeatedly, as a loose refrain, as a snapshot without a context, mysterious to the reader until the context that surrounds it locates its importance in the father–son relationship. This memory of his and Lorenzo's day separates Artemio from Catalina, who has no part in the life Lorenzo and he share at Cocuya, where Artemio has taken Lorenzo to live away from his mother. But it is also a memory of togetherness. The phrase that appears mainly in the first-person sections is not only without a context, it also interrupts the first-person singular with the first-person plural pronoun: we. The happiness that the phrase recalls is one of being together, a rare state of being, in the isolated life of Artemio Cruz, in the solitude of I, the distance of he. There is something then to be gained from this memory: "this place and his youth will let you remember your own youth, and you will not want to tell his how much this land means to you" (p. 161). The desire to remember is here the desire to remain within the memory—the future tense in the past captures hope: "you will remember in order to remember within your memory" (p. 161).

The past-as-future in the you-sections is thus not only a prediction that damns the choice. It also expresses hope for an imagined future, an imagination born from desire. Finally, the past as imagined future is motivated by regret, as Artemio recalls the letter from Lorenzo, sent by a friend after Lorenzo's death in Spain: "you will read and you will choose again: you will choose another life: / you won't force him to do what you did not do, rescue your lost life" (p. 237). A list follows where each entry is the other option, the road that Cruz did not follow, the man he did not become.

Faris claims that "Cruz uses his memory to fight against death: and that "Fuentes represents memory as power, how Cruz' memory triumphs (temporarily at least) over his surroundings."[12] I find it difficult to isolate one use of memory and especially to characterize that use as power. Cruz is a man at the mercy of memory rather than empowered with memory as a final instrument of mastery and domination. He is not at will to choose what to remember, but his memories master him and he must remember what condemns him, not only what pleases him or satisfies his desire.

In spite of the third-person sections being narrated in the past tense, that of memory, these sequences do not contain the personal remembrances of Artemio Cruz. They are rather public accounts of the man that others will remember. The memories that will no longer be kept in forgetfulness are called to Artemio's attention in the displays of a reflecting consciousness in the second person sections: "you will remember the self you left behind" (p. 12). The I that only wants to survive and escape the pain of the present is addressed by the other I that now insinuates itself as a splinter between and I and the he, "the cutting edge of memory that separates the two halves" (p. 12).

Time is used in many ways in *The Death of Artemio Cruz*. The present in the first-person sections is vital, lived time, hypostatized by the author, yet in flux: "Time that fills itself with vitality, with actions, ideas, but that remains always the inexorable flux between the past's first landmark and the future's last signpost" (p. 302). Such a time corresponds to Bergson's concept of pure duration or experienced time, an intensive magnitude, where each image is "permeating the other and [they are] organizing themselves like the notes of a time, so as to form what we shall call continuous or qualitative multiplicity with no resemblance to number."[13]

In the first-person sections of *The Death of Artemio Cruz* this sense of experienced time is, however, negative. The intensity of the awareness of time passing and passing away from him leads Cruz to struggle against time by thinking about what happened yesterday, by trying to forget the man he now finds himself to be. In conflict with this flight is the desperate wish to hold on to the present by holding on to awareness and reason. The sense of time as vital and lived time is negated also in the breakdown of the I as we witness the ending of lived time, the disintegration of vitality. The flux and flow become increasingly fragmented into disconnected thoughts and into unfinished and incoherent sentences.

The time in the second-person sections, both time lost and time recovered, is time reconstructed: "Time that will exist only in the reconstruction of isolated memory, in the flight of isolated desire" (p. 302). Time is recovered in Artemio's remembering the amorous hours with Regina. This is time relived in the return to a time filled with desire: "Desire will send you back into memory and you will remember, going back, back, never forward, in order to be satisfied: for memory is desire satisfied: and with memory you will survive, before it becomes too late/before chaos prevents memory" (p. 58). Descent into these memory images is an attempt both to regain time past and to gain time, to maintain awareness, and reason, to survive. Akin to this conception of time is the Bergsonian concept of scientific time, a quantitative process of counting simultaneities or successive oscillations. This is the sense of time as "the time you will create in order to survive, to feign the illusion of greater permanence" (p. 198).

The origin of measured time is located in the Cartesian *res cogitans*, the awareness of the self as a thinking thing. We measure time *because* we think. This operation is, according to Bergson, "native to the human mind; we practice it instinctively. Its recipe is deposited in the language."[14] This is not a time regained through memory, an individualized time, but, rather, the time we all share as conceptualizing beings: it is the invented measure of time. It is the sense of time that makes it possible to think, to perceive change, to retain images, "to hear the cyclical cries of animals on the mountain, to shout the changes of season, the howls of war, mourning and fiesta; in order, in short, to say time, speak time, and think the non-existent time of a universe that does not know time because it never began and will never end" (p. 198). There are clear echoes of this use of time in Octavio Paz' "The Dialectic of Solitude":

> Also, there was a time when time was not succession and transition, but rather the perpetual source of a fixed present in which all times, past and future, were contained. When man was exiled from that eternity in which all times were one, he entered

chronometric time and became a prisoner of the clock and the calendar.[15]

There is no sense of a Proustian eternal time in Fuentes' *The Death of Artemio Cruz*, of "fragments of existence withdrawn from Time."[16] The most highly valued sense of time in *Remembrance of Things Past* is the time regained that seems to lie outside of time, in such reminiscences as those of the madeleine dipped in tea, of the uneven stepping-stones at St. Mark's in Venice, and of the steeples of Martinville. The pleasure of the contemplation of these was, writes Proust, "the only genuine and fruitful pleasure that I had known."[17] The beauty of such moments, withdrawn from time, lies in their being regained in a work of art. Gilles Deleuze suggests that "The Search is oriented to the future, not to the past."[18] The voluntary memories that lead to thought and to art are essentially different from the involuntary figures of the imagination, "the sensuous signs of memory are the signs of life not of Art."[19] From such a Proustian perspective *The Death of Artemio Cruz* is oriented towards the past, in spite of the past-as-future tense of the second-person singular sections which signifies the desperate hope of a dying man as well as the lost time of a betrayed future. The recurrent memories of Artemio Cruz are signs of a wasted life, the life of an *hijo de la Chingada*, the fruit of a violation, if as Paz writes, "the *Chingada* is a representation of the violated Mother."[20] Artemio is, of course, the son of a violated mother, Isabel Cruz, violated by Atanasio Menchaca.

Remembrance of Things Past is oriented to the future in that we know that the end of *Time Regained* is the beginning of Proust's writing *Remembrance of Things Past* (with the exception of *Swann's Way*). As the three voices in *The Death of Artemio Cruz* stop sounding, however, there is no implication of a textual future. The sense of the future that Fuentes leaves the reader lies outside the text. It is the social and political state and future of a country that the anti-hero Cruz bequeaths his survivors. That the text serves this purpose is underscored by the author's dates at the end of the text: Havana, May 1960/Mexico City, December 1961; dates that locate the concern and evoke the hope for a different future inspired by the Cuban revolution. *The Death of Artemio Cruz* is not a Proustian text about a text; it is text about the character of Mexican reality compressed into a personality of one man. The disruption of language mirrors the disruption of mental continuity, but if the book is about Mexican reality, represented by one man, then the disruptive language is suggestive also of the disruption of social and political continuity. From this perspective, memory and time fill a social and historical function in *The Death of Artemio Cruz*.

NOTES

1. Carlos Fuentes, *The Death of Artemio Cruz*, tr. Sam Hileman (Farrar, Straus and Giroux, New York, 1964), p. 83. All subsequent references to *The Death of Artemio Cruz* are made in the body of the text.

2. Walter M. Langford, *The Mexican Novel Comes of Age*, (University of Notre Dame Press, Indiana, 1971, p. 136.

3. Ibid., p. 128.

4. Wendy Faris, *Carlos Fuentes* (Frederick Ungar Publishing Co., New York, 1983), p. 59.

5. Lanin A. Gyurko, "Structure and Theme in Fuentes' *La Muerte de Artemio Cruz*" (*Symposium*, 34 Spring 1980, 24–41), p. 30.

6. Ibid., pp. 33, 35.

7. I draw on Kierkegaard's *The Sickness Unto Death* here: "The self is a relation which relates itself to its own self, or it is that in the relation [which accounts for it] that the relation relates itself to its own self, the self is not the relation, but [consists in the fact] that the relation relates itself to its own self. Man is a synthesis of the infinite and the finite, of the temporal and the eternal, of freedom and necessity, in short it is a synthesis. A synthesis is a relation between two factors. So regarded, man is not yet a self." Soren Kierkegaard, *Fear and Trembling and The Sickness Unto Death*, tr. Walter Lowrie (Princeton University Press, Princeton, NJ, 1941) p. 146.

8. Joseph Sommers, *After the Storm* (University of New Mexico Press, Albuquerque, 1968), p. 156.

9. Faris, p. 61.

10. The translation reverses instead of repeats the reflections: "Soy esto. Soy esto." It also connects the repeated sentences with commas and finally signals the reflections with colons, as if the images were presented by the mirror, as if the I were introducing itself to the eye. The translation thus introduces a distortion in the reflected images of Cruz' face and eye, while in the original the image is merely repeated in square after square.

11. Gyurko, p. 31.

12. Faris, pp. 47, 58.

13. Henri Bergson, *Time and Free Will: An Essay on the Immediate Data of Consciousness*, tr. F. L. Dogson (George Allen & Unwin Ltd., London, 1916), p. 105.

14. Henri Bergson, *Duration and Simultaneity*, tr. Leon Jacobson (The Bobbs-Merrill Company, Inc., New York, 1965), p. 54.

15. Octavio Paz, *The Labyrinth of Solitude*, tr. Lysander Kemp (Grove Press, Inc., New York, 1985), p. 209.

16. Marcel Proust, *Remembrance of Things Past*, tr. C. K. Scott Moncrieff and Terence Kilmartin (Random House, New York, 1981), Vol. III., p. 908.

17. Ibid.

18. Gilles Deleuze, *Proust and Signs*, tr. Richard Howard (George Braziller, New York, 1972), p. 4.

19. Ibid.

20. Paz, p. 81.

RICHARD J. WALTER

Literature and History in Contemporary Latin America

Over the past several decades the literary "Boom" in Latin America has achieved a significant historical dimension. The leading figures of the movement have "made" history, not only in the way they have recreated the Latin American historical reality, but also through the indelible impact of their achievements throughout the hemisphere. The three novels considered here—Carlos Fuentes' *The Death of Artemio Cruz*, Gabriel García Márquez' *One Hundred Years of Solitude*, and Mario Vargas Llosa's *The War of the End of the World*—are essential reading for any historian of Latin American.[1] By the same token it seems to me equally essential for any reader of these works to appreciate and understand the historical context in which they are set, the approach to history of these three authors, and their contributions to the history of their continent.

The Mexican Revolution, the main backdrop for Fuentes' *Artemio Cruz*, began in 1910 as a confused rebellion against the dictatorship of Porfirio Díaz. Díaz, who had established his firm control over the country in the 1870s, was a politically skilled caudillo who forged a supporting coalition which included the Catholic Church, the Army, the wealthy landed elite, foreign investors, and creole bureaucrats called *científicos*, all of whom benefited directly from the Porfirian system.

The thirty-five year rule of Porfirio Díaz (1876–1911) brought some

From *Latin American Literary Review* 15, no. 29 (January–June, 1987): 173–182. © 1987 by *Latin American Literary Review*.

unquestionable gains to Mexico, foremost among them political stability and dramatic economic growth. By the first decade of the Twentieth century, however, the weaknesses of the Porfirian system had become patently obvious. Modernization had benefited foreigners and those at the top, who controlled most of the national wealth, but had done little if anything for the ninety-five percent of the population at the bottom. In 1910 and 1911 the various alienated and exploited sectors of Mexican society rose in a rebellion which lasted a decade and was the first great mass uprising of its kind in the Twentieth century.

For the purpose of better understanding *Artemio Cruz*, some essential characteristics of the Revolution should be noted. First, it lacked any single charismatic leader to provide it with coherence and continuity—no Lenin, Mao, or Fidel. Second, there was little ideological coherence, especially in the initial stages. Gradually, however, some revolutionary goals did emerge, finally codified in the new constitution of 1917. These included provisions for anti-clericalism, social justice, economic nationalism, and agrarian reform. Third, the Revolution was extraordinarily violent, many of the hundreds of thousands of deaths attributable as much to personal power struggles as to revolutionary passions.

By 1920 a new order was imposed on Mexico. A series of presidents, mostly from the north, controlled the nation until 1934. Under these leaders some progress was made toward fulfilling the goals of the Revolution, but it was slow and halting progress at best. In 1934 a new president, Lázaro Cárdenas, moved Mexico further on the path toward revolutionary achievement than had any other. Cárdenas greatly accelerated the process of agrarian reform, significantly strengthened the position of organized labor, and with the expropriation of foreign-owned oil companies in 1938 asserted Mexican control over Mexican national resources.

Mexican presidents since Cárdenas have tried to follow in his footsteps, but at a slower pace. Under their direction Mexico has made some notable advances in such areas as education, health care, and social services. Rapid industrialization and urbanization have been accompanied by marked improvements in transportation and communication facilities. Most significant, however, has been the political stability and continuity provided by the post-revolutionary leadership. Since 1920 Mexico has avoided any serious threat from either the left or the right and the military generally has remained only a negligible factor in Mexican politics, unlike the case in much of the rest of Latin America.

Nonetheless, the problems which confront present-day Mexico are staggering. Despite the gains made since the Revolution, severe social economic inequities prevail and millions of Mexicans live in abject poverty with little hope of relief. Unchecked urbanization threatens to overwhelm a capital city that contains a quarter of the country's total population. Mexico, along with Brazil, has amassed the largest foreign indebtedness in the Third World, producing widespread economic instability and uncertainty.[2]

Throughout the ups and downs of the postwar era, the government and the dominant *Partido Revolucionario Institucional* (PRI), two virtually indistinguishable institutions, have held high the banner of the Mexican Revolution as the touchstone of all official policy and action. At the same time, a growing number of critics have questioned the PRI's real commitment to the Revolution and argue instead that the original revolutionary impetus has not only slowed but has been abandoned altogether. Poverty, they note, still prevails and in some respects is worse than ever. While national control over certain resources, especially petroleum, has been assured, foreign investors since the 1940s have poured billions of dollars into Mexico and have realized handsome returns on their investments. Corruption has become an apparently ineradicable feature of all government operations. In sum, critics state, Mexico has returned in its essentials to the Porfiriato.[3]

Fuentes' *Artemio Cruz* fits into—and in many instances describes—the broad sweep of Mexican history. It also contributes to the debate over the course of the Revolution in recent decades. The main characters and the story are fictional, but there are references to actual personalities and events and the entire novel has about it, despite its structure and technique, an exceedingly realistic air. Artemio Cruz and others are presented as rather stark stereotypes, but, given our knowledge of Mexican history, rather believable stereotypes. Fuentes is sensitive to both the course and the nuances of Mexican history and expects the same of his reader. Although the story is told in a series of sometimes confusing flashbacks—perhaps as confusing and disjointed as the history of revolutionary Mexico itself—Fuentes' location of specific episodes in the life of Artemio Cruz in specific time periods is no accident. Fuentes uses this device to comment on different phases of Mexican history by describing the forces and circumstances existing at particular times and their likely effect on a man Cruz.

With an introduction to Mexican history, it is not difficult to place Cruz in the overall panorama. A revolutionary officer, he displays some courage and considerable shrewdness during his military career. Like so many involved in that experience, he seems caught up in events which are beyond both his control and his understanding. But he is clever, ruthless, and lucky enough to emerge from the Revolution unscathed and is able to use his wits and daring to take advantage of the new conditions created by the destruction of the Porfirian system to lay the groundwork for his own power and fortune. Gradually he makes the successful transition from revolutionary hero to powerful and wealthy figure in the mixed world of government and business. Allied with U.S.-based multinational corporations, he connives to break strikes and rob peasants of their land. He becomes in middle age that which he himself had fought against in his youth.

Forty years later, in his last hours, Cruz reflects back on his life and his legacy. In bitter self-awareness, he delivers a heritage to Mexico which consists of an unrelenting and damning indictment of the course of the Revolution:

> "You will bequeath them/future generations of Mexicans/their crooked labor leaders and captive unions, their new landlords, their American investments, their jailed workers, their monopolies and their great press, their wet-backs, hoods, secret agents, their foreign deposits, their bullied agitators, servile deputies, fawning ministers, elegant tract homes, their anniversaries and commemorations, their fleas and wormy tortillas, their illiterate Indians, unemployed laborers, rapacious pawnshops, fat men armed with aqualungs and stock portfolios, thin men armed with their fingernails: they have their Mexico, they have their inheritance."[4]

No one can doubt Fuentes' sophisticated and complete knowledge of Mexican history. His command of that history, combined with his literary genius, is what enables him to weave together fiction and fact in such a convincing and effective manner. No one can doubt either that in *Artemio Cruz* this politically-engaged writer has come down firmly on the side of those critics who have declared the Mexican Revolution, like the main character of the novel, if not dead, at least dying—falling apart from within. It is also significant that *Artemio Cruz* was written in the early 1960s when enthusiasm for the Cuban Revolution, the vitality and youth of which contrasted so strongly with the apparent petrification of the Mexican Revolution, was very high among Latin American intellectuals.

The value of *Artemio Cruz* for the historian, as is so often the case with literary works, is to bring great events and the large sweep of history down to the personal and individual level. Moreover, as a personal statement and interpretation of the author, it provides the historian with important evidence as to the state of mind of Latin American intellectuals at a particular point in history, in this instance when the left's euphoria over the Cuban Revolution collided with growing disillusionment over the failures of the Mexican experience. Nonetheless, the historian, as well as the general reader, must keep constantly in mind the fact that for all its realism, *Artemio Cruz* remains a work of fiction. Also, while *Artemio Cruz* illuminates many aspects of the Mexican historical experience, even with its unusual scope, it does not consider *all* aspects of that experience. The purposes of the author are clearly polemical. Fuentes is not striving for balance and objectivity, the goal of most historians. He is, instead, trying to make a particular point. One might fairly ask, for example, where are the undoubted accomplishments of the Revolution? Where are the honest and idealistic revolutionaries?

Unlike turbulent Mexico, Brazil, the setting for Vargas Llosa's *The War of the End of the World*, enjoyed a fair amount of political stability throughout the Nineteenth century. A constitutional monarchy, based on the wealthy planter class, itself based on black slavery, held the large and diverse country together and provided a favorable climate for foreign investment (mostly British) and economic growth. Eventually, however, social and economic changes led to the abolition of slavery in 1888 and the replacement of the monarchy with a republican form of government in 1889.

While these changes were accomplished with relative ease, the firm establishment of the republic proved complex, difficult, and time-consuming. The removal of the monarchy momentarily weakened central authority and led to several regional revolts. A series of military and civilian leaders struggled for better than a decade to establish a new central authority to restore political stability, continue economic growth, and move Brazil fully along the path of modernization. At all costs, the new leadership wanted to avoid the fragmentation, chaos, and confusion which had befallen the fledgling Spanish American republics at the beginning of the century.[5]

These events provide the larger context for Vargas Llosa's story. Briefly, in the 1880s and 1890s a backlands mystic, Antonio Conselheiro, "the Counselor," began to develop a following in the interior of the northeastern state of Bahia. Predicting the end of the present world and the beginning of a new one, he gradually became a symbol and leader for those who remained committed to the monarchy. In 1896 he and several thousand of his followers established a community at an abandoned cattle ranch called Canudos, where they planned to wait out the apocalyptic developments predicted by the Counselor, at the same time rejecting the advances of encroaching republican civilization by refusing to pay taxes and by serving as a haven for a large number of backland outlaws. The insecure new federal government eventually crushed this "revolt" in 1897, but only after sending several expeditions to Canudos and expending a significant amount of men, supplies, and prestige.

The events at Canudos were originally detailed in a classic of Brazilian historical literature, *Os Sertões* by Euclides Da Cunha.[6] Vargas Llosa, who dedicates *The War of the End of the World* to Da Cunha himself clearly draws on *Os Sertões* not only for inspiration, but also for much of the factual content of his novel. The story he tells is essentially the same story Da Cunha had told eighty years earlier. A reading of the two works finds many parallels in terms of characters, events, and themes. Antonio Conselheiro and Antonio Moreira Cesar (leader of the third expedition against Canudos) play major roles in both accounts. The details of the campaigns, including the savagery and destruction which accompanied them, are abundantly clear in both works. The themes of central authority versus local autonomy and of the modern versus the traditional are also prominent in both.

Vargas Llosa's novel, however, is more than just an echo of Da Cunha's. Fiction based on fact, the work embellishes and enriches the historical narrative through imaginative and evocative description and the introduction of new and different characters. These include Galileo Gall, a Scottish-born anarchist, who sees Canudos idealistically as the beginning of a revolution which will ultimately end the tyranny of the state; Epaminodas Goncalves, ambitious editor of the *Journal de Noticias* and leader of the "Progressivist Republican Party," who tries to use the rebellion in the backlands to bring ultimate discredit to the remnants of the Empire; and, the Baron de Canabrava, who represents the local elite and in response to the attacks from both sides attempts to turn matters to his own favor by accusing the republicans of fomenting the entire episode.

With these new characters, among others, Vargas Llosa also introduces some new themes to the story, most notably the presence of anarchism and the alleged intervention of Great Britain in the events surrounding the Canudos rebellion. Most likely, Vargas Llosa, who himself did extensive research on the larger historical context, employs these elements to provide his novel with a more contemporary framework. Foreign intervention and radical foreign ideologies were not prominent characteristics of Brazil's history in the late Nineteenth century and of little concern to Da Cunha, who saw the events at Canudos almost strictly in Brazilian terms. Interventionism and the impact of European-based radical ideas did become integral parts of the Brazilian and Latin American reality in the ensuing decades of the Twentieth century.

For the historian, then, *The War of the End of the World* brings to life again the events at Canudos and underscores and reflects their impact on Brazilian society as a whole. Vargas Llosa, like Da Cunha, uses his story to make some telling critical comments about the army, politicians, and the failures of successive governments to come to grips with the basic structural factors which led to rebellions such as that at Canudos. At the same time, the story also reflects Vargas Llosa's clear disenchantment with violent revolution, which, in the case of Canudos, led only to death and destruction. He is also severely critical of those who view revolution from the outside and in very romantic terms, with little real understanding of its causes or ultimate consequences.

From the viewpoint of the political historian, the most striking feature of García Márquez' Colombia is the long-lived two-party system, a system, with the exception of Uruguay, unique in Latin America. These two parties, the Liberals and the Conservatives, have dominated Colombian politics and government from the mid-Nineteenth century to the present day. Their persistence has been due to a host of complex factors, including effective organization, able leadership, and a willingness on occasion to compromise which has served to co-opt or preempt more extreme forces on the right and the left. The competition between the two parties historically has produced numerous revolts and attempted coups, especially in the Nineteenth century, but the moments of compromise when faced with common threats have also enabled the two parties to forestall the development of a Mexican or Cuban style revolution in Colombia.

Throughout the Twentieth century, except for a violent interlude in the late 1940s and early 1950s, the two parties have continued to alternate in and to share power, helping to make Colombia one of Latin America's most stable democracies. At the same time, Colombia, much like Mexico, faces enormous social and economic problems, which in the 1980s have been exacerbated by the challenges of revolutionary guerrilla organizations, the powerful and insidious influence of drug traffickers, and the devastating effects of natural disasters.[7]

Gabriel García Márquez' *One Hundred Years of Solitude*, for all its fantasy and "magic realism," is well-grounded in the history of Colombia.[8] A specific aspect of the experience which received particular treatment in the novel is the nature of the two dominant parties and their armed conflicts. In this regard, the author strives to make two main points. First, that while both parties seek to represent certain ideologies, most who follow them and are caught up in the interminable civil wars of the Nineteenth century do so without any clear idea as to why and for what they are fighting. In most instances, participants in these struggles follow a dynamic leader, like Colonel Aureliano Buendía, who himself may have no clear goal in mind other than to defend his own rights and privileges or to exact revenge on an opponent in a continuous cycle of attack, counter-attack, and frustration.

Second, García Márquez argues that for all their disagreements and disputes, Conservatives and Liberals are little different from one another in terms of basic beliefs and in the social background of their leadership. At one point, in disillusionment, Aureliano Segundo explains that "The only difference today between Liberals and Conservatives is that the Liberals go to mass at five o'clock and the Conservatives at eight."[9] At another point, Colonel Aureliano Buendía's revolutionary momentum is halted by a compromise between the leaders of the two parties. "It was," García Márquez writes, "the most critical moment of the war. The Liberal landowners, who had supported the revolution in the beginning, had made secret alliances with the Conservative landowners in order to stop the revision of property titles. The politicians who supplied funds for the war from exile had publicly repudiated the drastic aims of Colonel Aureliano Buendía ..."[10]

In sum, García Márquez believes that the two dominant parties represent only the elite and that their struggles for power have brought only suffering for most Colombians. This criticism echoes similar attacks from the left in Colombia (and elsewhere) and reminds us of Fuentes' condemnation of the Mexican Revolution in *Artemio Cruz*. As with Fuentes, however, this criticism fails to appreciate the relative political stability and continuity which Colombia has enjoyed, due in large measure to the two-party system and the abilities of the country's political leadership.

Despite the clear differences among these three novels, set in three different Latin American countries, the authors deal with some common themes which characterize the history of the entire region. All three, for example, refer to the consequences of modernization for traditional societies. All three, too, focus on the problem of revolution in Latin America, including the violence which accompanies such movements, the ideological confusion associated with revolution, the important role played by charismatic leaders, and the ultimate frustration of those who pursue a revolutionary cause.

All three authors were clearly influenced by what many Latin American writers and others consider the area's most successful revolution—that of Fidel Castro in Cuba. Moreover, all three seem to approach their historical material with revolutionary aims in mind. In these works, for example, they sharply attack the dominant traditional institutions and values of Latin American society. They argue, to one degree or another, that fundamental changes are required in Latin America or the familiar cycle of frustration, violence, and repression, so magnificently depicted in *One Hundred Years of Solitude*, will continue its relentless course. Vargas Llosa, it should be mentioned, perhaps reflecting his own disillusionment with the Cuban model and writing in the 1980s rather than the 1960s, suggests also that a romanticized view of revolution can produce more problems than it resolves.

Finally, all three works throw light on the historical evolution of Latin America and force the reader to confront the stark reality of that history.

Often the light they throw is a half-light, using history for the authors' fictional or political purposes. These works are novels, not scholarly accounts, and for all their power and insight should be read with discrimination and within the larger context of the overall historical framework. In the last analysis, the great value of these works from the viewpoint of the historian is their reflection of the attitudes and arguments of three of the most important Latin American writers and intellectuals of the postwar era.

NOTES

1. The editions used were Carlos Fuentes, *The Death of Artemio Cruz* (translated from the Spanish by Sam Hileman) (New York: Farrar, Straus and Giroux, 1964); Gabriel García Márquez, *One Hundred Years of Solitude* (translated from the Spanish by Gregory Rabassa) (New York: Avon Books, 1971); and, Mario Vargas Llosa, *The War of the End of the World* (translated by Helen R. Lane) (New York: Farrar, Straus and Giroux, 1984).

2. Some general works on Mexican History are Charles C. Cumberland, *Mexico: The Struggle for Modernity* (Oxford, 1968); Pablo González Casanova, *Democracy in Mexico* (Oxford, 1970); and, Michael C. Meyer and William L. Sherman, *The Course of Mexican History* (Oxford, 1979).

3. See Stanley R. Ross, ed. *Is the Mexican Revolution Dead?* (New York, 1966).

4. Fuentes, *op cit.*, p. 269.

5. General works on Brazil which cover these developments are José M. Bello, *A History of Modern Brazil, 1889–1964* (Stanford, 1966); Richard Graham, *Britain and the Onset of Modernization in Brazil: 1850–1914* (Cambridge, 1968); Clarence H. Haring, *Empire in Brazil: A New World Experiment with Monarchy* (Harvard, 1958); and, Rollie E. Poppino, *Brazil, The Land and People* (Oxford, 1968).

6. Euclides Da Cunha, *Rebellion in the Backlands* (Translated by Samuel Putnam) (Chicago, 1944).

7. Some general works on Colombia which stress the two-party dominance are Robert H. Dix, *Colombia: The Political Dimensions of Change* (Yale, 1967); John D. Martz, *Colombia: A Contemporary Political Survey* (North Carolina, 1962); and James L. Payne, *Patterns of Conflict in Colombia* (Yale, 1968).

8. See Lucila Inés Mena, *La función de la historia en 'Cien años de Soledad'* (Bogotá, 1979) and Raymond L. Williams, *Gabriel García Márquez* (Boston, 1985), pp. 82–86.

9. García Márquez, *op cit.*, p. 9.

10. Ibid., pp. 158–159.

SANTIAGO TEJERINA-CANAL

Point of View in The Death of Artemio Cruz: Singularity or Multiplicity?

The diversity of narrative voices is one of the most difficult and problematic aspects confronting the reader from the outset of *The Death of Artemio Cruz* (1962). In *Where the Air Is Clear* (1958) Carlos Fuentes had experienced problems with narrative technique due to its experimental nature and to complexity of plot.[1] He later skirted such difficulties in *The Good Conscience* (1959) by simplifying plot and by using a less innovative, more "traditional-Galdosian" narrative technique, as he himself recognizes.[2] Having learned from these two experiences, with *The Death of Artemio Cruz* Fuentes finally demonstrates his mastery of the experimental novel by successfully employing a complex technique, a synthesis of his past novelistic exercises.[3]

Such a narrative procedure is already suggestively "sketched out" in the third and fourth epigraphs, quoted from Stendhal and Gorostiza. In effect, these "pre-texts" (not merely pretexts) precede the text as generators of the novel's narratological organization.[4] The Stendhal epigraph defines the technical importance and method of the point of view: "I alone, I know what I can do. To others I am only a perhaps."[5] It is here that Fuentes pointedly introduces the problematics of linguistic expression and communication with others who, as mere spectators, have no reason to participate in the self-accounting of a life story. As A. A. Mendilow contends, the attainment of

From *The Review of Contemporary Fiction* 8, no. 2 (Summer 1988): 199–210. © 1988 by *The Review of Contemporary Fiction*.

self-knowledge may be possible solely from within the self: "We do not see ourselves as others see us. We are aware in ourselves of the whole pressure of the past in our present.... As regards others, however, we are mere spectators; ... We know only the resultant of the forces that work in them as it expresses itself in outward behaviour."[6] Analogously, Artemio's self, represented by the deictic "I," potentially remains a "perhaps" for anyone other than that same character. But in order to expose to the reader the narrating protagonist's mind, Fuentes availed himself of what Mendilow has termed "restricted point of view." With this, the "Arte-mío" ("my-art") inscribed in both the name of the protagonist and the title of the novel is fictively attributable to Artemio's consciousness, to the figurative "I" who observes that "I alone, I know what I can do." In the words of Carlos Fuentes as critic, "*The Death of Artemio Cruz* is the story of a personal, untransferable destiny that closes with the death of the protagonist.... It is a mirror-like dialogue among three persons, among three times which form the life of this tough and alienated character."[7]

Fuentes organizes his narrator's tale in twelve sections, each consisting of three parts which correspond to first-, second-, and third-person narrations respectively; an additional thirteenth section contains two subdivisions told in the first and second persons. The whole of Artemio's narrative act is carried out through a cohesive mental logic implicitly linked to the pronominal "I" of Artemio's present.

Since Spanish grammar affords no single verb tense capable of simultaneously expressing the psychological, chronological, and spatial dimensions of the tripartite Artemian personality, the "restricted point of view" of the "I as protagonist" must undergo a triple division, as suggested by Gorostiza's epigraph: "... of myself and of Him and of we three, always three!"; that is to say, into the consciousness of the Artemio-I of the present, the subconscious of the Artemio-YOU of the recent past and future, and the memory of the Artemio-HE of the distant past.

As the novel begins, we find Artemio Cruz struggling between life and death. The dying character renders an account of his immediate self-awareness, his genesis of knowledge: "I WAKE" (3), "I FEEL" (24), "I FEEL" (51), "I SMELL" (132), "I WAKE" (211), "I HAVE wakened" (262), "I KNOW" (297), "I DON'T know" (305). The Artemian "I" closely follows Jungian thought: "*The self is of an infinitely complex magnitude, somewhat like a condensed compilation of data and sensations*; firstly, there figures in the self the perception of the spatial orientation of the body, of coldness, heat, hunger, etcetera, and, secondly, the perception of the affective states."[8]

Following these fully lucid moments are periods of "half-darkness" (Jung, 7) and "half-sleep" (Jung, 57) narrated in the second person-YOU, during which structures emerging from Artemio's subconscious often bring about self-accusations. Further, the YOU represents the will to live, that is, the will to find the sentient, or the "lower half" of the brain (the I) which in turn "carries on the immediate tasks and thus frees the other, higher part [the YOU] for thought, imagination, and desire" (Jung, 57). Both narrative typologies embody the dichotomy Tzvetan Todorov posited as "themes of the self" (*thèmes du je*) and "themes of the other" (*thèmes du tu*); the former as "the relation between man and the world, of the *perception–consciousness system*," subsuming "the 'themes of vision' ... because of the importance which the sense of *sight* and *perception* in general assume." The latter, the "themes of the other," or "you," "concern, rather, the relation of man with his desire—and thereby with his *unconscious*.... If the themes of the self implied an essentially *passive* position, we note here, by way of distinction, a powerful *action* on the surrounding world."[9] The YOU apocalyptically prescribes the way to recapture time past. Thus, the narration moves from the YOU's will to the memory of the HE. Memory functions as the only means of survival, by "obtaining information and transmitting it from the front backward."[10] Life is memory, and a lack of that faculty is absence of life: "with memory you will survive, before it becomes too late, before chaos prevents memory" (58). When the YOU's will collapses, what follows will be chaos or death; accordingly, the novel ends in a second-person narrative section in which the YOU no longer wills memory.

The novel's narrative situation is surprisingly parallel to the example used by Ortega to illustrate distance and point of view in the section of his essay entitled "A Few Drops of Phenomenology": "A man is dying [*agoniza*]. His wife is by his bedside. A doctor takes the dying man's pulse. In the background two more persons are discovered: a reporter who is present for professional reasons, and a painter whom mere chance has brought here." In Fuentes's novel the reference is respectively to Artemio, Catalina, the examining doctor, and a medical team that is to perform surgery on him. Nor should we forget Pons and the reporters from the newspaper owned by Artemio, Padilla and his tape recorder, and, above all, the narrator and the "implied author," who, like Ortega's "painter" and "reporter," hide "in the background" of *The Death of Artemio Cruz* and move the narration's strings. In Ortega's situation "wife, doctor, reporter and painter witness one and the same event. Nonetheless, this identical event—a man's death [*agonía*]—impresses each of them in a different way." The closer the distance, the greater the sentimental participation in the scene (wife); and vice versa (painter). Still, Carlos Fuentes assumes a perspective not considered by Ortega: that of the dying man himself. It is he who experiences the immediate situation most intensely but at the same time remains most removed from it as he watches through the lens of memory. As source and ultimate focalizer of the narrative, Artemio assumes a role of a rather protean nature. He fabricates any number of subsidiary points of view, such as that of his wife, Catalina, where she acts as secondary narrator, or that of a practitioner of morality in second-person narration, or of a kind of "reporter" or narrator of memoirs. In this sense, Artemio plays the sole narrator-painter who provides the reader with apparently diverse points of view, which, nonetheless, are reducible to that of Artemio-I-of-the-present. Fuentes shows that a point of view whose distance is reduced to zero, rather than just to a minimum, as in his wife's case, can produce Ortega's "artistic art," of "inhuman" interest, but also art of "human" concern. Therefore, *The Death of Artemio Cruz*, though a work of "new art," has not only attracted the "select minority" but—something unforeseen in Ortega's aristocratic prophecy—has also appealed to that "majority" of the "bristling masses."[11]

The novel's formal pattern of first-, second-, and third-person narrations is fictively generated by this single narrator whose feelings and perceptions focus his "mind's eye," and constitute the overarching "restricted point of view" in *The Death of Artemio Cruz*. The remaining characters in the work are perceived through this narrator-protagonist.[12] Theoretically, this type of perspective would fit Friedman's "I as Witness" category, insofar as it is limited almost exclusively to Artemio's own thoughts and perceptions, his field of action having been severely reduced in comparison with the traditional omniscient third-person narrator. Nonetheless, his "mobility" must be taken into account. Artemio is not as "restricted" as might be supposed since Fuentes, through the mind of this narrator, presents conversations his focal character had participated in or overheard, as well as the visions and feelings of other characters. Thus, Artemio directs his senses—sight, hearing, touch, taste, and smell—and his thoughts in every direction. At times he couches his perceptions and thoughts in dialogue and scenes, and these passages might well be labeled "dramatic method or mode" under Mendilow and Friedman's classification. Whereas in "pure narration" the raconteur controls and often ironizes the story, in the more "dramatic mode" an author—Fuentes in this instance—narrows the gap between reader and story thereby drawing the reader, who senses a sharp immediacy, into the fictional event. Interior monologue, and stream-of-consciousness, subcategories of Friedman's "Selective Omniscience," are also employed, especially in order to delve into the lower depths of the mind whose subverbal level breaks up linguistic forms.

The problem Fuentes faced in employing first-person narration was that the narrator could neither properly characterize himself nor sufficiently analyze his own biases or subconscious reactions. Mendilow observes that the narration of memories in first person and past tense is ineffective since the reader is made to feel that events are distant in both time and effect. Narration in the third-person past tense, however, is felt by the reader as contemporaneous to him. Fuentes seems to have found a very appropriate solution to this problem. Just as Artemio's single facial image is turned into multiple reflections in the small mirrors adorning Teresa's purse, so the one "I-as-protagonist" becomes reflectively three narrative persons, in what appears to be a Cubist rendering, in narrative form, of the classic mirror image. The use of the future tense in both its apocalyptic and familiar second-person form brings Artemio's psychic depths closer to the reader; further, this technique places the reader in the protagonist's position, making him what Gerald Prince calls the "narratee."[13]

If Artemio's first- and second-person narrators respectively provide an exterior and circumstantial account of himself and his immediate surroundings, and a deep view of his psychological intimacy, his third-person narrator portrays the political, religious, economic, and historical background of his life.[14] The effect achieved by using Artemio as both main character and omniscient narrator is a highly dramatic one: far from being seemingly detached from the work, he stands out as the protagonist of both the story and its telling. What separates storyteller from his narrated self in the second- and third-person accounts is distance in time and space, so that there is a former Artemio Cruz who is both the same and distinct from the present narrating one. Just as the "real author" differs from the implied author, so in this case the "I," "YOU," and "HE" unfold and unite in an "I–YOU–HE" configuration or "Implied Narrator," in Booth's terminology. The first-person narrator would be "dramatized" ("homodiegetic" for Genette), and the second and third persons "undramatized" ("heterodiegetic").[15] At any rate, the "Implied Narrator" recounts his own life from his unique Artemian perspective. The narrator-protagonist's vision of the past is colored by his present and by the accumulation of all that has happened posterior to the events he remembers. The veil of objectivity is necessarily tenuous since Artemio is judging his own life story. He offers a self-interested "point of view" designed to justify his own behavior before himself and the reader. The narrator's continual modulations suggest the appearance of objectivity by showing characters from distinct "points of view," though these omniscient, pseudo-objective, and pseudo-distanced techniques only conceal a refined subjectivity designed to dispose the reader's opinions to those of Artemio.

The YOU's will is the origin and conscious motive for remembering, and its subjective nature is evident: "you will close your eyes and you will see only what your brain wants you to see: more than the world, yet less: you will close your eyes and the real world will no longer compete with the world of your imagination" (55). What seems to be the "point of view" of other characters, given on countless occasions in the novel, remains that of the only apparently "limited" narrator that is Artemio himself.

Take for example the episode in which the relationship between Artemio and Catalina is recounted, June 3, 1924 (87–109): The third-person narration of a conversation between Artemio and Ventura in revealing the former's deceitful takeover of the peasants is mixed with Catalina's thoughts explaining the end of her intimate relationship with Artemio. It is doubtful that this is a question of "Catalina's intrusion into the narrative from her own point of view," as Daniel de Guzmán claims.[16] On the contrary, Artemio remains the same protean narrator who pretends to deliver Catalina's point of view in order to affect objectivity. In this third-person episode, three separate forms of narration exist: one similar to other third-person narrations; another, in italics, simulating Catalina's personal diary; and a third, in parentheses and quotation marks, recording the dialogue between Artemio and Ventura. A salient feature of this passage is the evident connection, by virtue of common words or thoughts, among the three seemingly separate narrations which finally dissolve into one: that of the omniscient narrator. This episode's multiple points of view lead the reader to believe in Catalina's guilt and Artemio's bravery. But the eventual fusion of perspectives reveals this section's underlying subjective and self-interested nature. The explanation for this final soldering of voices is offered in the immediately preceding second-person section of the novel where memory, "unconscious, beyond your will, returns involuntarily to slip through the chinks in the wall of pain, and repeat to you, now, words you did not hear then ... 'I let myself go'" (85–86). These last four words lead into the June 3, 1924 episode and function as a leitmotiv in both the omniscient narration and in Catalina's diary. The latter case illustrates the superimposition by the mind of the first-person narrator-protagonist on what is only in appearance Catalina's account of the events of that third day of June. One of the second-person narrative sections playfully offers osmosis as an explanation for Artemio's omniscience: "... and perhaps with the stroke of her fingers there will come to you words that will mix with that recurrent memory ... her pale fingers will touch your fevered forehead, they will want to still your pain, they will want to say to you today what they have not said for forty-three years" (85–86).

Another clue to the novel's narratological singularity emerges from a consecutive reading of three sections: the Lorenzo episode of February 3, 1939 (220–33), and the narrations following it in first and second person. In this episode, the adventures, loves, and mishaps of Lorenzo, Artemio's son, are rendered in a rather traditional omniscient and detailed account except for a series of scattered and mysteriously puzzling quotes which "trouble" the narrative. The next two sections retrospectively reduce the strangeness of these quotes by identifying their origin and, indeed, explain the fictive genesis of the whole third-person passage. On one hand, the source of the quotes is revealed as Lorenzo's last letter to his father, mailed posthumously by the youth's friend Miguel who also included a note to the elder Cruz; on the other—as the following piece of first-person narration suggests—the third of February episode comes to be no more than Artemio's fictive, passionate elaboration of the missive:

> ... he rode away on horseback, that morning; this I remember: I received a letter with foreign stamps.... I dreamed, I imagined, I knew those names, I remembered those songs, *ay* thanks, but to know, how can I know? *I don't know*, I don't know what that war was like, with whom he spoke before he died, what the men's names were, who were killed with him, nor the names of the women, what he said, what he thought, how he was dressed, what he ate that day, *I don't know: I make up a country-side: I invent cities, I imagine names, and now I don't remember.* (235; my emphases)

The narrator inventively embellishes that correspondence so as to exalt and justify his own behavior with respect to his son, with whom Artemio identifies by means of another narratological deceit: the narrator-protagonist uses the deictic HE referring not to himself, as in the rest of the third-person passages of the novel, but to Lorenzo. Thus, the single narrator ties up the informational loose ends of Lorenzo's letter and Miguel's notes, and reveals as was the case in Catalina's pseudo-narration—pure novelization on his part as an "Implied Narrator," whether "dramatized" or "undramatized," "homodiegetic" or "heterodiegetic," "protagonist" or "witness." Artemio, like the hero of Italo Svevo's *La coscienza di Zeno*, "thinking that he can be the novelist of his own life, learns that to recapture the past is to structure it, to falsify it, to invent it, in short, as if it belonged to someone else."[17] Artemio as sole narrator recaptures his own life and justifies himself in the fiction of his memory. Nobody else within the novel exists as an autonomous narrator; rather, they are part of this narrator's fiction.

Consequently, as the narrator is one, so is the resultant "point of view."[18] In first-person sections Artemio is at once protagonist and narrator who in the second- and third-person sections puts aside his role as protagonist to offer two different facets and moments of his life and personality: the "yesterday" and the "today" of the YOU's unconscious, and the HE's memory of the distant past.

The Death of Artemio Cruz resists easy placement within the numerous typologies of "point of view" developed in the fifties, sixties, and seventies; however, the terminology they developed aids in making clear and concrete the work's technical narrative constructs and establishes the very identity and originality (or singularity) of Fuentes's novel. Nevertheless, as Susan B. Lanser contends in *The Narrative Act*, "point of view" is not simply a technical and aesthetic instrument but an ideological one. Theoretical innovation by itself cannot be divorced from Fuentes's social and ideological protest and this facet could have been the detonator which unleashed some of the most bitter attacks against the novel. Lanser states:

> It may not be surprising that works that perpetuate the status quo most uncritically ... are often formally imitative, tightly constructed around a formula, creating a closed world. In texts where ideological assumptions prevalent in the "culture-text" are explicitly or implicitly challenged or undermined, the form may be more likely to reflect the conflicts inherent in this very attempt. It is possible that new forms emerge not simply, as Lukács imagined, from new content, but from the attempt to reject ideology.[19]

The Death of Artemio Cruz is one such attempt. The main character embodies the "point of view" of the ruling class, which is of a monolithic, unscrupulous, and decidedly masculine character, endemic to a Mexico ruled by a "power elite": from Montezuma to Cortés, Santa Anna, and Porfirio Díaz; from Irineo to Atanasio, Gamaliel, and Artemio. Artemio's sway over point of view could therefore be taken as a metaphor of his absolute dominion over his world. The novel's dedication to a U.S. sociologist, transcribed in the form of a pyramid in the original Spanish edition, graphically and semantically acts as a generator of the Mexican society's pyramidal structure in the text:

A

C. Wright Mills

Verdadera voz de Norteamérica,

amigo y compañero en la lucha de Latinoamérica.

"For C. Wright Mills, true voice of North America, friend and comrade in the Latin-American struggle." Charles Wright Mills, the famous U.S.

activist, who had died the very year of the publication of the novel, introduced a conflictive sociology, focused on problems of power and its unequal distribution in society.

The real America, portrayed through Artemio's "point of view," is a dictatorial America, corrupted by economic, political, and religious interests. The reader familiar with American and Mexican history can perceive, through this "tough and alienated" narrator-protagonist, the implicit author's continuous condemnation of cultural, economic, and religious colonialism, be it from the Spanish past or the U.S. present. Such colonialism is upheld by the powerful for their own benefit (Artemio) and tolerated by the indifferent well-to-do, while the helpless masses endure poverty, humiliation, and deceit, all of which is emblematically portrayed in the dominant and deceptive point of view.

In *The Power Elite*, C. Wright Mills observes, on one side, the power, prestige, and riches of the elite formed by big corporations, "warlords," top politicians, and media barons, of whom Artemio would be a compendium: he owns corporations, commands the army, participates directly or indirectly in the political direction of Mexico. At the base of the social pyramid, Mills places the masses without any say in public affairs and forever subject to forces beyond their control, as happens in our novel to Indians, farmers (*campesinos*), and working masses, controlled by the "cacique de turno," be his name Irineo, Atanasio, Gamaliel, Pizarro, or Artemio.

C. Wright Mills interprets the social sciences in a macrosociological way; that is, he tries to study humans not in a little corner of reality but in history, establishing connections between history and biography.[20] The similarity with Fuentes's socio-novelistic study is also remarkable in this respect: we are offered Artemio's biography within the historical framework of the Mexican Revolution. The continuous comparisons between biography and history set up an equation of biography and history, the identification of Artemio with the Mexican Revolution: "Artemio Cruz. So that was the name of the new world that had risen from the ashes of civil war" (45). Artemio's account is a story of death, that is, the history of Mexico. Furthermore, Artemio's own fictionalized life story is the true synthesized history of America, from North to South, Precolombian, Colonial, and Independent. This is the America as expressed by C. Wright Mills as the "true voice of North America."

In this same way we arrive at still another generator, "Artemio Cruz": "the eleven letters of my name, which can be written a thousand ways, Amuc Reoztrir Zurtec Marzi Itzau Erimor, but which has as its key, its pattern, Artemio Cruz" (111). These eleven letters in Artemio Cruz's name anagrammatically generate and condense the same idea: *Americo Truz* ("truth"). This bilingual combination is neither arbitrary nor capricious. The novel uses English continuously in the original Spanish edition, and Catalina's preoccupation with accurate pronunciation is apposite:

> "Joan Crawford," said the daughter. "Joan Crawford."
> "No, no, it isn't pronounced like that. Crow-fore. Crow-fore. They pronounce it like that."
> "Crau-fore."
> "No, no. Crow, crow, crow. The 'a' and 'w' together are pronounced like 'o.' I believe that's how they pronounce it." (18)

Analogously:

> "Americo Truth. Americo Truth."
> "No, no, it isn't pronounced like that. Truz. Truz. They pronounce it like that."
> "Trus."
> "No, no. Truz, truz, truz. The 't' and 'h' together are pronounced like Castillian 'z.' I believe that's how they pronounce it."

That is to say, the "true America": *Americo Truz*. Certainly "Americo" and not "America": "Americo" in its Spanish masculine form, because in reality, America—or Mexico and its Revolution—is dominated by Artemios, by men "with balls" (as the text repetitively emphasizes), by powerful men who use women as sex objects or as ornaments in brilliant political careers, or perhaps as intermediary agents in the conquest of economic, social, or territorial advantages. This is the function of most of the feminine characters in *The Death of Artemio Cruz*: Ludivinia, Baracoa, and Isabel Cruz, Regina, Laura, Catalina, Lilia, and the Indian woman used by Artemio when Catalina is pregnant or upset, his own daughter, his granddaughter Teresa, and Gloria, whom he rejects as opposed to Lorenzo (his son), a beloved active masculine model. In opposition to masculine aggressiveness and manliness, which "is never to 'crack,' never to back down," never to "open oneself up," the woman is presented as a passive victim, "submissive [*rajada*] and open by nature" because of "the misfortune of her 'open' anatomy," as Paz writes.[21]

As in many other aspects, Octavio Paz's *The Labyrinth of Solitude* seems to mark the guideline for this perception of the feminine in which the woman is instrument and means, never end. There is a passage in Paz's important essay that seems an accurate model for this novel's feminine world:

Whether as prostitute, goddess, *grande dame* or mistress, woman transmits or preserves—but does not [create (*crea*)]—the values and energies entrusted to her by nature or society. In a world made in man's image, woman is only a reflection of masculine will and desire. When passive, she becomes a goddess, a beloved one, a being who embodies the ancient, stable elements of the universe: the earth, motherhood, virginity. When active, she is always function and means, a receptacle and a channel. Womanhood, unlike manhood, is never an end in itself.[22]

In the Artemian world, women are objects and means of masculine power, never subjects or protagonists. For that same reason, again according to Paz, a woman is not an individual but a species: "the woman with four names whom you have loved" (115), as Artemio Cruz says. In the woman Paz and Fuentes find the woman-symbol, queen and slave, mother and lover, prostitute and virgin· Marina, la Malinche, la Chingada. In this context, America's name remains grammatically and referentially ironic, given that recorded history and Artemian technique and story both show her under masculine control: "America's Artemio."

The Death of Artemio Cruz is a complex work, but not a difficult one once the clues and critical devices to unravel it are found. The completeness, complexity, and simplicity of the work are announced by the graphics and phonetics at its center: Artemio Cruz: alpha and omega, "a" and "z," beginning and end of a carefully elaborated, circular, technical, and semantic novelistic structure; Artemio Cruz, "the eleven letters of [his] name, which can be written a thousand ways"—*Americo Truz* (Americo Truth), *Muera Crizto* (Death to Christ), *Te Cruzamos Rio* (We Crossed the River), *Cuezo Mártir* (Broil Martyr), *Cortés Moria* (Cortés Was Dying), *Moctezuma Ir* (Moctezuma go), *Trío me Cruza* (Trio Crosses Me), *Zurcia Temor* (He Was Wearing Fear), *Urtar Mézico* (Robbing Mexico), *Morir Cuatez* (Die Brothers), *Temió Cruzar* (He Feared Crossing), *Azteca Murió* (Aztec Died), *Crear Mitoz* (Creating Myths), all combinations of essential relevance and meaning cabalistically encoded within that name, Artemio Cruz:[23] "the eleven letters of [his] name, which can be written a thousand ways" but which require twelve spaces in parallel with its twelve episodes; Artemio Cruz, total and ordered compendium of the vocalic Spanish system which we learn to sing (*tatarear*) with our first walking steps: A E I O U, AEIO U, ArtEmIO crUz.

A name, Artemio, a dedication to C. Wright Mills, and a narrator-protagonist of today, of yesterday, of the day before yesterday, and of tomorrow: that is to say—ending with the epigraphs that introduce this novel—"of myself, and of Him and of we three, always three" (Gorostiza). An example of apparently three or more separate principal narrators and main characters who are only one: the powerfully elitist and masculine "I" who mediates the various pseudo-independent narrations and who recounts his own story, which in its turn, is the history of Mexico and America, since "I alone, I know what I can do. To others I am only a perhaps" (Stendhal).

NOTES

1. The work's apparent chaos has been solidly rejected by critics in favor of recognition of its intentional artistic order. See, as a sampling, Mario Benedetti, "Carlos Fuentes: del signo barroco al espejismo," in *Letras del continente mestizo* (Montevideo: Arca, 1967), 155–70; René Jara, "El mito y la nueva novela hispanoamericana. A propósito de *La muerte de Artemio Cruz*," in *Homenaje a Carlos Fuentes: Variaciones interpretativas en torno a su obra*, ed. Helmy F. Giacomán (New York: Anaya–Las Americas, 1971), 147–208; Nelson Osorio, "Un aspecto de la estructura de *La muerte de Artemio Cruz*," Giacomán 125–46. I am most grateful to Daniel M. Murphy and to Julia and Howard Wescott (also to Claire E. Martin) for their invaluable and patient help in the word-by-word translation and discussion of my study, originally in Spanish. Spanish texts are given in my translation.

2. Emmanuel Carballo, *19 protagonistas de la literatura mexicana del siglo XX* (Mexico: Empresas Editoriales, 1965), 433.

3. Fuentes learned how to "assimilate influences" (Carballo, 442). The novel is not a "convulsive disordering," as Alone contends in *El Mercurio*, Santiago de Chile, 1 December 1968; nor is it a work lacking in naturalness and unity as Keith Botsford says in "My Friend Fuentes," *Commentary* 39.2 (Feb. 1965): 64–67; neither is it a Faulknerian and Joycean grafting (Manuel Pedro González in "La novela hispanoamericana en el contexto de la internacional," in *Coloquio sobre la novela hispanoamericana*, ed. Ivan Schulman, et al. [Mexico: Fondo de Cultura Económica, 1967], 96). Perhaps the bitter attacks directed at this novel are owing to its technical innovations and/or the sociopolitical protest explicit in the text and implicit in the very daringness of its technique.

4. As an introduction to generative theory see Jean Ricardou, "Naissance d'une fiction," in *Nouveau Roman, Hier, Aujourd'hui*, vol. 2 (Paris: Union Generale d'Editions, 1972), 379–92, and Bruce Morrissette, "Post Modern Generative Fiction: Novel and Film," *Critical Inquiry* 2.2 (1975): 253–62. To see a different interpretation of the epigraphs, refer to Liliana Bofumo Boschi and Elisa Calabrese, *Nostalgia de futuro en la obra de Carlos Fuentes* (Buenos Aires: Fernando García Cambeiro, 1974), 114–15; and also Lanin A. Gyurko, "Structure and Theme in Fuentes' *La muerte de Artemio Cruz*," in *Symposium* 34 (1980): 35 and 39.

5. Carlos Fuentes, *The Death of Artemio Cruz*, trans. Sam Hileman (New York: Farrar Straus Giroux, 1964). All future quotations of the novel are given parenthetically.

6. A. A. Mendilow, *Time and the Novel* (London, 1952; rpt. New York: Humanities Press, 1965), 114–15.

7. Carballo, 437, 441.

8. Carl G. Jung, *Los complejos y el inconsciente*, trans. Jesús López Pacheco (Madrid: Alianza, 1979), 96.

9. Tzvetan Todorov, *The Fantastic: A Structural Approach to a Literary Genre*, trans.

Richard Howard (Cleveland: Case Western Reserve Univ. Press, 1973), 139. My emphases.

10. Ibid., 199.

11. José Ortega y Gasset, *The Dehumanization of Art and Other Essays on Art, Culture and Literature*, trans. Helene Weyl (Princeton: Princeton Univ. Press, 1968), 14–19.

12. Similarly, Bienvenido de la Fuente takes "the first narrations ... as foundation of the whole work," in *"La muerte de Artemio Cruz*: Observaciones sobre la estructura y sentido de la narración en primera persona," in *Explicación de Textos Literarios* 6 (1978): 147.

13. Gerald Prince, "Introduction à l'étude du narrataire," in *Poétique* 14 (1973): 178–96. For a study of previous examples and development of second-person narration, see Richard Reeve, "Carlos Fuentes y el desarrollo del narrador en segunda persona: Un desarrollo exploratorio," Giacomán 75–87. Jaime Alazraki, "Theme and System in *Aura*," in *Carlos Fuentes: A Critical View*, eds. Robert Brody and Charles Rossman (Austin: Univ. of Texas Press, 1982), 103–04, shows the "dualism" and immediacy the use of the second-person narrator-protagonist attains in Aura, which could also pertain to *The Death of Artemio Cruz*.

14. Paul di Virgilio, in *"La muerte de Artemio Cruz*: The Relationship between Innovation in the Role of the Personal Pronouns in Narrative and Reader Expectancy," in *Revista Canadiense de Estudios Hispánicos* (1980): 99, is correct in affirming that "Artemio Cruz encompasses the impossible ontological dimensions of a man who is his own subject, object and observer in the narrative."

15. Gérard Genette, *Narrative Discourse: An Essay in Method*, trans. Jane E. Lewin (Ithaca: Cornell Univ. Press, 1980), 161–62.

16. Daniel de Guzmán, *Carlos Fuentes* (New York: Twayne, 1972), 115. Juan Loveluck, "Intención y forma en *La muerte de Artemio Cruz*," Giacomán 209–28, sees the work's dynamic point of view as a complete vision made up of a multiplicity of narrators.

17. Linda Hutcheon, *Narcissistic Narrative: The Metafictional Paradox* (Ontario: Wilfrid Laurier Univ. Press, 1980), 90.

18. Gerald W. Petersen, "Punto de vista y tiempo en *La muerte de Artemio Cruz* de Carlos Fuentes," in *Revista de Estudios Hispánicos* 6 (1972): 85–95, does not seem to find chronological or narratological unity in the novel.

19. Susan B. Lanser, *The Narrative Act: Point of View in Prose Fiction* (Princeton: Princeton Univ. Press, 1981).

20. For this section, see C. Wright Mills, *The Power Elite* (New York: Oxford Univ. Press, 1956); G. William Domhoff and Hoyt B. Ballard, eds., *C. Wright Mills and "The Power Elite"* (Boston: Beacon Press, 1968); Irving Louis Horrowitzs, ed., *The New Sociology: Essays in Social Science and Social Theory in Honor of C. Wright Mills* (New York: Oxford Univ. Press, 1964).

21. Octavio Paz, *The Labyrinth of Solitude: Life and Thought in Mexico*, trans. Lysander Kemp (New York: Evergreen, 1961), 29–46.

22. Ibid., 35–36.

23. For a cabalistic-onomastic approach, see second chapter of my *"La muerte de Artemio Cruz"*: *Secreto generativo* (Boulder: Univ. of Colorado Press, 1987).

ROBIN FIDDIAN

Carlos Fuentes:
La muerte de Artemio Cruz

Carlos Fuentes is Mexico's most prolific, versatile and commercially successful living writer, and the recipient of numerous literary prizes which testify both to the constancy of his creative powers over a period spanning more than thirty years, and to the prestige which he enjoys throughout the Spanish-speaking world. The Biblioteca Breve prize of 1967 for *Cambio de piel*—the fourth in a total of more than a dozen novels or novellas that have been published to date—was followed a decade later by the Rómulo Gallegos prize for *Terra nostra* and then in 1987 by the equally prestigious Premio Cervantes which, all but coinciding with the publication of *Cristóbal Nonato*, set the seal on a career which has been notable as much for its tireless self-renewal as for its author's assiduously cultivated public profile and international projection. For Fuentes, like García Márquez and Vargas Llosa, is rarely out of the public eye, whether in Latin America, where he lived as a child—in Panama City, Quito, Montevideo and Rio de Janeiro between 1928 and 1934 and in Santiago and Buenos Aires from 1941 to 1943—the United States of America, where his father served as counsellor of the Mexican Embassy from 1934 to 1940 and where Fuentes has held a series of academic positions at Harvard, Princeton and other universities, or in Europe, where he has lived in London and Paris and held a professorship at the University of Cambridge in 1986–7.

From *Landmarks in Modern Latin American Fiction*, Philip Swanson, ed. © 1990 by Routledge.

A former ambassador of his country under the presidency of Luis Echeverría (1970–6), Fuentes has regularly represented the political and cultural interests of Spanish America in the world at large, assuming a continental persona which was already apparent in the early 1960s. According to José Donoso, when Fuentes attended a congress of intellectuals at the University of Concepción in 1962 his articulate enthusiasm for the nascent values of the Cuban Revolution served as a catalyst for a wider response: 'Su entusiasmo por la figura de Fidel Castro en esa primera etapa, su fe en la revolución, enardeció a todo el Congreso de Intelectuales, que a raíz de su presencia quedó fuertemente politizado'. The impact of the Cuban Revolution throughout Latin America, its liberating and agglutinative effect on political opinion, are well-known facts of mid-twentieth-century history. Equally important for an understanding of the literary currents of the period is an acknowledgement of the role of individuals like Carlos Fuentes who through their public demeanour and professional example helped to create an *esprit de corps* among those who would shortly find themselves in the vanguard of the so-called Boom of Latin American fiction. 'No sólo por el estímulo literario de sus primeras novelas, sino también por su generosidad en forma de admiración y de ayuda', Donoso wrote, 'Carlos Fuentes ha sido uno de los factores precipitantes del *boom*.' Exploiting his considerable diplomatic and promotional skills, Fuentes became 'el primer agente activa y consciente de la internacionalización de la novela hispanoamericana de la década de los años sesenta'.[1]

Over the course of that heady and expansive decade which saw the publication of future classics like *Rayuela* (1960), *La ciudad y los perros* (1963), *La casa verde* (1966) and *Cien años de soledad* (1967), Fuentes himself produced no fewer than five novels or novellas: *La muerte de Artemio Cruz* and *Aura* (both in 1962), *Cambio de piel* and *Zona sagrada* (1967) and *Cumpleaños* (1969), as well as an important essay, *La nueva novela hispanoamericana* (1969), which surveyed the literary trends of an entire continent from the communal perspective—clearly defined in the opening pages of the text—of 'nosotros, los hispanoamericanos'. Through the 1970s in interviews like the one with Herman Doezema, and into the 1980s when he addresses audiences at UCLA, California, and Cambridge, England, Fuentes continues to speak for a continental body of opinion whose shared concerns include the threat posed to national sovereignty by North American espionage and military intervention, the prospects of the Southern nations for peace and prosperity in a world moving from a bipolar to a multipolar order, and the pressure on national governments constantly to reassess social, political, economic and cultural imperatives in an age of unequalled and unequal technological progress.[2]

The function of the writer in such circumstances, Fuentes believes, is to contest officially sponsored systems of thought and organisation of reality, to unsettle and subvert orthodox perceptions of the world. Searching for a literary form suited to that purpose, the writer discovers a powerful and versatile tool in the novel: from Cervantes, through Sterne, Balzac, Flaubert and Dostoevsky, down to Joyce, Kafka and present-day writing, the novel has served consistently to call the world into question ('pone en duda el mundo'), successfully resisting fixity and closure, '(la) pretendida autosuficiencia y... (la) segura reducción'.[3] In 1980 Fuentes declared, 'Yo creo mucho en la vitalidad de la novela, en su misión, en su función, su vigencia',[4] reaffirming a long-held belief in the novel's capacity to accommodate tragedy, dialectic and dissent, to confront society with evidence of its own alienation and to expose the vulnerability of liberal democratic ideals in a dehumanised world:

> Something we are seeing every day, it is mass communications, it is the atom bomb, it is AIDS, it is a million things that destroy the formal, formative bearings of the individual that is so precious a creation of Western civilization. The novel has always jumped ahead and shown its concern for this central problem.[5]

In Latin America, where writing and politics go hand in hand, ideological protest has often been accompanied by linguistic iconoclasm in the novel. Works by the Cuban Lezama Lima and also Roa Bastos, Cortázar and Fuentes, among others, exemplify a search for new norms of literary expression which are intended to deconstruct 'una larga historia de mentiras, silencios, retóricas y complicidades académicas'. If, as Fuentes suggests, 'Todo es lenguaje en América Latina: el poder y la libertad, la dominación y la esperanza', it follows that a creative departure from accepted standards of verbal decorum constitutes a revolutionary act: 'Nuestra literatura', Fuentes affirms, 'es verdaderamente revolucionaria en cuanto le niega al orden establecido el léxico que éste quisiera y le opone el lenguaje de la alarma, la renovación, el desorden y el humor. El lenguaje, en suma, de la ambigüedad'.[6]

Fuentes's own experiments with the forms and language of fiction match this blue-print very closely. Originally misinterpreted as gratuitous exercises in self-indulgence and the 'puerile' imitation of alien (European Modernist) models,[7] the narrative fragmentation, syntactic disruption and discursive openness of novels like *La región más transparente* (1958) and *Cambio de piel* effectively figure forth suppressed, alternative dimensions of experience which belong to the category of 'the Other'. In *Aura, Cumpleaños* and *Una familia lejana* (1980), the Other manifests itself in the themes of reincarnation and the double; in *La muerte de Artemio Cruz* and *Terra nostra*, it is constituted by the possibilities which have been negated in the lives of an individual and the Mexican nation, respectively; in *Gringo viejo* (1985), it is latent in the potentialities of a historical mystery (that of the disappearance of a retired North American soldier during the Mexican Revolution) which conventional historiography has failed to articulate. In *Gringo viejo*, as in *La muerte de Artemio Cruz* and the futuristic pages of *Terra nostra* and *Cristóbal Nonato*, Fuentes is particularly interested in investigating the relationships of alterity, antagonism and complementarity between Mexico and the United States of America. The later novels debate issues of national identity and integrity on a grand scale: in relation to the values and traditions of post-Renaissance Europe (*Terra nostra*) and against the hypothetical backdrop of a North American occupation of Acapulco, Veracruz and other provinces of Mexico (*Cristóbal Nonato*). The broad perspective of these narratives complements the narrow focus, found in earlier works such as 'Chat Mool' and *La region más transparente*, on 'subterranean' indigenous elements which survive in contemporary Mexican culture, contributing something vital and disruptive to a national identity which has engaged Fuentes's attention throughout his career.

La muerte de Artemio Cruz is generally regarded as his first major novel and a landmark in Mexican and Latin American fiction. Written between May 1960 and December 1961 in Havana and Mexico City, it absorbs many of the energies released by the Cuban Revolution, feeding consciously on a newly awakened spirit of solidarity and commitment to the struggle for greater freedom and self-determination in Latin America. Like *Rayuela*, it is a conjunctural text, and one which made an immediate impression on fellow writers like García Márquez and the Mexican Gustavo Sainz. García Márquez incorporated a reference to its protagonist in the final sections of *Cien años de soledad*: Sainz admitted that 'this book changed me, as the fall from the horse changed Funes the Memorious, in a provocative and highly stimulating fashion'.[8] Translated into some fifteen languages, *La muerte de Artemio Cruz* continues to be read in many parts of the world a quarter of a century after it was first published.

Essentially, the novel explores the legacy of the Mexican Revolution of 1910–17, filtered through the fragmented consciousness of Artemio Cruz whom we visualise lying on his death-bed on 10 April 1959. Cruz is 70 years old and the owner of a huge personal fortune amassed without scruple or restraint over the past forty years. The major events of his life are recounted in retrospect, in a disjointed series of twelve fragments that are narrated in the third person; the remainder of the narrative comprises twenty-six fragments divided equally between a first person—YO—and a second person—TO—whose interaction provides the necessary dynamics of narrative progression. In part a showcase of technical experimentation, *La muerte de Artemio Cruz* more importantly explores themes of individual psychology and morality, national history and identity, and certain regional and continental concerns. In this essay I shall examine each of these aspects of the novel in turn, paying attention to technical features of the writing when they seem to have a direct bearing on points of interpretation.

As a starting point for discussion, we may consider *La muerte de Artemio Cruz* as a novel of the psyche focused primarily on the maze-like mind of the dying Cruz. Access to this world of jumbled thoughts, memories, perceptions, sensations, feelings and desires provides insights into the minds and motivation of secondary characters including his wife, Catalina, and their daughter, Teresa, but these are strictly subordinate to Cruz's ego, as they have been throughout his life. Cruz's conscious and subconscious minds may usefully be visualised as the site of innumerable conflicts, a theatre in which are played out complex preoccupations with self and identity, affirmation and the will to power, pride and courage, frustration and guilt. These clusters of themes are presented systematically within the broad parameters of an Existentialist enquiry which highlights notions of responsibility and commitment, alienation and authenticity, freedom and identity, chance and destiny.

Beginning *in media res*, the novel depicts Cruz's interior struggle to salvage something of value from a life characterised by political opportunism, intimate personal failure and the abuse of human relationships. After a childhood which is reconstructed by memory as an idyllic age of innocence and ambiguous promise, the teenage Cruz becomes enmeshed in 'el tejido de lo incierto'[9] which obliges him to define himself and choose between multiple courses of action. Armed with indestructible self-confidence and a Nietzschean will to power which drives him ever onwards—'siempre había mirado hacia adelante desde la noche en que atravesó la montaña y escapó del viejo casco veracruzano' (p. 189)—he proceeds to impose himself on his natural and social surroundings, sweeping obstacles aside and creating new rules 'como si nada hubiese sucedido antes, Adán sin padre, Moisés sin tablas' (pp. 103–4). Just minutes before he is whisked away by ambulance to be operated on in hospital, he finds the spiritual strength to reaffirm his will to live and to feel pride once again in a sexual relationship which had been the source of an ecstatic 'encuentro con el mundo' almost half a century ago (p. 67). Through a selective operation of memory, Cruz contrives to forget the horror of Regina's death, an event which provoked 'su primer llanto de hombre' (p. 81) and coincided with his first experience of a sense of shame, during a battle in the military phase of the Mexican Revolution when he

deserted from his regiment and abandoned a wounded companion whose life
he could, and should, have saved. In the overall pattern of his life, this is a
crucial turning point when he lost a sense of direction, symbolised by the
'hilo perdido': 'El hilo que le permitió recorrer, sin perderse, el laberinto de
la guerra. Sin perderse: sin desertar.... El hilo quedó atrás' (p. 78).

Cruz's desertion is the first in a series of reactions to specific test-
situations where he fails to live up to standards of conduct which his son
Lorenzo's example proves are a wholly attainable ideal. It is a lapse which has
immediate and inescapable consequences, both for the subsequent direction
of his life and for the reader's evaluation of him. Straightaway it narrows the
range of options open to Cruz, on the basis that a choice between alternative
forks on the path of life simultaneously creates and denies experiential
possibilities: 'decidirás, escogerás uno de los caminos, sacrificarás los demás:
lo sacrificarás al escoger, dejarás de ser todos los otros hombres que pudiste
haber sido' (p. 209). And it projects a shadow onto his entire future which
will forever be contaminated by the past.

In this latter respect, his experience resembles a fall from grace into a
state of existential inauthenticity which is illustrated in various ways. Since
1947 Cruz has led a double life, grudgingly devoting time and attention to
his family in their house in Las Lomas, and cohabiting with Lilia in a
residence in Coyoacán which he regards as 'mi verdadera casa' (p. 31). The
retrospective episode of Lilia's sexual infidelity in Acapulco at the beginning
of their relationship pointedly reveals its foundation in artificiality and
pretence. Flanked by two scenes in which Cruz contemplates his reflection
uneasily in a mirror, it awakens in him feelings of vulnerability, world-
weariness, impotence, suspicion and rage:

> No podía tenerla más. Esta tarde, esa misma noche, buscaría a
> Xavier, se encontrarían en secreto, ya habían fijado la cita. Y los
> ojos de Lilia, perdidos en el paisaje de veleros y agua dormida, no
> decían nada. Pero él podría sacárselo, hacer una escena... Se sintió
> falso, incómodo y siguió comiendo la langosta ... (p. 159)

Cruz's embarrassment is plainly visible shortly after, when, as he prepares to
shave, he turns to the mirror 'quer(iendo) descubrir al mismo de siempre',
and sees an image of himself stripped of comforting illusions: 'Al abrirlos, ese
viejo de ojos inyectados, de pómulos grises, labios marchitos, que ya no era
el otro, el reflejo aprendido, le devolvió una mueca desde el espejo' (p. 162).
The motifs of the mask and the mirror are constant reminders of the
fragmented and inauthentic basis of his life.

That lack of wholeness manifests itself in Cruz's inability to establish integrated relationships with other people. The relationships on which he embarks after his personal Fall characteristically pit one person's will and needs against those of another, excluding any harmonious resolution of contraries. His marriage to Catalina is an extreme example. Locked in a conflict of self-assertion and mutual mistrust, Artemio and Catalina are twinned in complex ways: they are identical in their pride, their disenchantment and sense of loss (Catalina senses that they have both been expelled from their respective 'paradises'); they are potential complements to each other, 'quizás dos mitades y un solo sentimiento' (p. 222); yet, they are sadly unable to communicate when the occasion demands and remain unreconcilable in their antagonism.

At a further level of psychological analysis each of these characters embodies contradictory features. On the critical night of 3 June 1924, Catalina feels torn between an instinctual sexual desire for Cruz and a vengeful rejection of the man who was responsible for her brother's death: 'Me vence de noche. Te venzo de día', she reflects, later lamenting the division of her life 'como para satisfacer a dos razones' and imploring '¿Por qué no puedo escoger una sola, Dios mío?' (p. 105). For his part, at this stage of their relationship Cruz is still convinced of his love for Catalina and would openly beg her: 'Acéptame así, con estas culpas, y mírame como a un hombre que necesita.... No me odies. Tenme misericordia, Catalina amada. Porque lo quiero' (p. 114). But, he lacks the courage to admit his weakness and culpability, and responds to Catalina's recriminations by taking a frightened, compliant Indian girl to his bed, thus reinforcing the barriers between them.

The sequence of events under consideration illustrates Cruz's tragic inability not only to compromise in his relationship with Catalina but also to integrate opposing sides of his personality. This applies particularly in respect of the feminine side of his nature which he resolutely denies, both figuratively and literally, in his relations with his daughter, Teresa. Fuentes probably had the mythological character of Artemis in mind when he chose his protagonist's Christian name. Artemis, a redoubtable huntress renowned for her vindictive and bloodthirsty nature, was a virgin who refused any contact with the opposite sex, in dramatic contrast to the conduct of her brother and alter ego, Apollo. In Fuentes's novel the name 'Artemio' is at once ironic, inasmuch as it reverses the gender of the mythological referent and a telling comment on Cruz's suppression of half of his sexual being. The surname 'Cruz' reinforces this interpretation: among its many connotations is that of a coin (the Spanish equivalent of English 'Heads or tails' is 'Cara o Cruz') flipped to decide who wins and who loses a contest. Here, Cruz turns out to be simultaneously a winner in life's contest for material gains and a loser in the moral and spiritual stakes. A faceless man who has fulfilled only half of his potential, he might also be described as 'Cruz sin cara'.

Cruz reacts to his circumstances in a variety of ways. One reaction consists in redoubling his challenge to the established moral order, in a triumphant reassertion of pride: 'Les gané a muchos. Les gané a todos', he boasts on his death-bed (p. 32). This diabolical egotism, coupled with cunning and perversity, provides a yardstick with which Cruz may be judged. Crucially, it establishes a perspective from which to evaluate some of the more positive traits of his character such as the courage that he displays on occasions throughout his life (for example, at a political rally when he was fired on by Don Pizarro's thugs and stood his ground, or on the flight from Sonora to Mexico City where a mechanical failure causes consternation amongst all of the passengers except him); the dignity which informs some of his personal relations; and his capacity for experiencing emotions of love, nostalgia and regret, as in a memorable moment, steeped in pathos, when he wishes he could recall every feature of his dead son, Lorenzo: the smell of his body, the colour of his skin.... It is a measure of Fuentes's grasp of the subtleties of Existentialist morality that he recoils from presenting any of these qualities in a pure, unadulterated state. It may be that Artemio's courage is no more than the mask of aggressive bravado associated with the Mexican *chingón*: his pride is double-edged ('Nos salvó el orgullo. Nos mató el orgullo', he mentally confesses to Catalina (p. 204)); his nostalgia may be a cover for cowardice. Overall, Fuentes's presentation of Cruz captures the internal contradictions of a man who is 'capaz... de encarnar al mismo tiempo el bien y el mal' (p. 33).

Cruz's nostalgia for a lost garden of Eden (cf. 'jardín', 'paradiso') is a second reaction to his Fall, and one which invariably leads to disappointment because, as Catalina learns from experience, there can be no return to the source of purity, no recovery of innocence (pp. 113–14). Cruz's private realisation that this is so intensifies the pathos of his nostalgia. Yet, the suspicion is never dispelled that his nostalgic attitude may not be yet one more aspect of a general bad faith. That objection does not hold for the third of his reactions, which consists of a mature acceptance of guilt. For, ever since he abandoned the anonymous soldier in December 1913, Cruz has harboured feelings of guilt which he has so far managed to suppress by dint of will and self-deceit. Years of living 'como si no hubiera atrás, siempre atrás, lápidas de historia e historias, sacos de vergüenza, hechos cometidos por [Catalina], por él' (p. 158) have effectively numbed 'la herida que nos causa traicionarnos' (p. 267), and protected Cruz from the provocations of conscience. However, on 10 April 1959 the voice of that conscience—the TÚ voice—breaks through his defences and visits on him spectres of the past, from which there is no escape. As the twelve sets of narrative fragments unravel like a ball of twine, we witness the gradual return of the repressed, orchestrated by a mind which is straining to come to terms with its history. In the first YO fragment, a minimal and uncontextualised reference to 'Regina. Soldado' sets in motion a process of recovery which is sustained in the fourth fragment through a simple repetition, and expanded in the eighth and eleventh with the recitation of a full list of 'nombres muertos' of people who died in order that Cruz might survive: 'Regina ... Tobías ... Páez ... Gonzalo ... Zagal ... Laura, Laura ... Lorenzo' (p. 271). The exhumation of these names gives Cruz the chance to relive events which took place on days 'en que tu destino ... te encarnará con palabras y actos' (p. 17) and enables him to face up to the truth about his relationships with other people

Fuentes seems to envisage a positive outcome to Cruz's experience, 'hoy que la muerte iguala el origen y el destino y entre los dos clava, a pesar de todo, el filo de la libertad' (p. 279). A prefatory quotation from Montaigne, 'La préméditation de la mort est préméditation de la liberté', had already anticipated the possibility of a secular form of redemption. Yet the message of salvation contained in *La muerte de Artemio Cruz* is a conditional one which allows contradictory interpretations: on the one hand, it asserts the possibility of finally attaining freedom, while on the other, it is shot through with a streak of irony redolent of Jorge Luis Borges's speculations about imminent revelation and mystical enlightenment at the moment of death, as illustrated in the story of Jaromir Hladík in 'El milagro secreto'.

In any case, the promises held out in Fuentes's novel must be weighed against much more sombre insights into the human condition, encapsulated in two other quotations which make up the Preface: these are an *estribillo* from a popular Mexican song which claims that 'No vale nada la vida, La vida no vale nada', and a quatrain from *El gran teatro del mundo* by Pedro Calderón de la Barca which reads 'Hombres que salís al suelo / por una cuna de hielo / y por un sepulcro entráis, / ved como representáis...'. Elaborating on these ideas in the text of his novel, Fuentes conveys an often overwhelming impression of the utter worthlessness and fragility of life. The scene in which a fat policeman plays Russian roulette with Cruz illustrates a horrifying contempt for life which is supposed to typify the Mexican outlook, as examined by Octavio Paz in *El laberinto de la soledad* and dramatised by Malcolm Lowry in the *cantina* episode of *Under the Volcano*.

Elsewhere in *La muerte de Artemio Cruz*, the human body is the focal point of Fuentes's wholly conventional but nonetheless striking thoughts about suffering and death. The opening fragment spares Cruz few indignities as it records his physical collapse into a dehumanised state:

Los párpados me pesan: dos plomos, cobres en la lengua,
martillos en el oído, una... una como plata oxidada en la
respiración. Metálico todo esto. Mineral otra vez. Orino sin
saberlo. (p. 9)

This graphic picture of physical disorder confirms TÚ's prophecy that 'serás
un depósito de sudores nervios irritados y funciones fisiológicas
inconscientes' (pp. 14–15), at the same time as it emphasises Cruz's
vulnerability to the ravages of time and sickness. Having previously taken the
workings of his body for granted ('vivirás y dejarás que las funciones se las
entiendan solas' (p. 90)), Cruz now experiences their ephemerality and
acknowledges the shocking vulnerability of what Fernando del Paso in a
central chapter of *Palinuro de México* terms the body's 'sacred symmetry'.[10] In
this regard, Cruz's perception of fragmented images of an eye, a nose, an
unshaven chin and a sunken cheek which are reflected on the surface of his
wife's handbag, and his piecemeal account of the sensations he feels in
various other parts of his body, underline the vanity of his thoughts about the
unity of 'El propio cuerpo. El cuerpo unido' (p. 10).

A similar mood of disenchantment informs Fuentes's evalution of
human life in relation to the astronomical duration of the universe. At a point
when approximately two-thirds of the narrative have elapsed, the TÚ voice
insists on the futility of Cruz's previous attempts to stall and buy time,
assuring him that 'tu quietud no detendrá al tiempo que corre sin ti, aunque
tú lo inventes y midas, al tiempo que niega lo inmovilidad y to somete a su
propio peligro de extinción' (p. 207). And, near the end, it evokes the chilling
emptiness of interstellar space where 'los inmensos astros ... giran en silencio
sobre el fondo infinito del espacio' (p. 312), anticipating the ultimate
degradation of the universe on a day when 'no habrá ni luz, ni calor, ni vida'
(p. 313). Reminiscent of the final section of James Joyce's *Finnegans Wake* and
of Spanish writing of the Baroque generally, these themes reveal a deep-
seated pessimism which is at odds with the requirements of humanistic and
Marxist philosophies alike.

Turning to Fuentes's treatment of Mexican themes, we note the same
acuteness and breadth of vision and the same spirit of passionate debate as
evidenced in his exploration of Existentialist concerns. Collective
psychology, race, history and culture are the principal foci of an enquiry
which is conducted at all three levels of the narrative: the YO voice acts as
the vehicle of ancestral memory and collective desire; the TÚ voice ranges
over two thousand years of Mexican history and transcends the bounds of
national and regional geography; the narrative fragments in the third person,
besides following the course of Cruz's life from the cradle to the grave, also

survey the history of his family over four generations. These expansive patterns of the narrative are supplemented by allegorical and figurative procedures which serve to deflect the reader's attention away from the particular aspects of Cruz's experience to a broader frame of reference where his behaviour has a more general significance. For, as well as being the protagonist of an individual biography, Cruz represents a class—of bourgeois entrepreneurs—an age—that of burgeoning capitalist investment in mid-twentieth-century Mexico—and successive periods of the nation's history from the late *porfiriato*, through the years of the Revolution to the narrative present when President López Mateos is in charge of the country's affairs.

In the very first fragments of *La muerte de Artemio Cruz*, Fuentes reveals the extent of his character's financial holdings and gives a detailed description of the social values, aspirations and way of life of a bourgeois parvenu. Multiple business interests allied to the political status quo support a life-style which we are asked to believe was typical of the Mexican bourgeoisie after 1940. Cruz's conspicuous consumerism and sophisticated tastes in food, clothes, music, painting and so on, characterise a social type which compensates for its insecurities by aping foreign life-styles and values, in particular those of white urban society in North America. The TÚ voice observes:

> Desde que empezaste a ser lo que eres, desde que aprendiste a apreciar el tacto de las buenas telas, el gusto de los buenos licores, el olfato de las buenas lociones, todo eso que en los últimos años ha sido tu placer aislado y único, desde entonces clavaste la mirada allá arriba, en el norte, y desde entonces has vivido con la nostalgia del error geográfico que no te permitió ser en todo parte de ellos. (p. 32)

The admiration which Cruz and those like him feel for the social and economic achievements of North America is shot through with jealousy and remorse: 'te duele saber que por más que lo intentes, no puedes ser como ellos, puedes sólo ser una calca, una aproximación' (p. 33). Yet, Fuentes suggests, few Mexicans acknowledge the deep-seated motives and implications of their behaviour as they routinely order waffles with Pepsi Cola or Canada Dry from a waitress 'vestida de tehuana' at Sanborn's; in effect, they are collaborating in their own economic and cultural colonisation (p. 22).

Fuentes's most pungent satire of the mental set of the Mexican bourgeoisie is contained in the ÉL fragment which describes 'la fiesta de San Silvestre' celebrated on New Year's Eve 1955 in Cruz's house at Coyoacán.

This grotesque tableau, worthy of Hieronymus Bosch, portrays the collective greed, pettiness, vanity and *mauvaise foi* of those whom in another context the author deprecatingly calls 'los de arriba'.[11] Antedating the narrative present by only four years, it sharpens the historical perspective of Fuentes's novel.

The actual death of Artemio Cruz occurs at a critical moment in a turbulent period of Mexican history which Fuentes examines in his essay, 'Radiografía de una década: 1953–1963'. There, Fuentes surveys political events in contemporary Mexico and records 'las luchas obreras de 1958 y 1959, la represión brutal contra el sindicato ferrocarrilero de Demetrio Vallejo y el deterioro de las condiciones de vida y de trabajo de la gran mayoría de los mexicanos'.[12] On the day before he dies, Artemio Cruz flies into Mexico City and is driven to his office along streets impregnated with mustard gas, 'porque la policía acabará de disolver esa manifestación en la plaza del Caballito' (p. 15). The bloody repression of striking railway workers, which will shortly provide the backdrop to *José Trigo* by Fernando del Paso (1966), is referred to in a conversation between Cruz and a North American, Mr. Corkery, who would like to use Cruz's newspaper to discredit 'los ferrocarrileros comunistas de México' (p. 118). Cruz manages the interview with Corkery shrewdly and acts quickly to protect his own financial interests by sanitising reports about 'la represión de la policía contra estos alborotadores' (p. 87). He is thus inextricably implicated in contemporary events.

Delving into the past, the novel traces the immediate roots of Cruz's political and financial influence to the new order which arose out of the Mexican Revolution. When Cruz visits the Bernal household in Puebla in 1919, don Gamaliel, the failing patriarch, reflects: 'Artemio Cruz. Así se llamaba, entonces, el nuevo mundo surgido de la guerra civil: así se llamaban quienes llegaban a sustituirlo' (p. 50). Don Gamaliel's judgement turns out to be prophetic: Cruz wheedles his way into the home and, by marrying Catalina Bernal, becomes master of the family estate.

Don Gamaliel's lapidary assessment uncovers an allegorical dimension in Cruz's character and fortunes: he is the personification of the Revolution, an emblem of its origins, course and results. Several commentators have documented coincidences between the fictional life of Cruz and the process of the Revolution, positing a common progression from an initial stage of idealism, through corruption and betrayal to an institutionalised atrophy. They accordingly identify the young Cruz with Francisco Madero's principled opposition to Porfirio Díaz's re-election, and chart his faltering course through late December 1913 (the temporal setting of the third ÉL fragment) and October 1915 (the seventh ÉL fragment) up to May 1919 (the second ÉL fragment) when he arrives in Puebla. As the Mexican critic, Maria Stoopen, observes, '1913 es el año de] fin de la revolución y del gobierno de Madero; es el año del golpe de Huerta y del ascenso del traidor; es el año de las lealtades y de las traiciones'. Significantly, Cruz's biography is similarly ambivalent at this time:

> Es Artemio Cruz, en estos momentos, como tantos otros participantes de la lucha armada, un representante del pueblo que no posee una conciencia clara de movimiento, pero que tiene la intención justa de 'llegar a México y correr de la presidencia al borracho de Huerta, el asesino de don Panchito Madero'. (in the words of the text, p. 70)[13]

By 1915 the Revolution has entered a third phase of partisan military activity which effectively destroys any chance of its radical potential being realised. At this stage of the conflict, Cruz is fighting for General Alvaro Obregón in alliance with the troops of Venustiano Carranza, and is taken prisoner by the *villista* colonel, Zagal. In the circumstances, he appears to face certain death, along with his wounded Indian companion, Tobías, and Gonzalo Bernal, 'enviado del Primer Jefe Venustiano Carranza' (p. 186), who shares their cell in the prison at Perales. But, a combination of treachery and good fortune allows Cruz to escape, leaving behind the corpses of his two cell-mates along with that of Zagal whom he kills in a duel made possible when *carranclán* troops launch a surprise attack on the town.

Maria Stoopen interprets Cruz's behaviour in this episode as a triple betrayal, of (1) the Indian peasant class, represented by the *yaqui* Tobías, (2) the popular cause championed by Villa, and (3) untainted revolutionary idealism personified by Gonzalo Bernal who, according to his father, 'Fue siempre tan puro' (p. 36). Yet, when he learns that Tobías is to be shot, Cruz asks Zagal to spare his life (p. 198); also, he does not kill Zagal, as he could have, by shooting him in the back during the confusion of the *carranclán* attack, but grants him the chance to fight a duel with loaded pistols across an imaginary line in the prison courtyard. It is therefore wrong to accuse Cruz of blanket treachery: plainly, his treatment of the three men involves different degrees of culpability. His treachery is greatest with Bernal who represents the moral and intellectual direction of the Revolution, a value nicely illustrated in the image of his corpse lying next to that of Zagal: 'El brazo muerto del coronel Zagal se extendió hacia la cabeza muerta de Gonzalo' (p. 201). In abandoning Bernal to his fate, Cruz simultaneously sacrifices that part of himself which comprises 'ideas y ternuras' (p. 197) and destroys the integrity of the Revolutionary movement.

So, when he visits Gonzalo's family in Puebla in 1919, Cruz is already the standard-bearer of betrayed ideals 'en el mundo destruido y confuso que dejaba la Revolución' (p. 43). He is also the prototype of instinctive opportunism: 'Todo el camino de Puebla: cuestión de puro instinto' (p. 43), ready to exploit the embattled position of don Gamaliel whom he finds locked in 'una lucha pasiva' with the recalcitrant local peasantry (p. 48). As soon as they meet, don Gamaliel, who 'se imaginaba a sí mismo como el producto final de una civilización peculiarmente criolla: la de los déspotas ilustrados' (p. 50), seals a 'pacto tácito' with the self-possessed Cruz who, he tells Catalina, can save the old order—'Este hombre puede salvarnos'—by accommodating it within the new regime of land tenure, political influence and power being forged in the early days of post-Revolutionary Mexico. From this point on, the fortunes of the Bernal family and those of Artemio Cruz merge and become a mirror of the motley affairs of the nation.

Cruz's semiotic status as a type is signalled repeatedly throughout the narrative. In an early section; the TÚ-voice, wondering 'cuáles datos pasarán a tu biografía y cuáles serán callados', answers: 'No lo sabrás. Son datos vulgares y no serás el primero ni el único con semejante hoja de servicios' (p. 17). Near the end of the novel, the same voice considers Cruz's legacy to the nation in terms which confirm his role as a personification of Mexico: 'legarás este país; legarás tu periódico, los codazos y la adulación, la conciencia adormecida por los discursos falsos de hombres mediocres; tengan su México: tengan tu herencia' (p. 277).

Other allegorical dimensions of *La muerte de Artemio Cruz* centre on Cruz's family history and origins, which are the subject of the last two fragments narrated by the ÉL voice. At this late stage we discover that Cruz is the illegitimate child of a black servant-girl known as Isabel Cruz, and Atanasio Menchaca, the elder son of a *criollo* family settled since the early nineteenth century on a large estate in Cocuya in the province of Veracruz. Atanasio's father, Ireneo, had been an associate of General Santa Anna—the supremo of Mexican politics during the 1830s, 1840s and 1850s—and had lived 'una vida de azar y loterías como la del país mismo' (p. 293). His wife, Ludivinia, is a symbolic counterpart, having been born in 1810, the year in which Mexico broke its colonial ties with Spain. In January 1903, which is the temporal setting of the penultimate ÉL fragment, Ludivinia still occupies the dilapidated remains of the family estate, whose doors she remembers opening 'al largo desfile de prelados españoles, comerciantes franceses, ingemeros escoceses, británicos vendedores de bonos, agiotistas y filibusteros que por aqui pasaron en su marcha hacia la ciudad de México y las oportunidades del país joven, anárquico' (p. 291). Clearly, Cocuya is a microcosm of nineteenth-century Mexico, and the Menchacas typical representatives of the nation's tendency to accept *caudillo* figures and submit to colonising forces. It is no accident that these faults reappear in the character of Artemio Cruz a century later: in Fuentes's diagnosis, they constitute a *damnosa hereditas* which hangs like a dead weight around the country's neck.

In the case of Artemio, that heritage is handed down through his father Atanasio, a violent man who drove Isabel Cruz off his estate as soon as she gave birth, and would have killed the baby if Lunero had not made himself available as surrogate father. Interestingly, Atanasio had a brother, Pedro, who differed markedly from him in character and behaviour, striking up a contrast which the narrative mediates through the thought processes of their mother, Ludivinia:

> Ah— suspiró Ludivinia, encaramada en su lecho revuelto—, ése no es Atanasio, que era como la prolongación de su madre en la virilidad. éste es la misma madre, pero con barba y testículos— soñó la vieja—, no la madre como hubiese sido en la hombría, como fue Atanasio. (p. 296)

In a brilliant analysis of this aspect of the novel, Steven Boldy has explained Pedro and Atanasio's role as the first pair in a series of brothers or doubles of opposing tendencies, who represent stark moral and political alternatives between which the nation must choose at crucial moments in its history. Following the sequence through to the fictional present, Pedro and Atanasio are succeeded by Gonzalo Bernal and Artemio Cruz who stand respectively for revolutionary commitment and cynical self-interest; their antagonism, which acquires its most dramatic expression in the prison sequence at Perales, is reproduced in the following generation in the relation between Lorenzo and Jaime Ceballos. As Boldy sees it, this cyclical scheme is intended to evoke 'the unfulfilled, censured promises of the Mexican heritage'.[14] Yet, one might argue just as convincingly that Fuentes paints a profoundly dispiriting picture of recurrent frustration and determinism in Mexican history since 1810: looked at from the vantage point of 1959, Artemio Cruz seems to have been fated to repeat the excesses and shortcomings of his grandfather, Ireneo, and his uncle Pedro. What is more, prospects for the future are glum, since the death of Lorenzo in the Spanish Civil War leaves the way open for the unscrupulous and scheming Jaime Ceballos to inherit Cruz's legacy, setting in motion a new cycle of injustice and sterility.

Cruz's status as Atanasio's illegitimate child yields a further set of meanings which have relevance here. First and foremost, his illegitimacy

marks him as an 'hijo de la chingada' who is the very type of his nation, born
in 1519 of the conjunction between imperial Spain—its power delegated to
Hernán Cortés—and the Aztec empire of Anáhuac to whose seat Cortés
gained access by using the political, linguistic and sexual services of an Indian
woman known as La Malinche. According to Paz and Fuentes, modern
Mexican man's obsession with legitimacy and betrayal follows directly from
that founding event which is pictured as a violation of the national psyche
and body politic.

In complicated ways, Cruz stands for all three terms in the equation
Spain + Anáhuac = Mexico. He is portrayed as a *conquistador* setting foot on
Mexico's Gulf Coast at Veracruz (p. 35), like Cortés in a famous mural
painted by Diego Rivera. A New World Atlas, he carries on his shoulders the
whole of Mexican antiquity, including its landscapes, languages, customs and
civilisations (p. 275). And, he embodies the Mexican nation's two-pronged
obsession with sexual betrayal and abuse, which is summed up in the
repertoire of phrases featuring variants of the verb 'chingar'. The immense
referential range of this 'palabra de honor' makes it the 'blasón de la raza ...,
resumen de la historia: santo y seña de México' (pp. 143–4). Used by the
malevolent *chingón*, the word is a weapon that can hurt and humiliate, but
also one that can be turned against its user. This is exactly what happens in
La muerte de Artemio Cruz where the TÚ voice turns on the protagonist and
reminds him that 'Eres un hilo de la chingada / del ultraje que lavaste
ultrajando a otros hombres' (p. 147). The ÉL fragments also conspire to
shatter Cruz's pretensions to power and respectability, tracing his origins
back to the day when he was born and, imaginatively, to the moment of his
conception during one of 'los mil coitos feroces, descuidados, rápidos [de
Atanasio Menchaca]' (p. 299). The overall pattern of the narrative thus tends
towards the revelation and reenactment of a violation in which the origins of
Cruz's personal identity and that of modern Mexico reside.

Comparisons of Cruz with the archetypal figures of Quetzalcóatl and
Jesus Christ enhance his significance as an emblem of the nation. In *Tiempo
mexicano* (1970) Fuentes represents the Conquest of Mexico as a process of
interaction between one mythical and religious type identified with the
Mesoamerican tradition, and another central to European culture. Fuentes
recalls how in 1519 the Mexican Indians were awaiting the return of their
chosen god, Quetzalcóatl, who had earlier fled the country in disgrace.
Fortuitously, on the very day when he was expected to return, Hernán Cortés
disembarked at Veracruz and instigated a chain of substitutions which caused
native Mexicans subsequently to confuse Quetzalcóatl and Jesus Christ:
'México impuso a Cortés la máscara de Quetzalcóatl. Cortés la rechazó e
impuso a México la máscara de Cristo. Desde entonces', Fuentes writes, 'es

imposible saber a quien se adora en los altares barrocos de Puebla, de Tlaxcala y de Oaxaca'.[15]

This psycho-historical analysis of the Conquest provides an insight into processes of cultural syncretism in sixteenth-century Mexico and establishes a context for understanding the symbolic portrayal of Artemio Cruz as both a Christ-figure and an avatar of Quetzalcóatl. Parallels between Cruz and Christ are varied and oblique. In the opening pages of the novel Cruz suffers '[un] dolor del costado' which brings to mind Christ's suffering on the Cross (p. 12). The surname 'Cruz' contributes a vital element to the comparison, connoting the weight of collective guilt which rests on the character's shoulders like the sins of the world on those of Jesus. Indeed, the sum of 'hechos cometidos por todos' is a burden that Cruz finds intolerable: 'La era la palabra intolerable. Cometidos por todos' (p. 158). In a complicated set of equivalences, Cruz is also likened to God the Father, at the moment when his daughter Teresa remarks, apropos of his relationship with Lorenzo, '¿No envió a la muerte a su propio hijo mimado?' (p. 242). That the analogy is meant seriously and not ironically is confirmed by the author's declaration to Walter Mauro that he was moved to write *La muerte de Artemio Cruz* partly by 'una obsesión trinitaria de la que siempre he sufrido'.[16] In narrative terms, that obsession translates into the three levels of Cruz's consciousness which correspond to the Holy Trinity of God the Father (YO), God the Son (ÉL) and God the Holy Ghost (TÚ). The figure of Cruz combines aspects of all three in a heretical synthesis which challenges conventional notions of moral authority.

The role of Quetzalcóatl is assigned most conspicuously in the novel to Lorenzo Cruz who is identified with fertility and self-sacrifice and other positive values. As he leaves Mexico to go and fight for freedom on the side of the Republic in the Spanish Civil War, Lorenzo follows in the fabled footsteps of Quetzalcóatl who, in the author's words, 'Huyó, hacia el oriente, hacia el mar. Dijo que el sol lo llamaba'. The manner of Lorenzo's death is suitably heroic, making him a worthy successor of Quetzalcóatl. However, to emphasise Lorenzo's positive attributes and achievements is to overlook the ambivalence of Quetzalcóatl and of Mesoamerican deities in general. For the fact is that Quetzalcóatl symbolises vice as well as virtue, lust as well as chastity, shame as well as honour. Fuentes incorporates these negative traits into the character of Artemio Cruz who cuts a cowardly figure no less reminiscent of Quetzalcóatl than his son Lorenzo. Referring to a legendary event in the god's experience, Fuentes relates how Quetzalcóatl, faced with the reflection of his body in a mirror, 'Sintió gran miedo y gran vergüenza ... Presa del terror de sí mismo—del terror de su apariencia—Quetzalcóatl, esa noche, bebió y fornicó. Al día siguiente, huyó

...'. Cruz's experience overlaps with this account in some important details: he indulges in repeated acts of self-contemplation which cause him to feel disgusted with himself and anxious about his identity; also, he has a substantial record of adultery. In short, he resembles the mortal and fallible Quetzalcóatl whom Fuentes elsewhere compared interestingly to more familiar archetypes: 'Quetzalcóatl, protagonista simultáneo de la creación, la caída y el sacrificio: Yavé, Adán y Cristo de un mundo sin secuelas históricas, mítico'.[17]

This hybrid characterisation of Artemio Cruz conforms to the dominant patterns of the cultural history of Mexico. Yet it should not be forgotten that the worship of Quetzalcóatl was a regional phenomenon, extending beyond the territorial boundaries of modern Mexico. Similarly, the fusion of Christian and Amerindian traditions was not unique to the colony of New Spain, but typified the cultural *mestizaje* of the New World generally. With these points in mind; we may briefly consider the regional and continental resonances of Fuentes's novel.

A Caribbean perspective linking the Eastern seaboard of Mexico with the 'archipiélago tropical de ondulaciones graciosas y carries quebradas [de las Antillas]' (p. 278) is defined in the final sections of *La muerte de Artemio Cruz*, tying the history of that part of Mexico in with the slave trade emanating from 'las islas del Caribe' (p. 292) and identifying the Gulf as an important point of intersection where the pre-Colombian civilisations of Meso-America met with a multiplicity of cultures arriving from Africa as well as Europe. The Menchaca estate in Veracruz exemplifies a synthesis of historical, racial and cultural factors which set it apart from the 'Mexico seco [del] altiplano' (p. 278). In that setting, the figure of Lunero is of special importance. Described by Helmy Giacomán as '[el] primer gran personaje mulato de la novela mexicana',[18] he may be regarded as a fictional cousin of Carpentier's Ti Noel and other black characters who populate the literary landscape of the Caribbean, particularly that of Cuba.

Cuba is in fact a prominent point of reference in *La muerte de Artemio Cruz*. At one moment in the narrative a tape-recording is played back of a conversation between Cruz and Mena in which Cruz comments on the changes that have taken place in Cuba since Batista's departure; the same conversation also mentions General Trujillo whose presidency of the Dominican Republic came to an end in 1960 (see p. 140). At another point on the tape, a citizen of the United States who is visiting Cruz's office announces his Ambassador's intention 'to make a speech comparing this Cuban mess with the old-time Mexican Revolution' (p. 206)—a project which reflects ironically both on Cruz, who had seen active service in the Mexican Revolution, and on the Revolution itself, now largely institutionalised and ineffectual. In a very real sense, Fuentes, as he writes from Havana, invites his Mexican readers to look at the achievements of their own revolution through the prism of the new Cuba of 1959–61.

As stated earlier in this essay, events in Cuba sent reverberations all over the Americas, altering political perceptions and creating new perspectives on areas of common interest. In such circumstances it was inevitable that certain writers of the period should register a sense of community and take it upon themselves to represent continental opinion. Fuentes's dedication of *La muerte de Artemio Cruz* to C. Wright Mills, whom he salutes as the 'verdadera voz de Norteamérica, amigo y compañero en la lucha de Latinoamérica', indicates a clear and conscious intention to pitch the message of his novel beyond local boundaries, onto a wider plane of significance.

While the text of *La muerte de Artemio Cruz* makes overt references only to Cuba and the Dominican Republic outside Mexico, a supra-national perspective may readily be inferred from a range of historical data which are valid for the entire subcontinent. At a general level, these include the experiences of conquest, colonial and neo-colonial status and the consequences of political and economic dependence. More specifically, they embrace the phenomena of *caciquismo* or bossism, government repression of labour organisations, financial corruption and social inequality. As he denounces these and other ills in Mexican society under President López Mateos, Fuentes articulates the grievances of people throughout Latin America, prefiguring his systematic treatment of some of the same themes in *La nueva narrativa hispanoamericana*.

The climax of that essay is an analysis of linguistic alienation north and south of the Rio Grande, where the name of C. Wright Mills is invoked once again to exemplify continental experience. In Fuentes's opinion, the linguistic falsification of reality 'is an enormous fact in Latin America',[19] which he describes as a 'continente de textos sagrados' requiring immediate 'profanation' by writers of an iconoclastic disposition.[20] On the evidence produced in this essay, *La muerte de Artemio Cruz* is a seminal contribution to that enterprise. In it Fuentes mounts a vigorous and coherent assault on moral and political dogmas, with the aid of formal and linguistic procedures which shortly become common currency in the writing of the Boom. A quarter of a century later, when other writers have renounced their faith in formal experimentation, Fuentes retains an unswerving commitment to exploration and iconoclasm, forever producing new and unsettling novels. Histories of the Boom and after will remain incomplete as long as he continues to write there.

Notes

1. See José Donoso, *Historia personal del 'boom'* (Anagrama, Barcelona, 1972), pp. 56–7.

2. See Herman P. Doezema, 'An interview with Carlos Fuentes', *Modern Fiction Studies*, vol. 18 (1972–3), pp. 491–503; 'Carlos Fuentes at UCLA: an interview', *Mester*, vol. 11 (1982), pp. 3–15; and John King, 'Carlos Fuentes: an interview', in *Modern Latin American Fiction: A Survey* (Faber & Faber, London, 1987), pp. 136–54.

3. Carlos Fuentes, *La nueva novela hispanoamericana*, 5th edn (Joaquín Mortiz, Mexico, 1976), p. 49.

4. 'Carlos Fuentes at UCLA', p. 15.

5. John King, 'Carlos Fuentes: an interview', p. 143.

6. Carlos Fuentes, *La nueva narrativa hispanoamericana*, pp. 30–2.

7. For a hostile reaction, see Manuel Pedro González's comparison of *La muerte de Artemio Cruz* with James Joyce's *Ulysses* in his *Coloquio sobre la novela hispanoamericana* (Fondo de Cultura Económica, Mexico, 1967), pp. 90–7.

8. Gustavo Sainz, 'Carlos Fuentes: a permanent bedazzlement', trans. Tom J. Lewis, *World Literature Today*, vol. 57, no. 4 (Autumn, 1983), p. 569.

9. Carlos Fuentes, *La muerte de Artemio Cruz* (Fondo de Cultura Económica, Mexico, 1978), p. 62. All subsequent page references are included in the text.

10. Fernando del Paso, *Palinuro de México* (Alfaguara, Madrid, 1977), p. 578.

11. Carlos Fuentes, 'Radiografía de una década: 1953–1963', in *Tiempo mexicano*, 4th edn (Joaquín Mortiz, Mexico, 1972), pp. 75–9.

12. Ibid., pp. 86–7.

13. Maria Stoopen, *La muerte de Artemio Cruz: una novela de denuncia y traición* (UNAM, Mexico, 1982), pp. 113–15.

14. Steven Boldy, 'Fathers and sons in Fuentes' *La muerte de Artemio Cruz*', *Bulletin of Hispanic Studies*, vol. 61 (1984), p. 39.

15. Carlos Fuentes, 'De Quetzalcóatl a Pepsicóatl', in *Tiempo mexicano*, p. 22.

16. Walter Mauro and Elena Clementelli, 'Carlos Fuentes', in *Los escritores at poder* (Luis Caralt, Barcelona, 1975), p. 185.

17. Carlos Fuentes, 'De Quetzalcóatl a Pepsicóatl', p. 24.

18. Helmy Giacomán (ed.), *Homenaje a Carlos Fuentes* (Las Américas, New York, 1971), p. 12.

19. Herman Doezema, 'An interview with Carlos Fuentes', p. 499.

20. Carlos Fuentes, *La nueva novela hispanoamericana*, p. 30.

CURRIE K. THOMPSON

The House and the Garden:
The Architecture of Knowledge and
La muerte de Artemio Cruz

Described in environmental terms, *La muerte de Artemio Cruz* is a study of the house in the garden. The garden in its various manifestations—the Veracruz plantation where the protagonist is born or the fragrant chestnut trees shading the dwelling he temporarily shares with Catalina, for example—is the setting for the house; it is the background. The house—the ruined mansion inhabited by Ludivinia or the restored monastery where Artemio Cruz lives separated from his wife and daughter and from the guests he entertains annually—is the foreground. Because it occupies the foreground, readers are more aware of the house, as evidenced by critical comment on its meaning. Speaking of the Coyoacán house, Lanin Gyurko remarks, "It is no accident that Cruz chooses to restore [for his home] an ancient monastery in ... the very same section of Mexico City where Hernán Cortés had his headquarters after the collapse of Mexico-Tenochtitlán" (34). In a similar vein, Meyer-Minnemann interprets Cruz's annual gatherings at his Coyoacán residence in the context of Mexican history, which he describes as caught in a vicious circle of repeating "ciclos de poder" (98). The house is indeed significant. The restoration of the Coyoacán edifice is symptomatic of the frustrated aspirations of the Mexican Revolution, which could be described in architectural terms as an unsuccessful effort to demolish the foundations of Mexican society and to construct a new order in place of the

From *Hispania* 77, no 2 (May 1994): 197–206. ©1994 by American Association of Teachers of Spanish and Portuguese.

old one. One should not overlook the background, however, for the house is in the garden. More precisely, as Frank Lloyd Wright remarked of the house and the hill, the house is *of* the garden.[1] One cannot separate the house from the garden, which is, in the broadest sense, its foundation. If the house is structurally flawed, it is a search in the garden that will reveal any flaws that may exist in its foundation.

La muerte de Artemio Cruz draws attention to the garden. Living in conflict with Catalina, Cruz looks out the window at "los árboles del jardín" (115). As he suffers on his deathbed, his second-person self tells him he will smell the enclosed garden: "olerás el jardín cerrado" (122). The fragrance of incense when a priest is hidden in his home makes him recall that "también ascendió del jardín un olor de castaña" (128) and remember that "el jardín había sido plantado con hortalizas de adorno" (128). He imagines that, in Spain, his son Lorenzo described Mexico as a tropical garden: "El le contó que venía de México y que allá vivía en un lugar caliente, cerca del mar, lleno de frutas" (238). Before entertaining his guests at Coyoacán, he gazes at his reflection "en las puertas de cristal que conducían al jardín" (256).

Some of Artemio Cruz's thoughts suggest a flaw in the garden. On his deathbed, recognizing his alienated condition, which is reflected in a more generalized separation of subject and object "las cosas y sus sentimientos se han ido deshebrando, han caído fracturadas a lo largo del camino" (17)—, Artemio sees existence as a fruit sliced in half—"la fruta tiene dos mitades" (17)—and concludes that he has been expelled from a garden: "allá, atrás, había un jardín: si pudieras regresar a él, si pudieras encontrarlo otra vez al final ... estás sobre la tierra del jardín, pero las ramas pálidas niegan las frutas" (17). This passage apparently reflects the protagonist's memory of the garden-like plantation in Veracruz where he was born and to which he would like to return to begin his life again. It also brings to mind another story of alienation and expulsion from a garden: the Genesis myth of the tree of knowledge. In this context, it is interesting to note that Catalina believes that she, like Artemio, has been expelled from a garden—and that she equates expulsion from the garden with the loss of innocence: "Perdiste tu inocencia.... Quizás tuviste tu jardín. Yo también tuve el mío, mi pequeño paraíso. Ahora ambos lo hemos perdido" (113).

The relationship between the garden and Biblical myth is more explicit in Catalina's reflections and her identification of the garden with a "pequeño paraíso" than it was in her husband's meditation. But Artemio also associates the garden and paradise. In a blasphemous version of the myth of the virgin birth he supposes that Mary kept white doves hidden between her thighs: "las palomitas blancas entre los muslos ... las palomitas escondidas entre las piernas, en el jardín bajo las faldas" (30). His intended meaning is clear: the garden—"paradise"—is to be found between a woman's legs in sexual intercourse. But his words also evoke standard psychoanalytic readings of the Genesis myth, according to which the paradise that all humans lose is the ecstatic union—*participation mystique* (mystic participation) or *jouissance* (extreme joy)—experienced prior to birth. According to these readings, we have all been expelled from the existence of blissful ignorance (one of the meanings of *inocencia* in Spanish) in "the garden under the skirts" into the broken world of awareness or knowledge.

Cruz lives in this broken world, banished from the "jardín cerrado" (122) and seeking to regain the lost paradise, or garden, which he recalls repeatedly. In Acapulco, scorned by Lilia, he observes the bed they have shared, feeling that "la almohada, aún hundida, era jardín, fruta" (161). During the revolution, when he attempts to escape from Zagal by fleeing into the labyrinth—matrix or uterus—of an abandoned mine, he crawls through its passages like an Edenic serpent as he imagines the taste of a forgotten fruit:

> Así fue arrastrándose, sin saber a dónde conducía su carrera de reptil. Vetas grises, reflejos dorados ... iluminaban su lentitud de culebra.... Sintió la boca llena de tamarindos: acaso el recuerdo involuntario de una fruta que aun en la memoria agita las glándulas salivales, quizá el mensajero exacto de un olor desprendido de una huerta lejana. (181)

The memory of his son's death brings to his mind the passage from Genesis that associates the fruit of the tree of knowledge with death: "Porque el día que de él comas ciertamente morirás" (247–48).

By evoking in this manner the Biblical myth of the tree of knowledge, *La muerte de Artemio Cruz* invites its readers to consider it in the light of an intertextual tradition that has elaborated the meaning of this Biblical mytheme (or "savage thought").[2] In the context of this tradition, the garden, agriculture, evokes culture in general, and nature becomes representative of human nature—especially, the nature of human knowledge. Examined against this background, Artemio's flaws and, implicitly, the failure of the Mexican revolution are not just defects of an individual and a nation. Rather, they are the consequence of a basic and fundamental flaw (original sin) that is shared by the entire human race and that undermines all mortal endeavor. If the nature of human knowledge is defective, the text implies, it is only logical that the enterprises constructed upon that knowledge will be similarly flawed, for it is as impossible to base sound actions on faulty knowledge as it is to erect a solid edifice upon an unsatisfactory foundation.

Such are the initial implications of the attention accorded in the text to the house and the garden and its evocation of the myth of the Garden of Eden. As already noted, however, the treatment of this myth occurs in the context of several other explications of it which prove enlightening. One is a meditation on the tree of knowledge authored by Swiss psychoanalyst Carl Jung in 1934; another is a more complex elaboration of the myth made written by Jacques Lacan several decades later.

Jung views knowledge or consciousness as fragmentation but nevertheless affirms his faith in its reconciling powers:

> Not for nothing did the Bible story place the unbroken harmony of plant, animal, man, and God, symbolized as Paradise, at the very beginning of all psychic development, and declare that the first dawning of consciousness ... was a fatal sin.... It was the Luciferian revolt of the individual against the One. It was a hostile act of disharmony against harmony, a separation from the fusion of the all with all....
>
> And yet the attainment of consciousness was the most precious fruit of the tree of knowledge, the magical weapon which gave man victory over the earth, and which we hope will give him a still greater victory over himself. (*Civilization in Transition* 139–40)

In this passage Jung does not explain how he expects knowledge to bring humanity its victory over itself, but in the context of his other writings, one may logically conclude that he has in mind a type of mysticism or gnosis based upon the presumed recovery of a primitive transcendent vision: the archetype.[3] Similar ideas inform *La muerte de Artemio Cruz*, although they do so in a negative way. As we will see, it is precisely the visionary nature of Artemio Cruz's attempts to come to terms with his environment that explain his greatest errors.

For this reason, one may consider Artemio's shortcomings in the context of the distinction Jacques Lacan establishes between the types of knowledge represented by the imaginary and the symbolic orders and in light of the contrast between his and Jung's meditations on the tree of knowledge. In a passage that is fundamental to understanding the adaptive nature of his thought, Lacan has observed, "Repetition demands the new. It is turned towards the ludic.... Whatever, in repetition, is varied, modulated, is merely alienation of its meaning" (*The Four* 61). In this context, his meditation on the tree of knowledge may entail a revision or correction of Jung, whom he apparently knew and to whom he refers on three different occasions in the *Ecrits* (116, 195, 233). On the other hand, it is well established that much of Lacan's thought involves a revisionary repetition of Hegel, who published the following meditation on the tree of knowledge in 1837 in *The Philosophy of History*:

> Man, created in the image of God, lost it is said, his state of absolute contentment by eating of the Tree of the Knowledge of Good and Evil. Sin consisted here only in knowledge.... This is a deep truth, that evil lies in consciousness.... Consciousness occasions the separation of the Ego, in its boundless freedom as arbitrary choice, from the pure essence of the Will—i.e. from the Good.... Sin is the discerning of Good and Evil as separation, but this discerning likewise heals the ancient hurt, and is the fountain of infinite reconciliation. (321–23)

Lacan's commentary on the tree of knowledge myth evokes not only the protagonist's last name—Cross or *Cruz*, but his first name, seemingly related to Diana or Artemis,[4] as well:

> Let us take our word "tree" again ... and see how it crosses the bar of the Saussurian algorithm. (The anagram of "*arbre*" [tree] and "*barre*" [bar] should be noted.)....
>
> Drawing on all the symbolic contexts suggested in the Hebrew of the Bible, it erects on a barren hill the shadow of the cross. Then reduces to the capital Y, the sign of dichotomy.... Circulatory tree, tree of life of the cerebellum, tree of Saturn, tree of Diana ... it is your figure that traces our destiny for us ... that causes that slow shift in the axis of being to surge up from an unnameable night into ... language: *No! says the Tree, it says No!* (*Ecrits* 154–55)

To the Jungian celebration of a grand design, Lacan opposes the play of the linguistic sign, and in keeping with the open-ended nature of discourse, his meditation avoids the closure that Jung appears to suggest. Declining to limit his linguistic play even to "all the symbolic contexts suggested in the Hebrew of the Bible," Lacan juxtaposes the Biblical myth of the tree with various other classical myths. In his meditation, knowledge continues to reside in the unconscious but is no longer an eternal and immutable idea or visionary archetype hidden beneath the flux of the contingent. Rather, it is an arbitrary system of differences based on binary oppositions. Lacan emphasizes the alienating nature of knowledge by noting that the tree is shaped like the letter Y, representative of the binary nature of language, and by evoking the myth of Artemis, who caused Actaeon to be torn asunder. Lacan also abandons Jung's optimistic conviction that consciousness will bring infinite reconciliation. Rather, by allowing the tree to speak a single, negative word, he suggests that one may only aspire to better adaptations (in every sense of that word) through an ever continuing negation of the negation.

La muerte de Artemio Cruz's elaboration of the myth of the tree of knowledge has much in common with Lacan's. Like the latter, it emphasizes both the central role of language in knowing and the relationship between knowledge and separation or difference. In this text, knowledge is not ideal or archetypal knowledge. Rather, it is a constructive adaptation based on binary oppositions. Fuentes' text concurs with Jung in recognizing the power knowledge provides, but the paean it sings to the power of knowledge is in a minor key. "Tú sobrevivirás" (206), it declares as it begins to enumerate a long list of accomplishments that have made human survival possible. A close examination of the accomplishments listed reveals that all of them are "fruits" or products of the dividing power of the intellect. The first of the tools of survival examined by this passage is the ability to measure time, and the text attributes this achievement to the conscious separation of light and darkness:

> el tiempo que inventarás para sobrevivir ... el tiempo que tu cerebro creará a fuerza de percibir esa alternación de luz y tinieblas ... a fuerza de gritar los signos del tiempo ... a fuerza, en fin, de decir el tiempo, de hablar el tiempo. (207)

As the final words make clear, the achievement discussed here is a linguistic one: humanity learns, quite literally, to "tell time." Through this achievement, which is based upon a binary opposition, humanity adapts by separating itself from an indifferent and undifferentiated universe:

> de pensar el tiempo inexistente de un universo que no lo conoce porque nunca empezó y jamás terminará: no tuvo principio, no tendrá fin y no sabe que tú inventarás una medida del infinito, una reserva de razón. (207)

The indifference and inability to differentiate are illustrated by the animals with which humanity is forced to struggle:

acabarás por pensar lo que no tendrá otra realidad que la creada
por tu cerebro, aprenderás a ... espantar a las bestias que no te
distinguirán, que no diferenciarán tu carne de la carne de otras
bestias y tendrás que construir mil templos, dictar mil leyes,
escribir mil libros. (207)

Humanity survives its predators through separation—through the
linguistic oppositions discussed earlier and by creating a more fundamental
binary opposition between its organism and the environment:

harás todo eso porque piensas, porque habrás desarrollado una
congestión nerviosa en el cerebro, una red espesa capaz de
obtener información y transmitirla ... sobrevivirás, no por ser el
más fuerte, sino por el azar oscuro de un universo cada vez más
frío en el que sólo sobrevivirán los organismos que sepan
conservar la temperatura de su cuerpo frente a los cambios del
medio. (208)

Human linguistic ability as well as the ability to separate our warm bodies
from the cold environment are, moreover, products of the separation of the
organism into specialized parts and of the ability to separate the present from
the future: "sobrevivirás con tus células cerebrales diferenciadas, tus
funciones vitales automatizadas ... libre para pensar más allá de los sentidos
inmediatos y las necesidades vitales" (208).

This extensive and important catalogue of human achievement
constitutes an unqualified paean to the productive power of the mental and
physical ability to separate, except for its mention of one type of separation
or splitting: "tendrás que ... fabricar mil máquinas, dominar mil pueblos,
romper mil átomos" (207). The splitting of the atom introduces a sobering
note in this hymn to progress. Basing himself on the "victory over the earth"
that consciousness's breaking of harmony had produced, Jung, as we have
seen, predicted "a still greater victory" of humanity over itself. *La muerte de
Artemio Cruz*, with its awareness of the implications of atomic fission,
suggests a significantly less optimistic view of the future—one in which
humanity, if it is not itself destroyed, will destroy all the achievements of
civilization and return to a primitive, uncivilized existence: "romper mil
átomos para volver a arrojar tu tea encendida a la entrada de la cueva" (207).

The tone of the passage is a balanced one, however. Although its
anticipation of eventual atomic destruction, rather than a Jungian conquest
over both universe and self, stresses the finite dimension of human existence,
it also takes into consideration the temporarily adaptive consequences of

humanity's creation of "una reserva de razón" (207) in its being toward death. In this respect, it does not reflect the protagonist's customary view of knowledge.

Although Artemio Cruz is aware of and preoccupied with the linguistic nature of knowledge, he prefers the imaginary order and regards language as an exclusively negative phenomenon—a fundamental human defect or "original sin" from which there is no redemption. Immediately before his first meditation on the garden and the divided nature of his being, in a passage that recalls Adam's responsibility for assigning names, Artemio considers the inadequacy of language as an instrument for his memory: "Son días que ... rotulados por el recuerdo ... fueron y serán algo más que los nombres que tú puedes darles" (17). This evokes the name-giving role of Adam in the Garden of Eden. Later he recalls his conversation with a priest prior to his first visit to Gamaliel Bernal (perhaps an evocation of Bernal Díaz del Castillo) and the priest's negative description of words: "las palabras, malditos rosarios de sílabas que encienden la sangre y las ilusiones" (46). He remembers the priest's description on his death-bed: "basta repetir mil veces una palabra para que pierda todo sentido y no sea sino un rosario ... de sílabas ... huecas" (272).

In Artemio's view language is not only inadequate and empty, but it also separates humans from one another. The protagonist believes that speakers of different languages may not remember in the same way: he comments, referring to the Yaqui Indian sharing the cell with him and Gonzalo Bernal, "Puede que en su lengua no se recuerde igual" (191). Artemio insists that even speakers of the same language are separated by the word. His long meditation on "the order of the screwed" which deals specifically with the word *chingar* is, as Floyd Merrell has observed, a reflection on "the word" in general.[5] In this meditation Cruz refers to the word as "la chingada que divide, la chingada que separa" (146) and wishes, despite his recognition of the impossibility of returning to "el terror sin nombre del origen" (145), to destroy the word: "asesínala con armas que no sean las suyas: matémosla: matemos esa palabra que nos separa, nos petrifica, nos pudre con su doble veneno de ídolo y cruz" (146).

Considering the separating properties of the word, Artemio recalls with nostalgia the silence that he believes united him with Lunero in the garden-like plantation in Veracruz:

> No hablaban. Pero el mulato y el niño sentían esa misma gratitud alegre de estar juntos que nunca dirían ... porque estaban allí no para decir ... sino para comer y dormir juntos y juntos salir cada madrugada, sin excepción silenciosa. (281)

On several occasions during his life, Artemio attempts to recover his lost garden—his lost paradise—by recreating this silence. When he is with Regina he does not wish her to speak, because he is afraid that speech will destroy the bond between them: "Si Regina hablara: él sintió el aliento cercano y le tapó los labios con la mano. Sin lengua y sin ojos: sólo la carne muda, abandonada a su propio placer" (64). Similarly, he strives to overcome his alienation from Catalina through silence. Wishing to communicate his love for her—"hacerle creer que la había amado desde el momento en que la vio pasar por una calle de Puebla" (101)—he attempts to do so through silence:

> Pudo habérselo dicho, pero una explicación obligaría a otra y todas las explicaciones conducirían a un día y un lugar, un calabozo, una noche de octubre. Quería evitar ese regreso; supo que para lograrlo sólo podía hacerla suya sin palabras; se dijo que la carne y la ternura hablarían sin palabras. (102)

With Regina and Catalina, Artemio attempts through silence to muster against the separating word weapons other than its own. In both cases, his effort to achieve a silent jouissance meets with failure. Ironically, Artemio recognizes the need for speech. Reflecting on his relationship with Catalina, he says: "Sólo un acto podría ... deshacer este nudo de la separación y el rencor. Sólo unas palabras dichas ahora o nunca más" (114). Although Artemio does not wish to speak, he yearns to be spoken to; he wants Regina and Catalina to speak to him. Yet the protective silence he creates to keep from confronting an alienating truth also makes it impossible for him to hear the words he wants them to speak.

In Regina's case, silence functions paradoxically through (empty) speech. Regina invents an idyllic story in which she and Artemio met and made love on a deserted beach, and her "hermosa mentira" (82) enables Artemio to silence the alienating truth of their meeting: "No era verdad que aquella muchacha de dieciocho años había sido montada a la fuerza en un caballo y violada en silencio en el dormitorio común de los oficiales, lejos del mar" (82–83). Unfortunately for him, however, the same fiction also silences the forgiveness he wishes Regina had spoken: "No era cierto que él había sido perdonado en silencio por la honradez de Regina" (83).

Catalina's more conventional silence is similar to Artemio's. Like Artemio, she refuses to speak in order to maintain her dignity. On his deathbed, feeling her (silent) caress, Artemio recognizes that, ironically, both of them were ultimately condemned by the silence they hoped would save them:

Qué inútil, Catalina. Me digo: qué inútil, qué inútil caricia. Me
pregunto: ¿qué vas a decirme?, ¿crees que has encontrado al fin
las palabras que nunca te atreviste a pronunciar? Ah, ¿tú me
quisiste? ¿por qué no lo dijimos? Yo te quise.... El orgullo. Nos
salvó el orgullo. Nos mató el orgullo. (204)

We may begin to understand the paradox involved in this passage if we
recognize that the aspect of Artemio and Catalina that was saved was an
illusion of integrity and independence: the part of the self Lacan identifies as
the specular (mirror-image) *moi* ("me") and contrasts with the symbolic *je*
("I"), the broken or "castrated" self, which is subject to and mediated
through language.

The mirror image, representing the specular *moi*, is a recurrent motif
in *La muerte de Artemio Cruz*, which Lino García has aptly referred to as a
"dialógo de espejos" (106–13).[6] From the text's first page in which Artemio
opens his eye and sees it "reflejado en las incrustaciones de vidrio de una
bolsa de mujer" (9), the protagonist is preoccupied with mirrors and
identifies, like Lacan's infant, with his mirror image: "Soy esto. Soy esto....
Soy este ojo" (9). When his image disappears (because his daughter Teresa
moves her purse away from him), Artemio begins to perspire, anxious
because he feels that his face and body (and his very being) have been taken
away from him: "¿Y el rostro? Teresa ha retirado la bolsa que lo reflejaba....
Me corre el sudor por la frente. Cierro otra vez los ojos y pido, pido que mi
rostro y mi cuerpo me sean devueltos" (10).

In the context of Lacan's theory, according to which the specular *moi* is
the defensive creation of the unspeaking infant, and in light of Artemio's
efforts to overcome his alienation through silence, it is significant that the
protagonist's memories of both Catalina and Regina involve mirror images.
In Catalina's case, Artemio recognizes that he and she are captured by an
illusion that overpowers, or drowns, their attempts at intimacy:

en ese espejo común, en ese estanque que reflejará los rostros de
ambos, que los ahogará cuando traten de besarse, el uno al otro,
en el reflejo líquido de sus rostros: ... ¿por qué tratas de besarla en
el frío reflejo del agua?, ¿por qué no acerca ella su rostro al tuyo,
por qué, como tú, lo hunde en las aguas estancadas ...? (92)

By identifying the mirror in this case with water, which like their relationship
is stagnant, the passage emphasizes the narcissistic nature of Artemio's and
Catalina's vanity and suggests that, like Narcissus, they are destroying
themselves because of their pride in an illusion.

The mirror associated with Regina also consists of water. In her "pretty lie" Regina imagines that she saw Artemio's reflection appear in "una laguna entre las rocas [donde] uno puede mirarse en el agua blanca. Allí me miraba y un día apareció tu cara junto a la mía" (66). Later, thinking of Regina, Artemio, like Narcissus, admires his own reflection in the water of a spring:

> Se detuvo junto a un ojo de agua y llenó la cantimplora.... quiso mirarse reflejado en el ojo de agua. Ese cuerpo no era de él: Regina le había dado otra posesión: lo había reclamado con cada caricia. No era de él. Era más de ella. Salvarlo para ella. Ya no vivían solos y aislados; ya habían roto los muros de la separación. (76)

This repeated use of the term *ojo de agua* in this passage to refer to the spring in which Artemio observes his reflection lends itself to at least two interpretations. On one hand, it suggests that he has been captivated or hypnotized by Regina's gaze. It is more likely, however, that the eye that meets his gaze in the spring is, like the eye reflected by Teresa's purse, his own—as is the illusion that he has found *jouissance*—has overcome the alienating "muros de separación"—and his desire to save (only for Regina's sake, he tells himself) the body he is admiring.

With both Catalina and Regina, Artemio's reflection offers him a reassuring illusion of integrity. Breaking the silence that characterizes his relationship with them would entail shattering that illusion.[7] This is a sacrifice he is unwilling to make until, on his deathbed, he is forced to do so when "los órganos del dolor, más lentos, vencerán a los de la prevención refleja" (61), when "los órganos del dolor ... más lentos ... vencen a los de mi reflejo" (307).[8] Only then does he recognize that his silence, which saved him, also condemned him.

Until then Artemio constructs a silent illusion of integrity and independence and resists subjecting himself to language. He avoids knowledge, because he believes that it will weaken him: "darse cuenta debilita, nos convierte en victimas" (61). He insists that he has already been victimized by language—by the world's conflicting codes—and is, therefore, not responsible for the way he has lived:

> pensarás que no se puede escoger ... que aquel día no escogiste: dejaste hacer, no fuiste responsable, no creaste ninguna de las dos morales que aquel día te solicitaron ... porque el mundo sólo te ofrecerá sus tablas establecidas, sus códigos en pugna. (122–23)

As this passage demonstrates, Artemio believes that differences cannot be reconciled—that when there are conflicting claims to truth, one must win out over the others. Unable to accept the differences—and deferrals—of language, he clings to the immediacy of the visual. By doing so, like most visionaries, he denies the temporal, and his (silent) love for Regina is, as Wendy Faris has remarked, a utopian "imagining [of] cosmic unions taking place outside time" (70). But as Faris observes, *La muerte de Artemio Cruz* emphasizes the incompatibility of the utopian drive with history:

> Fuentes is ... an imperfect utopianist, mainly because he is too good a historian. Full erotic love is a dream, a counterpart to the real nightmares of history from which we are wishing to awake....
> For Fuentes, man dreams in a space outside history, but lives within it. (73)

Faris sums up the protagonist's dilemma succinctly: Artemio's dream of full erotic love—his desire for *jouissance*—is an integral aspect of, a counterpart to, the nightmarish history of his life.

In this context, one may wonder whether Artemio's life might have been different if he had recognized the illusory and destructive nature of his utopian drive toward an imagined integrity, if he had recognized— acknowledged, spoken—his own broken and fragmentary nature. Would he then have written himself differently? Might he have discovered that language's "doble veneno" (146) holds, like Plato's *pharmakon*, curative as well as mortal effects?[9] Perhaps he would have discovered that language does not only divide, that it also joins together—that in its fullest manifestation it balances engagement and distance, "that to the obsessional intrasubjectivity is to be opposed hysterical intersubjectivity.... The realization of full speech begins here" (Lacan, *Ecrits* 46).[10]

Artemio's view of language focuses exclusively on its intrasubjectivity (its dividing properties). He does not take into consideration its hysterical intersubjectivity (its capacity to join together) and rejects the first-person plural as useless: "Teresa. Nuestra hija. Qué difícil. Qué inútil pronombre. Nuestra" (28)—because, in his view, integrity must be singular. It is ironic that it is precisely his favoring of the singular pronouns—*yo, tú,* and *él*—that underlies his radical split or disintegration into opposing and conflicting voices. It is equally ironic that Artemio's one exceptional memory of grace or self transcendence—his memory of a morning he spent with his son— involves the use of the first-person plural form, which he rejects as useless: "Cruzamos el río" (29, 56, 88, 162, 206, 221, 222). In fact, recalling the meaning of the protagonist's surname and the translation of the name of the city Veracruz, we may conclude that Artemio is more true to himself when he is open to others—when he uses the plural *nosotros* rather than the singular *yo*, *tú*, or *él*: "*Cruz*amos el río a caballo. Y llegamos hasta la barra y el mar. En Veracruz" (143, my emphasis).

There is a sticky point here, however: "Y llegamos hasta la barra." Reading these words, one hears an echo of the remarks by Lacan cited earlier: "Let us take our word 'tree' again ... and see how it crosses the bar of the Saussurian algorithm. (The anagram of '*arbre*' and '*barre*' should be noted)" (*Ecrits* 154). We note, however, a significant difference: Artemio Cruz reaches the bar but does not cross it. Language for him is only a barrier, division, separation, and he is incapable of rewriting *barre* as *arbre*—of transforming the barrier that separates and divides him into the tree of the garden he yearns for.

Unlike the text in which he is generated, Artemio is not adept at anagrams. As Santiago Tejerina-Canal's construction of meaningful anagrams as "combinations of essential relevance and meaning ... encoded within [the] name: *Artemio Cruz*" ("Point of View" 208) demonstrates, much of the beauty and complexity of this text depends upon our appreciation of "the graphics and phonetics at its center" ("Point of View" 208).[11] In contrast, the protagonist, despite his recognition that "mi nombre ... puede escribirse de mil maneras" (118), is convinced that it has a single pattern: "pero que tiene su clave, su patrón, Artemio Cruz, ah mi nombre, me suena mi nombre que chilla, se detiene" (118). Like all obsessional victims of the compulsion to repeat, Artemio fears castration—represented, in this case, by the need to break his name in order to rewrite it (and himself) more creatively. He believes that there is a single correct pattern (*patrón*) that must be obeyed or followed. Because he is committed to what he considers the true Cruz, he cannot cross the bar, as his son does; he remains in Veracruz.

In a sense, Artemio does not even know his name with its crucial acknowledgement of castration in a broken body—crucified, or torn apart by Artemis. Frightened and afraid to cross the bar—one of the anagrams of his name which Tejerina-Canal identifies is "temió cruzar" ("Point of View" 208), Artemio turns away from the utterance of a broken body to save (and condemn) himself with an illusion of a perfect and eternal wholeness.

Cognizant of the errors inherent in his strategy, we as readers would like to believe that we do not resemble Artemio and that we possess the integrity he lacks. Ironically, however, to deny our similarity to Artemio only causes us to resemble him more and to find ourselves reflected in his denial of his resemblance to us:

por más que lo intentes, no puedes ser como ellos ... porque ... di:
¿tu visión de las cosas, en tus peores o en tus mejores momentos,
ha sido tan simplista como la de ellos? Nunca. Nunca has podido
pensar en blanco y negro, en buenos y malos, en Dios y Diablo:
admite que siempre, aun cuando parecía lo contrario, has
encontrado en lo negro el germen, el reflejo de su opuesto....
Sabes que todo extremo contiene su propia oposición. (33)

The crux of the matter is that *La muerte de Artemio Cruz* will not grant us the
comfort of imagining that the flaws and failures it describes belong to
another epoch or to other individuals whose errors are unfamiliar. Rather, it
suggests that the only way we can, to some measure, not resemble Artemio
Cruz is to accept our similarity to him. If forces us to know Artemio Cruz
and to acknowledge him—to recognize that he and you and fare one. *La
muerte de Artemio Cruz* is a novel of the Mexican Revolution and a universal
one. Its universality consists of its bidding us to join together as we explore
the tree of knowledge in all its ramifications.

NOTES

1. "No House should ever be *on* any hill or on anything. It should be *of* the hill,
belonging to it so hill and house could live together, each the happier for the other." *An
Autobiography*, 1932 (Bartlett 729: 10).
2. The term "savage thought" is a literal translation of the title of Claude Levi-
Strauss's *La Pensée sauvage*, in which the French anthropologist analyzes myth as a set of
subconscious patterns organizing societies.
3. See, for example, Jung's definition of the archetype as a primordial image in
Psychological Types, 413, 443.
4. Santiago Tejerina-Canal, whose anagrams of the protagonist's name are considered
later in this essay, finds a relationship between this name and Cristo (Cristo) and notes that
Artemio Cruz "se cree hasta cierto punto Dios" (*La muerte de Artemio Cruz: Secreto
generative* 65). He further observes that this attitude has been inherited, at least in part, "...
de Ludivinia, la vieja diosa que se mantiene encerrada en su habitación, recinto sagrad....
Su hijo Don Pedrito comete el sacrilegio de profanar ese sagrario y pronto to paga con la
muerte. Es ella la que ha de salir de] sagrario para infundir su divinidad, su 'Luz divina,' al
nieto cuya sangre ya ha reconocido" (65). Although Tejerina-Canal does not mention
Artemis directly, his association of Ludivinia's name with "luz divina" [divine light] brings
to mind the Greek goddess of the moon and the hunt, just as the death sentence imposed
upon those who violate her sacred shrine brings to mind the story of Artemis and Actaeon.
5. As Merrell observes, "There is certainly a close tie between [the] words Artemio
and Catalina cannot speak and THE WORD (*chingar*...) .... THE WORD, metaphor of
metaphors ... marks the origin, if we follow the interpretation of Octavio Paz... (In the
beginning was THE WORD)" (354).
6. Since the text represents the discourse between different aspects of a fractured
personality, the phrase "monologue of mirrors" would be equally accurate.

7. As Potvin and Solomon have observed, one reason Artemio resists brokenness relates to his macho identity. Males—perhaps especially in Mexico, where "el hombre no se raja"—are encouraged by society to strive for an image of integrity and to be less open to others than are females.

8. These two significant passages are virtually impossible to render gracefully into English and are omitted from the English translation. (See Hileman 57, 297.)

9. This reference to the "double poison" of language anticipates Derrida's discussion of Plato's *pharmakon* in *La Dissémanatión*. Derrida's text is a deconstruction of the opposition established by Plato's treatment of the myth of King Thamus between the presumedly authentic knowledge of speech as opposed to its counterfeit imitation in writing. In Artemio Cruz's mind, a similar opposition exists between the integrity of silence and the brokenness of language. *La muerte de Artemio Cruz* undermines or deconstructs this opposition, however, and one way it does so is by emphasizing the meaning of "doble veneno." One page after Artemio's repetition of the Genesis mandate that whoever eats of the fruit of knowledge will die, he recalls, "Laura que hablaba de estas cosas ... dice que todo puede sernos mortal, aun lo que nos da vida" (248–49). Of course, one can reverse (Artemio's memory of) Laura's words: as in the case of Plato's *pharmakon*, that which kills also gives life.

10. In a similar vein, Lloyd Merrell in his study of *La muerte de Artemio Cruz*, identifies "a dialectical conflict between the need to propiate the transindividual Other and the need for autonomy" (354). Although Merrell does not cite Lacan, he bases many of his ideas on a reading of Kojève, who, as previously noted, was a major influence on Lacan's thought. It is not surprising, in this context, that his study of the breakdown of communication between Artemio and Catalina reaches conclusions that could accurately be described as Lacanian.

11. Tejerina-Canal also includes an extensive treatment of anagrams of Artemio Cruz's name in *La muerte de Artemio Cruz: secreto generativo* (57–80).

WORKS CITED

Bartlett, John. *Bartlett's Familiar Quotations*. Ed. Emily Morison Beck. Boston: Little Brown, 1980.

Derrida, Jacques. *Dissemination*. Trans. Barbara Johnson. Chicago: U of Chicago P, 1981.

Faris, Wendy B. "'Without Sin, and with Pleasure': The Erotic Dimensions of Fuentes' Fiction." *Novel: A Forum on Fiction* 20 (1986): 62–77.

Fuentes, Carlos. *The Death of Artemio Cruz* Trans. Sam Hileman. New York: Farrar, Straus and Giroux, 1964.

———. *La muerte de Artemio Cruz*. México: Fondo de Cultura Económica, 1985.

García, Lino, Jr. "Diálogo de espejos: *La muerte de Artemio Cruz*." Hernández de López 105–13.

Gyurko, Lanin A. "Structure and Theme in Fuentes' *La muerte de Artemio Cruz*" *Symposium* 34 (1980) 29–41.

Hegel, G. W. F. *The Philosophy of History*. Trans. J. Sibree. New York: Wiley Book Company, 1944.

Hernández de López, Ana María. *La obra de Carlos Fuentes: Una visión múltiple*. Madrid: Editorial Pliegos, 1988.

Jung, C. G. *Civilization in Transition*. Trans. R. F. C. Hull. Princeton: Princeton UP, 1978.

———. *Psychological Types*. Trans. R. F. C. Hull. Princeton: Princeton UP, 1976.

Lacan, Jacques. *Ecrits: A Selection*. Trans. Alan Sheridan. New York: W. W. Norton &
    Company, 1977.
————. *The Four Fundamental Concepts of Psychoanalysis*. Ed. Jacques-Alain Miller. Trans.
    Alan Sheridan. New York: W. W. Norton & Company, 1977.
Levy, Isaac Jack and Juan Loveluck. *Simposio Carlos Fuentes: Actas*. Columbia: U of South
    Carolina, 1978.
Merrell, Floyd. "Communication and Paradox in Carlos Fuentes' *The Death of Artemio
    Cruz*: Toward a Semiotics of Character." *Semiotica* 18 (1976): 339–60.
Meyer-Minnemann, Klaus. "Tiempo cíclico e historia en *La muerte de Artemio Cruz* de
    Carlos Fuentes." Levy and Loveluck 87–98.
Potvin, Claudine. "La política del macho en *La muerte de Artemio Cruz*." *Canadian Journal
    of Latin American and Caribbean Studies. Revue canadienne des études latino-américaines
    et caraibes* 9 (1984): 63–74.
Solomon, Irvin D. "A Feminist Perspective of the Latin American Novel: Carlos Fuentes'
    The Death of Artemio Cruz." *Hispanófila* 33 (1989): 69–75.
Tejerina-Canal, Santiago. *La muerte de Artemio Cruz: Secreto generativo*. Boulder, Colorado:
    Society of Spanish and Spanish-American Studies, 1987.
————. "Point of View in *The Death of Artemio Cruz*: Singularity or Multiplicity?" *Review
    of Contemporary Literature* 8 (1988): 199–210.

CYNTHIA GIRGEN

The Magic Word in
Carlos Fuentes' The Death of Artemio Cruz

> Culture is the way we laugh, even at ourselves. It is the way we
> remember ... (Carlos Fuentes, *The Buried Mirror*).

In a seminal 1969 essay, one of the first to synthesize the new direction
Latin American literature was taking, Carlos Fuentes suggests that the use of
mythic or archetypal patterns must become important fictive devices because
they can serve essentially as new language strategies.[1] It is in this essay that
Fuentes first argues that by incorporating myth, Latin American writers can
learn a new language to replace the gaps he sees in traditional, bourgeois
literature of the past:

> A radical who confronts his own past, the new Latin American
> writer embarks on a revision that begins with a recognition: that
> a language is missing. The obligation to denounce converts into
> a task much more arduous: the critical elaboration of everything
> not said in our long history of lies, silences, rhetorics and
> convoluted academics. To invent a language is to say everything
> that history has silenced (30).[2]

However, as early as *The Death of Artemio Cruz* written in 1959,
Fuentes apparently already begins to give his own creative work the ballast

From *Hispanic Journal* 16, no. 1 (Spring 1995): 123–134. © 1995 by Indiana University of
Pennsylvania.

151

of a "new language" through archetype and myth. He elaborates a baroque structure for the book that allows the protagonist to vacillate between the traditional paradigms of time and space. I think the novel's elastic structure is fundamental to Fuentes' strategy to conflate the present and the past, myth and history. For this reason it is worthwhile to first consider how the novel's organization operates to support this stratagem. When the novel opens we know that the year is 1959, that Artemio Cruz is sixty-one years old, he apparently has suffered some kind of infarction after his return to Mexico City after a business trip to Sonora, and that now, twenty-four hours later, he is dying. But beyond the lean details of circumstance, we learn about Artemio Cruz only by disjointed narrative pieces: his past as it unfolds itself to a dying mind.

Fuentes uses stream of consciousness narratives, the cinematic effect of the frequent use of flashback and montage, exuberant word play, and most of all, the deliberate play Fuentes makes with point of view that attempts to simultaneously portray the past, present, and future of Cruz's consciousness. With adroit oppositions of consecutive first, second and third person narrative—what I will refer to as the *Yo* or I (first person), the *Tú* or You (second person), and the *Él* or He (third person) of Cruz's consciousness.

In the third person narratives, Fuentes writes a more traditional novel. Although they rely on flashback and montage to create cinematic effects, they are nonetheless the most straightforward of the three narratives. These *Él* phases function as exposition; they appear to be how Cruz relives episodes in his life, but they are told "objectively," through third person narration. Moreover, the *Él* offers the only coherence between the chaotic voice that swings in and out of delirium and the often hermetic voice of the guilty conscience present in the *Tú*, or second person narrative. Perhaps the *Él* is strictly Cruz's memory, and as such, probably less reliable than the *Tú* phases—it is in the *Él* that Cruz meets Catalina, the wife he has to "buy," has an affair in Acapulco with Lilia, and even recreates his memory of how he imagined his son Lorenzo's wartime experience and death in Spain. Cruz's memory often seems caught up in the details of scenes, in the minutiae of the moment in his memory—everything seems included, unsorted, unfiltered. However, these memories are biased by Cruz's own devotion to his ego and its expression through material objects. The montages that are part of each *Él* phase include multiple inventories of things, from furniture to food to shaving gear, all the highest quality—the best that money can buy, usually from the United States or Europe. It is as if Cruz's memories were being directed by the most scrupulous of set designers. It is in the third person narratives that Fuentes makes clear Cruz's obsessional memory in regard to the material, especially with material symbols of wealth. However, revealing the motivations for this kind of neurotic memory are left to the second and first person narratives.

> Death awaits us behind the fairgound, the carnival that overturns social categories and political fictions, the great egalitarian spectacle that dissolves the frontiers between stage and auditorium, player and spectator, viewer and viewed. (Carlos Fuentes, *The Buried Mirror*)

The novel begins and ends with first person narratives, the *Yo* phases, which reveal the activity of the dying man's present. The *Yo* exposes the reader to Cruz's pain and to his awareness of the other characters compelled to watch him die—the family, doctors, priests who attend him. In the *Yo* phase of each narrative, the text is often chaotic; Cruz's sensations mix with dream-like sequences of memory as Cruz re-lives key episodes of his life juxtaposed with the intervention of doctors and intravenous tubes.

> Now I'm waking up, but I don't want to open my eyes. Even so, I see something shining near my face. Something that turns into a flood of black lights and blue circles behind my closed lids ... I open my right eye, and I see it reflected in the squares of glass sewn onto a woman's handbag. That's what I am ... I am that eye. I am that eye furrowed by accumulated rage, an old, forgotten, but always renewed rage. (MacAdam trans. 3)

In the *Yo* phase, too, Fuentes uses the device of particular repetitions of Cruz's semi-conscious thought patterns. One repetition is his constant desire to have the window open in his room, and another is "We crossed the river on horseback" which is a memory trigger, a symbol for Lorenzo, Cruz's son who had died years earlier in the Spanish Civil War. Both of these images function as *leitmotivs* across the sections, serving as markers of recognition in the disorderly text of the *Yo* sections.

The second-person narratives, however, consist of curious "futurizations." The *Tú* phases seem at times to be the voice of Cruz's conscience, and they frequently provide information about the protagonist's past. Nevertheless these narratives always unfold in future tense. The first *Tú* phase begins in the future of Cruz's most recent past—the events of the previous day—the hours before he collapses:

> Yesterday you did what you do every day. You don't know if it's worthwhile remembering it. You only want to remember, lying

back there in the twilight of your bedroom, what's going to
happen: you don't want to foresee what has already happened. In
your twilight, your eyes see ahead; they don't know how to guess
the past. (MacAdam trans. 7)

The *Tú* phases reveal most the temporal play Fuentes makes in the novel by
unraveling the life of Artemio Cruz not only through the character's own
first person stream of consciousness, but through another voice—one that
condemns Cruz by replaying the tapes of his past in a different way. The
voice behind the *Tú* gives us more than data, it reveals the options Cruz has
regarding the significant choices he makes in his life. The *Tú* judges Cruz by
reminding him that there were other options that were less selfish than the
ones he chooses, options that would have allowed his son to live to manhood,
allowed him to promote land division instead of exploitation after the
Revolution, allowed his marriage to Catalina to be more than dry ink on a
crumbling document.

     It is notable that the *Tú* strategy that appears in much of Fuentes' work
begins with *The Death of Artemio Cruz* and continues as a recurring stylistic
device throughout the novels of the decade that follows. In an interview
given in 1974, Fuentes asserts that the use of the second-person strategy was
related to his personal concept of the Revolution itself—one of those stories
from childhood that make intense impressions, a story for Fuentes to develop
in his imagination. He remembers well hearing the story of Zapata's troops,
the *campesinos* from Morelos who had entered Mexico City· in 1915 to
overthrow President Huerta, and how they took over palatial buildings and
hotels, and were thus exposed to unaccustomed luxury. According to
Fuentes' anecdote, the fact of the matter was that the *campesinos* who
suddenly found themselves lodged in a French hotel full of ornate mirrors
were seeing their own images for the first time in their lives.

     Never before had they seen themselves in a mirror. They spent
     hour after hour, and did nothing more than to stare at themselves
     and each other reflected there and they were saying, Look! It's
     me! Look! It's you! Look! It's us. I had this in mind when I wrote
     The Death of Artemio Cruz ... for me, the *Tú* was extremely
     important as a recognition of the other ... It is not just Artemio
     Cruz's double that speaks; it is perhaps the collective voice of the
     Mexican people that speaks to Cruz saying, *you, you, you.* (225)

The format of the novel, then, is a rather rigid one in regard to the
predictable oscillation among the points of view in Artemio Cruz's

consciousness. Britt Schiller suggests that this often criticized "rigidity" in the novel is not a device separate and imposed on the text, but instead the way Fuentes maintains "the tension between order and chaos, the chaos that Cruz fears and tries to hold off through the ordering and clarifying power of his mind" (94). Another purpose for Fuentes' play with rotating points of view might be his attempt to create spaces in the novel that will allow him not only to create a believable character, but to create one who can function as a victim on two distinct levels: the Cruz who sacrifices his integrity for power and at the same time the Cruz (the cross) that symbolizes Mexico, the implicit sacrificial victim of the Revolution. Cruz is Mexico's microcosm, the principle of the Revolution that transmogrifies into corruption, a *fiesta* for demagogues.

Ironically, it is the rigidity of the multiple point of view structure that allows Fuentes the freedom to broach from the surface of the text its sub-textual explorations of myth and archetype. Fuentes seems to be rewriting the myths; Lanin Gyurko suggests, for example, that Fuentes uses his fictions to challenge the notion of "progress" in post-revolutionary Mexico, with stories that expose the party line. Gyurko argues that what Fuentes does is "demythification"—exposing the reality of Mexico, where the benefits of the "new prosperity" of the 1960's (which seem little removed from the agenda of Nafta in the 1990's) are realized by only a select few, like Cruz himself, former revolutionaries who betray their countrymen in order to launch careers fueled by exploiting the poor (109).

> There is a very tall hotel in Mexico that has never been finished. Year after year builders add to its height, but one can always look right through its hive of gaping stones. (Carlos Fuentes, *The Buried Mirror*)

One of the most pervasive and important archetypes in Mexican mythologies is contained within one word, the verb *chingar*. Fuentes attempts to interrogate this archetype just as he does Revolution ideology itself by exposing it. It is notable that Fuentes chooses to grapple in this way with one word in Artemio Cruz's consciousness, but I believe this choice is very much within the Fuentes signature. For example, Octavio Paz has pointed out in the introduction to *Cuerpos y ofrendas* that in Fuentes' fictional landscape, "The world is not presented like a reality that one has to name, but rather like a word that we have to decipher" (9). Paz elaborates further,

> Every symbol evokes another symbol ... from novel to novel and from character to character. Interminable task and one which the

novelist [Fuentes] has to begin again and again: in order to decipher a hieroglyph one takes advantage of symbols (words) that immediately evoke another hieroglyph. (9)

What I will refer to as the *chingar* narrative occurs appropriately in one of, the *Tú* phases of the novel (where the voice of the collective conscience can speak), and it occurs precisely in the novel's center. The placement of this narrative immediately follows a *Yo* phase, a first person narrative, wherein Cruz experiences moments of self-realization: his first person consciousness expresses implicit guilt feelings and self-justifying responses to them. He needs to explain himself. More, Cruz has reached the point where he knows with certainty that he will not survive:

> What do they know, Catalina, the priest, Teresa ... What importance are their boasts going to have, or these statements of sympathy that will appear in the newspapers? Who will have the honesty to say, as I say now, that my only love has been material possessions, sensual acquisition? (Hileman trans. 132)

In this narrative, which prefigures the *chingar* passage that will follow, Cruz's stream of consciousness is a jumble of impressions; he speaks "mentally" to his wife, his daughter, his right-hand man. At the end of the passage, he speaks of himself as well—in the third person, admitting at last *"se chingó chingando a los demás"* (Fuentes 143). There is bravado mixed with guilt, and he manages to use three variations on *chingar* just before the voice of *Tú* takes over—*"se chingó, se chingó chingando, chinguen a su madre"* (Fuentes 143).

The second person narrative differs from the other *Tú* phases which have come before. This one veers from specific and deliberate commentary on the facts of Cruz's life to a voice laden with the knowledge of *chingar* and its effect on everyone. The *Tú* performs, for the next five pages of the text, an exhaustive linguistic analysis of the word. Cruz's mind purges itself of every meaning it associates with *chingar*. A brutal, verbal projection of his anguish is embodied in an explosive collection of meanings, uses, various conjugations, including at last a vehement rejection of the word itself. Cruz's mind seems to be reconstructing the formation of his own worldview through the word play in this *Tú* phase. It recreates itself in a spiral of delirious lucidity that Cruz's consciousness propels forward on the basis of this one word:

> You will say it, it is your word and your word is my word: word of honor, man's word, word that lasts, coin word that everyone

spends: imprecation, snapping greeting, man's extravagance, boss word, invitation to a brawl, call to labor, epigraph for love, bastards' word, threat, mock, oath, comrade word at fiesta and binge, claim to guts and balls, magic saber, height of chicanery, white word and nigger word, frontier barrier, resumé of our history ... (Hileman trans. 137)

Seeming like an outpour of every obscenity Cruz can conjure, Fuentes begins in this way a complex revelation of the meanings and the power of one word, the prohibited word, *chingar*—the most profane word a Mexican can use.

The origins of chingar remain mysterious, although it is speculated that its etymological roots lie in the Nahuatl (the language of the Aztecs) word *Xinaxtli* which means juice of the maguey or *xinachtli*, meaning garden seed.[3] There is, then, a wide usage of the word throughout Latin America that relates to beverages, particularly alcoholic ones. However, in Mexico, where the word originates, there is a proliferation of words based on *chingar*, many sexual, all violent, all negative. Octavio Paz asserts in "The Sons of La Malinche," a chapter of *The Labyrinth of Solitude*, that *chingar* is a "magical word" that can change entirely its meaning with a nuance of tone or inflection; however its ultimate meaning in Mexico is a denotation of violence and aggression, whether it is rape or wounding or murder—it means "to injure, to lacerate, to violate—bodies, souls, objects—and to destroy" (76).

Within the word *chingar* lies one of Mexico's fundamental mythical figures, Doña Marina, or La Malinche. In "The Sons of La Malinche" Pas also argues that implicit in any form of *chingar* is *la chingada*, the violated Mother, and "it is appropriate to associate her with the Conquest, which was also a violation, not only in the historical sense but also in the very flesh of Indian women" (86). Her origin begins with the Indian girl sold to Cortés who learns Spanish and serves as his principal translator. It is generally believed that if it were not for Cortés' ability to communicate with the Aztecs through Marina, he would not have defeated them so easily. Tzvetan Todorov's study of the cultural confrontations in the New World points out that for a time La Malinche was a person of great importance to both the Spanish conquerors and the indigenous people—so much so that the nickname the Aztecs gave to Cortés was also *Malinche* (101). Doña Marina bears Cortés a child, as well—the first mestizo. However, the story goes that when Cortés was through with her, he sent her away, as a gift to a captain in his army. *La chingada*, then, subsumes all that La Malinche represents today: she is a symbol of violation, treason, of conquest, of duality and the contradictory nature of Mexico's heritage.

However, I believe the *chingar* narrative relies in important ways not only on its historical contextualization of La Malinche but on its appropriation of Paz's conclusions about this fundamental archetype. In fact there appears to be a direct parallel between the development of the passage and the key points of "The Sons of La Malinche." For example, in this chapter of *Labyrinth*, Paz concentrates on the essential duality of the Mexican personality, the otherness expressed in the epithet *Viva México, hijos de la chingada!* He calls the phrase Mexicans' true battle cry because it affirms their identity in the face of "the others" "the bad Mexicans," who are "the sons of a mother as vague and indeterminate as themselves" (75). Paz argues also that *la chingada* is "the Mother forcibly opened, violated or deceived. *La hijo de la chingada* is the offspring of violation, abduction or deceit" (79). Notably, Artemio Cruz himself is Fuentes' quintessential *hijo de la chingada*—he is the "bad Mexican," the literal son of a vague and indeterminate mother, Isabel Cruz (or Cruz Isabel—no one knows which), a mulatto impregnated by Atanasio Menchaca, a rich Creole.

Clearly, Fuentes replicates the legend of La Malinche in the character Cruz: "Cruz without a real first or last name, baptized by the mulattos with the syllables of Isabel Cruz or Cruz Isabel, the mother who was *run off by Atanasio: the first woman on the property to give him a son*" (297–98; emphasis added). It is significant, too, that Artemio Cruz was born near Veracruz, where Cortés first meets Doña Marina and where she will have his child.[4]

Paz argues that La Malinche is *la chingada in person*; she has the quality of openness and trust which opposes the closed and stoic attitude that is so much a part of the Mexican cultural identity. Moreover, Paz suggests that it is this archetype that most influences the Mexican self-concept:

> The strange permanence of Cortés and La Malinche in the Mexican's imagination and sensibilities reveals that they are something more than historical figures: they are symbols of a secret conflict we have still not resolved. When he repudiates La Malinche ... the Mexican breaks his ties with the past, renounces his origins, and lives in isolation and solitude (87).

Fuentes characterizes Artemio Cruz in exactly this way. For example, Cruz lives in isolation and solitude, believing he loved Regina, but she was murdered in the Revolution. After he loses his son, the only *other* person he loves in his life, Cruz takes on, in an exaggerated way, the "closed" personality just as Paz delineates it. What is more, through the *chingar* narrative, Fuentes manages to "explain" why Cruz is as he is, just as Paz explains the impetus for the collective Mexican identity. When Paz tells us in

Labyrinth that what we really find in the word *chingar* is the dichotomy between the closed and the open, signifying the triumph of the closed, the male, the powerful, over the open (78), we are assaulted with the *experience* of the same argument in Fuentes' narrative wherein the *Tú* of Cruz's consciousness delivers a litany to the "sons of the word:"

> It faces you everywhere, it deals your hand, cuts your deck, covers your bet, disguises reticence and the double-cross, reveals cowardice and bravery, intoxicates, shouts, succumbs, lives in every bed, presides over the ceremonies of friendship, of hatred, and of power: our word, you and I, members of the lodge, the fraternity of the fucked: You are what you are because you know how to fuck 'em without letting them fuck you ... (Hileman trans. 138)

Fuentes shows through Cruz's agony how the word is strong with the power myth has given it. Obviously, Fuentes believes *chingar* descends from Mexico's colonial past, building a power of its own, as if it were the linguistic albatross responsible for the bifurcated Mexican identity Paz describes in *Labyrinth*. The testimony of the *Tú* illustrates, then, Paz's conception of *chingar* as a word that defines a great part of a Mexican's life, because to a Mexican "there are only two possibilities in life: either he inflicts the actions implied by *chingar* on others, or else he suffers them himself at the hands of others" (78):

> child of the children of the word, father of sons of the word: our word, looking out at us from every face, behind every gesture, yet an outcast ... the word provides your promises, secures your sacrifice ... You have no mother but you have your word ... you have your buddy: ass-hole buddies, you have your wives or your fists, your old women and your office chippies, and you have the word: with the word you rattle closet skeletons ... You advance with the word and with guts, you are as truthful as the word, you hang to the tit of the word ... (Hileman trans. 138)

However, Fuentes does more than illustrate through the dying Cruz the archetype and myth implicit in all the uses of *chingar* that Paz analyzes in *Labyrinth*. It appears that Fuentes essentially interrogates Paz's cultural assumptions as well. Midway through the *chingar* narrative, the accusing voice of the *Tú* changes; the anger and the profanity disappear; its tone becomes didactic. Moreover, this new voice no longer appears to illustrate or confirm the word's multiple connotations, it wants now to shape the future. And it is here that the burden of *la nueva novela* Fuentes constructs with *The Death of Artemio Cruz* unfolds its dominant purpose—to re-write history from the point of view of an active participant in imaginary events. The use of the past-as-future *Tú* at this point reveals, I think, Fuentes' desire to diffuse the power of the myth behind *chingar*. Fuentes himself explains in the *Kenyon Review* interview that the past is, after all, simply a function of memory, an imaginative construct: "history is only what we remember of history. What is fact in history? The novel asks this question ... Men and women, we create history, it is our creation; it is our creation; it is not the creation of God. Since we made history, we have to imagine history. We have to imagine the past" (Weiss 106). The voice in the *chingar* narrative seems to be asking the same question and delivering the same answer:

> oh mystery, oh, deception, oh, mirror facing a mirror: do you believe that you can go forward with the word, that you will affirm yourself? Forward to what future? Not to yours: no one wants to on to damnation, suspicion, frustration, resentment, hate, envy, rancor ... misery, abuse, insult, intimidation, false pride, bravado, with the fucking corruption of your fucking word. (Hileman trans. 139)

The voice of the *Tú* assaulting Cruz's consciousness here longs for a remembrance of a past that can reject the inheritance of *la chingada*. What appears to happen in the *chingar* narrative is really a disturbance of the myth; it questions the *force* of *chingar*—"The sons of the word are those beings you will change into objects for your employment, pleasure, mastery, despight, victory, your life" (Hileman trans. 139).

With all of its meanings folded back on each other through the voice of the *Tú*, Fuentes seems to want to relieve Mexico from the cultural oppression implicit in the *chingar* construct: the myth of its "traitor" Aztec mother and its "abusive" Spanish father. In place of repeated and reinforced antagonistic images that every use of *chingar* achieves, the voice of the *Tú* now suggests that the magical power of the word could somehow deflate if only Cruz would recognize it for what it is—a fraud. It is a word emptied of meaning: *el hijo de la chingada es una cosa que tú usas: peor es nada* (146). It is as hollow as a building never finished but forever elaborated. Here the narrative appears to once again echo "The Sons of La Malinche" where Paz asserts that *la chingada*, because of constant usage, contradictory meanings "wastes away, loses its contents ... It says nothing. It is Nothingness itself" (79). Paz reaches the conclusion in "The Sons of La Malinche" that all the negative feelings, images, and actions he associates with *chingar* are really paradoxical: they spring from the sham of a myth based on violation and a word dedicated to aggression.

Regardless of the similarities between Paz's *Labyrinth* and the *chingar* narrative in *The Death of Artemio Cruz*, Fuentes' *Tú* always challenges the certainty of Paz's assertions. In this case, the second person voice implies that wholeness will follow the word's erasure: "leave the word behind you, kill it with borrowed arms, destroy it: Murder the word that stands between us, makes stone of us, rots us with its poison mixed of idolatry and the cross: so that it cannot be either our reply or our destiny ..." (Hileman trans. 139). In this way Fuentes also challenges the imagination to be active, not passive, to language. The state of consciousness from which the *Tú* speaks can disregard a fundamental fact of language: we as individuals have no real power over it. We cannot alone neologize nor delete its vocabulary; we cannot changes the rules of its grammar or syntax or the cultural codes embedded within it. However, as Fuentes suggests, the *Tú* is Mexico's collective voice, and only collective awareness will subvert the influence of *chingar*.

NOTES

1. Carlos Fuentes, *La nueva novela hispanoamericana* (México: Fondo de Cultura Económica, 1969)

2. Elsewhere in the essay, Fuentes argues in the section titled "has the Novel Died?" that the novel itself is not dead, but rather its bourgeois form with its point of reference—realism—that imposes a descriptive style of observing individuals in personal and social relations. The death of the traditional novel signals for Fuentes the birth of a new and more powerful one. *La nueva novela* concerns itself with the totality of history. The new novel has the capacity to encounter and lift *above language* the myths and the prophecies of a historical period; it is not limited to the either/or of capitalism vs. socialism, not limited to the dichotomies the traditional novel engenders (16–22). All translation and paraphrase from the essay are mine.

3. In *The Labyrinth of Solitude* Octavio Paz ascribes these etymologies to a work by linguist Darío Rubio, *Anarquía del lenguage en la America española* (Mexico: Confederación Regional Obrera Mexicana, 1925). One of the first contemporary works to do so, this two-volume work reveals the influence of indigenous language on Spanish in Latin America.

4. Beatrice Berler's chapter notes from *The Conquest of Mexico: A Modern Rendering of William H. Prescott's History* (San Antonio: Corona, 1988), reveal that Veracruz was first names "Villa Rica de Vera Cruz, *The Rich Town of the True Cross*, a name which was considered as happily intimating the union of spiritual and temporal interests to which the arms of the Spanish adventurers in the New World were to be devoted" (140). The irony between these noble goals and the reality of Spanish exploitation of the indigenous people of Mexico seems to be implicit in Fuentes' play with his character's name and the name of his place of origin. The play with Cruz, Veracruz, and Cruz Isabel/Isabel Cruz serves to reinforce Cruz's role as the ironic "true cross" of Mexico—he sacrifices love, self, ideology in order to gain wealth and power.

Works Cited

Fuentes, Carlos. *The Buried Mirror*. New York: Houghton, 1992.

———. *The Death of Artemio Cruz*. Trans. Sam Hileman. New York: Farrar, 1964.

———. *The Death of Artemio Cruz*. Trans. Alfred MacAdam, New York: Farrar, 1991.

———. *La muerte de Artemio Cruz*. Mexico, D.F.: Fondo de Cultura Económica, 1962.

———. *Lo nueva novela hispanoamericana*. México, D.F.: Joaquín Mortiz, 1969.

Gyurko, Lanin A. "Myth and Demythification in Fuentes' *Aura* and Wilde's *Sunset Boulevard*." *Hispanic Journal* 7 (1985): 91–113.

Levy, Isaac Jack and Dale E. Enwall, eds. "Diálogo con Carlos Fuentes." Isaac Jack Levy and Juan Loveluck, eds. *Simposio Carlos Fuentes*. Columbia, SC: University of South Carolina P, 1978. 215–29.

Paz, Octavio. Prólogo. *Cuerpos y ofrendas*. By Carlos Fuentes. Madrid: Alianza Editorial, 1972. 7–15.

———. "The Sons of La Malinche." *The Labyrinth of Solitude*. Trans. Lysander Kemp, Yara Milos, and Rachel Belash. New York: Grove P, 1985. 65–88.

Schiller, Britt-Marie. "Memory and Time in *The Death of Artemio Cruz*." *Latin American Literary Review* 15 (1987): 93–103.

Todorov, Tzvetan. *The Conquest of America: The Question of the Other*. Trans. Richard Howard. New York: Harper, 1992.

Weiss, Jason. "An Interview with Carlos Fuentes." *Kenyon Review* 5 (1983): 105–18.

MAARTEN van DELDEN

Modes of Redemption

La muerte de Artemio Cruz is both a paradigmatic modernist text, with its nonlinear narrative and interiorist focus, and a culminating instance of the novel of the Mexican Revolution, with its broad historical and political concerns.[50] By situating his novel at the intersection of these two literary modes, Fuentes to a certain extent enriches them both: his use of modernist techniques grants greater interest and complexity to a subject-matter often treated in a straightforward, documentary fashion, whereas his historical and political concerns help Fuentes transcend the often narrowly subjectivist nature of modernist fiction.[51] Yet there is also a loss in Fuentes's translation of a modernist aesthetic into a Mexican context. For if an interest in the topics of time and consciousness is one of the elements that links *Artemio Cruz* to the modernist tradition, then it must be noted that Fuentes's need to provide his novel with a clear political message—that the Mexican Revolution was betrayed by the greed and selfishness of its protagonists—in fact places clear limits on his exploration of these topics. In the classic modernist novel of such writers as Marcel Proust, Virginia Woolf, and William Faulkner, consciousness is experienced as fragmented in large part because of the inherently destructive nature of time. Thus, Georg Lukács speaks in *The Theory of the Novel* of how "the sluggish, yet constant progress of time ... gradually robs subjectivity of all its possessions and imperceptibly

From *Carlos Fuentes, Mexico, and Modernity.* © 1998 by Vanderbilt University Press.

forces alien contents into it."[52] Of course, there is also a social context to this experience: for Lukács the volatility of consciousness is a direct consequence of the disorientedness and meaninglessness of modern society itself. In *Artemio Cruz*, however, the specific features of the protagonist's career and character make it much more difficult to read the novel as a broad meditation on the topic of time. Fuentes unfolds a series of devices with which to illustrate the splintered condition of Artemio Cruz's consciousness—the shifts between first-, second-, and third-person narrative, the winding interior monologues, the theme of the double—yet this fragmented self belongs to a character who, as Gerald Martin points out, is explicitly judged and condemned in the novel.[53] The result is that the reader holds Artemio at a distance, for we regard his disintegrated consciousness not as an aspect of modern subjectivity itself, but rather as a form of punishment for Artemio's opportunism, his lack of an ethical core.[54]

Many critics read *Artemio Cruz* as a powerful study of the split condition of the self.[55] But what must be emphasized is that the process of psychic fragmentation Artemio undergoes is meaningful only against the backdrop of an alternative image of an unfissured self. Artemio's plight has a certain element of contingency to it: his destabilized subjectivity is the result of the personal choices he has made in the course of his life, but things could clearly have been otherwise. It is this "otherwise" that is captured in the evocation of various ephemeral moments of plenitude Artemio has experienced. These moments constitute the norm against which the fundamentally fractured quality of Artemio's consciousness appears as a deviation. The insistent presence in *Artemio Cruz* of an ideal of transparency—in the constitution of the self and in the self's relations with the world—helps us see the links between the novel and Fuentes's journalistic writings of the late 1950s and early 1960s. In his political commentaries, Fuentes makes constant use of unified categories—such as the notion of "the people"—and appeals repeatedly to a utopian vision of a disalienated society—for which Cuba under the new revolutionary regime provides the model. On the surface, *Artemio Cruz*, with its ambiguous protagonist and jagged narrative line, appears to resist the ideal of transparency that animates Fuentes's political journalism. Yet *Artemio Cruz* is, in fact, informed by the same utopian impulse as Fuentes's political writings, the same desire for the restoration of a state of social and political wholeness.[56]

A brief examination of a number of literary essays Fuentes first published in the late 1950s and early 1960s can help bring this aspect of Fuentes's aesthetics to light. In these essays—on Jane Austen, Herman Melville, and William Faulkner—Fuentes puts forward a broad interpretation of the history of the novel, an interpretation that helps us see where Fuentes locates his own work.[57] Fuentes divides the genre of the novel into two broad categories: the classic and the modern. The former is the bourgeois realist novel, with its linear organization and its preference for unproblematic description. It is what Fuentes labels "the novel of recognition," a type of novel which confirms rather than subverts the order of the real. The prime example of this type of work is offered by Jane Austen: "In Jane Austen's novels the readers immediately recognized themselves: they saw themselves as they wanted to be seen" (29). Austen's novels serve to consecrate the new class in power—they provide the bourgeoisie with a portrait of itself, but above all they instill in it a good conscience about itself. Thus, the novelistic tradition Austen helped to establish presupposes a seamless relationship between text and reality, as well as between text and reader.

Fuentes rejects the Jane Austen type of novel, for it is far too cautious and conventional for his tastes. He clearly prefers what he sometimes calls the novel of radical modernity, and at other times the novel of tragic vision, a type of work of which the writings of Faulkner are a prime expression. For Fuentes, tragic vision, a quality he believes the modern world sorely lacks, is intimately related to the consciousness of something he calls "separation." In the essay on Austen, he defines "separation" as the opposite of "recognition," and suggests that William Blake, "in the midst of the victorious rise of the bourgeoisie" (28), offered the first powerful intuition of its meaning. Blake explored the reverse side of the safe and familiar world depicted by the bourgeois novelists. In the tradition of "poetic radicalism" (70) he inaugurated, identity is not held within a stable circumference, but rather discovers its own profound otherness. Faulkner belongs to this tradition precisely because his characters are not fixed and predictable figures, but rather "extreme, deep and secret possibilities" (70). In his discussion of Faulkner, Fuentes relates this discovery of the abyss within the self to man's paradoxical and tragic relationship to nature. Man, dependent upon nature for his survival, must use it, but in doing so he also violates it. He introduces evil into the natural order; he divides the earth, but as a result also divides himself, for the need to exploit nature signals the impossibility of living in harmony with nature. This, says Fuentes, explains why Faulkner gave the name Yoknapatawpha County to the imaginary world of his novels, for Yoknapatawpha means "the divided earth" in Chickasaw (64).

This tragic vision is embodied in Faulkner, but also in Dostoyevsky and Kafka, and in Poe and Melville, in an aesthetics of estrangement. These novelists all reject the familiar, and seek the unknown. They are in opposition to a world dominated by what Fuentes calls "a double rationality, of the reconciliation of man and God in Christianity, and of man and reason in history" (70–71). Against what we would now call the grand narratives of Christianity and the Enlightenment, Fuentes proposes a giddy vision of unremitting conflict, contradiction, and incompleteness. Against the novel of recognition, he proposes the novel of separation. Yet, interestingly enough, at several points in Fuentes's argument, the opposition between the two types of novel is erased.

Toward the end of his essay on Austen, Fuentes suddenly reverses direction, suggesting that, in light of certain traits inherent to the genre of the novel, Austen's work, almost in spite of itself, possesses a subversive dimension. Octavio Paz's definition of the novel as the "epic of a society in conflict with itself," and so as "an implicit judgement of that same society,"[58] leads Fuentes to the conclusion that even Austen's work—true as it must remain to the fundamental impulses of the genre—leaves "a space for doubt, for reflection, for the reader's alarmed consciousness" (31). Yet in the same way as Fuentes ends by discovering an unsuspected sense of openness in Austen's novels, his reading of Faulkner—and of the tragic vision in the modern novel—finally emphasizes a paradoxical sense of closure. Although the notion of "separation," as Fuentes uses it in *Casa con dos puertas*, appears on one level to denote the irremediably exilic nature of human existence itself, on a different level the terra seems to allude to what is merely a stage in the development of human consciousness, or of human society. When Fuentes suggests that what Blake called "separation," Marx would later call "alienation" (28), the implication is that "separation," a condition denied and suppressed by the bourgeois realist aesthetics of "recognition," is discovered, but also overcome, in the Romantic visionary tradition embodied by Blake. Indeed, in the work of Blake and his successors (Fuentes mentions Brontë, Novalis, Hölderlin, Büchner, Marx, Nietzsche, Dostoyevsky, and Kafka) the aesthetics of estrangement serves ultimately to lead to a higher form of recognition—a kind of "other-recognition" to which Jane Austen remained immune (32). In his discussion of Faulkner, Fuentes describes an analogous process, though here he places it in a Christian framework: "Where formerly there was only being and contemplation, men introduce sin, and hence redemption; violation, and hence love; responsibility, and hence grace; grief, and hence happiness" (64). In this narrative, separation is merely a prelude to redemption. When, elsewhere in the same essay, Fuentes argues that in the work of James Joyce, William Faulkner, Hermann Broch, and Malcolm Lowry, the novel becomes poetry, he states his utopian vision, now shorn of its Christian connotations, with even greater force, for Fuentes draws his definition of poetry from surrealism: "For the surrealists, poetry and revolution were one and the same thing: both, in a fusion of identities, were to destroy all forms of alienation and reveal the complete reality of mankind, the vital correspondences between fact and dream, reality and desire, nature and the individual: between all the separated halves" (60).

Whether couched in a Christian or in a surrealist vocabulary, the promise of redemption constitutes one of the informing principles of Fuentes's aesthetics. This is clear not only in Fuentes's literary essays, but also in *Artemio Cruz*, where the protagonist is measured specifically in terms of his distance from the ideals of fusion and integration so vividly evoked in *Casa con dos puertas*. One of the key words used in the novel to capture Artemio's condition is the word "separation." On one level, the word captures the tragic truth about Artemio's life, a truth which his social self, oriented toward status and recognition, would prefer not to admit. From this perspective, Artemio's willingness to face this truth, at least in the inner recess of his self, grants a degree of depth and dignity to his character. Yet "separation" also emerges as the cost of Artemio's success, and therefore as the mode in which the novel expresses its condemnation of him.

"Separation" defines Artemio's relationship to his wife Catalina, who never forgives Artemio for having failed to save the life of her brother Gonzalo, with whom Artemio had shared a prison cell during the Revolution, nor for the ruthless way in which Artemio seized her along with her father's wealth after the Revolution. Near the beginning of the novel the narrator describes Catalina and Artemio listening to each other's movements through a door that separates their rooms. "Who will live in that separation?" he wonders (34/28). When, in an episode set in 1941, the narrator alternates between descriptions of Artemio conducting his business from his office, and Catalina and their daughter Laura going shopping, the point of the very modernist device is to show how husband and wife live in separate orbits. This dreadful sense of separation haunts Artemio's relations with all the women in his life: Regina meets a violent death during the Revolution, Laura slips away when Artemio—worried about appearances—refuses to divorce his wife, and Lila is only interested in Artemio's money. But Artemio's unhappy romances are a symptom, not a cause. Artemio is like Captain Ahab, of whom Fuentes writes in his essay on Melville that "rooted in the freedom of his own self, he ends by transgressing the freedom of his fellow human beings" (47). Artemio has a similarly immoderate conception of his own freedom: "Perhaps her hand speaks to you of an excess of freedom that defeats freedom. Freedom that raises an endless tower that does not reach heaven but splits the abyss, cleaves the earth. You will name it: separation" (85–86). But Artemio's pathologies also have a specifically Mexican genealogy. After all, Artemio corresponds very closely to the figure of the *chingón* so vividly described by Octavio Paz in *El laberinto de la soledad*.

The *chingón* is the active, aggressive male who imposes his will on the passive, inert female.[59] According to Paz, Mexicans venerate the *chingón*; the result is to turn society into a battlefield, where all that counts is the ability to lord it over one's fellow human beings.[60] In a passage from *Artemio Cruz* that is clearly indebted to Paz, Fuentes describes the poisonous effects of such values: "the *chingada* who poisons love, dissolves friendship, smashes tenderness, the *chingada* who divides, who separates, who destroys, who poisons" (146/138). The irony in *Artemio Cruz* is, of course, that the *chingón* becomes the victim of his own violence. Artemio owes his social and financial success to his determination to climb to the top, and to his willingness to sacrifice others for the sake of his personal advancement, but his fate is to be haunted by feelings of inner division and incompleteness. The *chingón* masks a fragmented self, his willful separation from his fellow human beings results in a separation from himself. And so, Artemio's life, as he experiences it in retrospect, becomes a kind of protracted death. Near the end of the novel, with his life hanging by a thread, Artemio is rushed to the hospital for an operation. "I'm separated ... I'm dying" (270/262) he thinks to himself. When, on the next page, Artemio reflects that "living is another separation" (271/263), the phrase does not so much undermine the earlier identification of separation with death as suggest that Artemio's life has, in fact, amounted to a kind of death-in-life. The idea of the identity of life and death is, of course, implied in the very title of the novel: *La muerte de Artemio Cruz* is, after all, the story of the *life* of Artemio Cruz.

Artemio is a social climber, but he is also a seeker after some form of redemption. However, given that the supreme form of redemption in the novel is achieved in the act of revolution, it is clear that Artemio is doomed to fail in his search. On his deathbed, Artemio remembers the Revolution: "Those faces you saw in Sonora and Chihuahua, faces you saw sleepy one day, hanging on for dear life, and the next furious, hurling themselves into that struggle devoid of reason or palliatives, into that embrace of men separated by other men" (276/268). But it is also at this moment that Artemio realizes that he has lived his entire life fearing a new revolution: "You feared it each of your days of power. You will fear that the amorous impulse will burst again" (276/268). Revolution as the highest form of eroticism: this conception also informs the role of Artemio's son Lorenzo in the novel. Lorenzo is the hero his father failed to be, for he dies fighting for his ideals, whereas Artemio let others die so that he could survive, but he is also his father's heir, for he explains his decision to join the Republican forces in the Spanish Civil War by telling his father that he is merely following in his footsteps.[61] In this way, Lorenzo reveals Artemio's ambivalence: Artemio both identifies with the revolutionary ideal of fraternity, yet fears the threat this ideal poses to his social and economic position.

The chapter that narrates the day of Lorenzo's death in Spain is the only chapter in the novel in which the protagonist is somebody other than Artemio. Yet the narrator says to Artemio that the day of Lorenzo's death is "one day that is more yours than any other day" (228/219). It is Artemio's day not only because he experiences the death of his son as the death of a part of himself, but also because Lorenzo's experiences cast a sharp light on Artemio's own trajectory. In this section, the image of the unfissured self, which helps the reader place Artemio's experience of psychic fragmentation in the proper perspective, obtains its clearest expression. The state of wholeness achieved by Lorenzo is linked in the first place to his ability to bring the private and public dimensions of his experience into conjunction with each other. The story of Lorenzo suggests that private fulfillment is only available to the individual who participates in some significant collective venture. Artemio ruthlessly disregards the claims of others in the course of his social ascent, and is punished, as it were, in the form of a series of stunted relationships with the women in his life, whereas Lorenzo dedicates himself to a noble cause and is, in effect, rewarded with a fulfilling, though brief, love affair with a Spanish woman named Dolores. Through the depiction of the amorous encounter between Lorenzo and Dolores, Fuentes creates an imaginary space in which love and politics, the private and the public, are fused into a harmonious whole. Lorenzo's and Dolores's lovemaking is preceded, and, in fact, enabled, by a joint act of courage that constitutes a clear political gesture. Fleeing for France along with a number of their companions, they are faced with a bridge that offers them their only means of escape, but that may well have been mined by the enemy. One member of the group, a man named Miguel, is ready to admit defeat. It is at this moment that Dolores takes Lorenzo's hand into her own. Slowly, hand in hand, they cross the bridge, risking their lives to prove to their comrades that it is safe. Their bravery is an expression of political hope; it refutes the temptation of despair reflected in Miguel's words. On the night following their daring walk across the bridge, Lorenzo and Dolores consummate their love. The two stages of the narrative are closely intertwined with each other: the burgeoning love between a man and a woman inspires them to an act of public heroism; their act of public heroism deepens their mutual attraction and prepares the way for the sexual consummation of their love. The fact that Lorenzo dies shortly afterward in a Fascist air attack is more than anything else a confirmation of the unity of love and politics, for the implication is that the kind of personal fulfillment Lorenzo and Dolores discover through each other is finally doomed in a world without social justice.

Doris Sommer has described *Artemio Cruz* as the most programmatic of the attacks by the writers associated with the Boom on the "romanticized history" of what she calls Latin America's "foundational fictions."[62] These fictions, ranging from José Mármol's *Amalia* (1851) to Rómulo Gallegos's *Doña Bárbara* (1929), fused romance with nation-building through the depiction of erotic unions that constituted idealized projections of the coming together of a people otherwise divided by race, class, region, or party line. Fuentes subverts this tradition by describing a nation-builder—for that is what Artemio is—whose "foundational love affairs ... are revealed as rapes, or as power plays that need to traffic in women."[63] I think Sommer overstates the extent to which Fuentes in *Artemio Cruz* departs from his precursors, for the story of Lorenzo reveals how Fuentes continues to rely on romance as a way of imagining a political community. Thus, the encounter between Lorenzo and Dolores represents the rapprochement between Mexico and Spain—and so, in a broader sense, between Mexico and its Hispanic heritage—that resulted from the Mexican government's support for the Republic during the Spanish Civil War. The fact that the political community Fuentes imagines in *Artemio Cruz* with the help of Lorenzo and Dolores is not a *national* community does not diminish the novel's links with the tradition described by Sommer. It merely reflects the more internationalist orientation of political mobilization in the period in which Fuentes wrote *Artemio Cruz*, a tendency reflected in the first place in the impact of the Cuban Revolution throughout Latin America. Indeed, the Cuban Revolution is a strong presence in Fuentes's novel, for if the Lorenzo episode harks back to the Mexican Revolution, it also looks forward to the Cuban Revolution. Fuentes sketches a narrative in *Artemio Cruz* in which the revolutionary ideal, betrayed in Mexico, and defeated in Spain, now experiences a new dawn in Cuba. It is of crucial significance that Fuentes wrote part of *Artemio Cruz* in Cuba in the year alter the Revolution, and that he wants his readers to know this, as we can see from the dates and place names that appear at the close of the text. In this sense, Roberto Fernández Retamar was right when he stated that *Artemio Cruz* was written "from the Cuban Revolution."[64] It is also for this reason that Gerald Martin need not be troubled—as he claims to be—by what he describes as "Fuentes's unfavourable comparison of the Mexican Revolution with the Spanish Civil War, as exemplified through his treatment of Cruz's son Lorenzo, who, unlike his lather before him, dies heroically in the Iberian conflict, as if Mexico is inherently incapable of the 'true' ideals which are put into practice elsewhere."[65] Martin overlooks the passages in *Artemio Cruz* that present the revolutionary spirit in Mexico as a perennial threat to the status quo; what is more, he hails to see that the Mexican Revolution and the Spanish Civil War are presented in *Artemio Cruz* as stages in a historical development that culminates for now in the Cuban Revolution. It is wrong, therefore, to compare the Mexican Revolution and the Spanish Civil War as if they were discrete episodes, rather than part of a larger narrative (hat encompasses them both.

Lorenzo is perhaps the most important person in Artemio's life, for it is through his son that Artemio hopes to achieve a form of redemption from his own injured life. On his deathbed, Artemio repeatedly evokes a scene in which he goes horseback riding with Lorenzo. The scene is not fully described until we are well into the novel, yet Artemio condenses his recollection of it into two sentences, "That morning I waited for him with joy. We crossed the river on horseback," which he murmurs to himself over and over again in the novel's present-tense scenes, evidently delighting in the fact that his wife cannot decipher the meaning of his words. Filled with a private, enigmatic significance, the words gradually come to symbolize Artemio's true self, or, at least, the self he would have wanted to be. In the image of Artemio and his son riding across a river on their horses are compressed all of the old man's longings for a fulfilled, joyous existence.[66] The image is especially resonant because it foreshadows Lorenzo's walk across the bridge with Dolores. At the same time, as we will see later, it harks back to Artemio's childhood. Thus, the scene reveals Lorenzo's mediative role in the novel: he shows the path to the future, but he is also a bridge to the past. But we need to ask at this point what kind of weight is attached to the image of *crossing*. Why is the hope for redemption in this novel figured in precisely this fashion?

In a review, published in 1962, of Luis Buñuel's *The Exterminating Angel*, Fuentes wonders why human beings are so reluctant to *cross the threshold* that separates them from happiness. It is worth quoting at some length from this passage, inasmuch as it shows very clearly how the idea of crossing (a barrier, a divide) acquires in Fuentes's imagination at this point in time the significance of a profoundly transformative experience, an experience that opens the way to a utopian remaking of the world:

> Buñuel's question—the question of humanism—is clear and all-encompassing. Why do we not cross the threshold? ... Why, if man is finally master of the possibility of overcoming, once and for all, poverty, sickness and ignorance, why does he not cross the threshold? Why, if he can see the gates of a terrestrial paradise, does he not pass through these gates, preferring to remain in the inferno of the past? Why, if he needs to take but one step in order to enter a humane world, the world of the future promised by

science and technology, does he remain a prisoner of an old, inhumane, alienated existence? Why does man not cross the threshold?[67]

The various crossings described or imagined in *Artemio Cruz* do not immediately introduce the individuals who engage in them into a perfect world, but they clearly articulate the *hope* for a better life. It is surely also significant that Artemio's own last name is inscribed in the verb *cruzar* (to cross), as if to suggest that in the act of crossing he becomes his name, and therefore is finally most truly himself. In this act of self-realization, moreover, Artemio also manages to cancel the original, negative meaning of his name. For Artemio takes his last name from his mother, Isabel Cruz; in fact, as a child, he is known simply as "Cruz." But "Cruz" probably derives from the mark illiterate people use as a signature, so that more than a name it is a sign of Artemio's anonymity. He lives his childhood "without a real first or last name" (306/297–98), bearing only the mark of his missing identity. But when the *cruz* of Artemio's obscure origins becomes the *cruzamos* of his bond with his son, the name sheds its blankness, and instead reveals a rounded, completed self.

This interplay between emptiness and fullness also emerges from the way Artemio's last name links him to Christ. On the whole, of course, Artemio is a mock Christ-figure. To the extent that Artemio has built his career upon the sacrifices of others, his life is a parodic version of the life of Christ, who sacrificed himself for the sake of humanity. Yet the crossing of the river, viewed as a sign of Artemio's bond with his son, who, unlike his father, does sacrifice himself for a higher cause, reveals how Artemio's name, as well as his life, contains at least the shadow of a redemptive significance.[68]

The scene in which Artemio and Lorenzo go horseback riding takes place at the hacienda of Cocuya, near Veracruz, the very place, that is, where Artemio was born and grew up. The scene—reiterated in fragmentary form throughout the novel—expresses then a desire to return to the past. Yet this past turns out to be so violent and turbulent that we can see that Artemio wishes to restore what he has lost, but perhaps also to overcome what was done to him. Artemio, it turns out, is the product of the rape of his mother Isabel Cruz, a mulatto woman who lives on the Cocuya estate, by Atanasio Menchaca, the master of the property. Ireneo Menchaca, Atanasio's father, had built up a fortune thanks to his alliance with General Antonio López de Santa Anna, a man who held the office of president of Mexico eleven times between 1833 and 1854, and who, as Fuentes writes in *The Buried Mirror*, came to represent "the prototype of the comic-opera Latin American dictator."[69] When, in 1867, in the last days of Maximilian's empire, Santa

Anna makes a final attempt to seize power, Ireneo joins his old comrade, only to be dragged down in Santa Anna's defeat, meeting the end of "a life of chance and spins of the wheel of fortune, like that of the nation itself" (293/285). Having thrown in their lot with the losers in Mexico's protracted post-Independence political struggles, the Menchacas must now watch their properties being seized, just as the Menchacas themselves had once taken the land away from its rightful owners. For a while, the will to conquer survives in Atanasio, who is remembered many years later by his ninety-three-year-old mother "galloping over the fertile land, his whip in his hand, always ready to impose his decisive will, to satisfy his voracious appetites with the young peasant women, to defend his property, using his band of imported Negroes" (292/284). But Atanasio is killed in an ambush, and the Menchaca family must face utter ruin. Ireneo's widow Ludivinia (like a character out of Faulkner) locks herself in her room to brood upon the past, while her sole surviving son, the cowardly and dissolute Pedro, takes to the bottle. Against this background of decay and collapse, Artemio grows up. Yet in describing the peaceful rhythms of Artemio's childhood life, the novel presents us with its most extended and eloquent vision of a paradisiacal existence.

Artemio's mother is chased off the property by Atanasio, so Artemio is raised by his maternal uncle Lunero. Even as the hacienda falls further and further into ruin, Artemio's childhood transpires in a realm that appears to exist outside of time. He lives with Lunero in a shack by a river (the same river Artemio and Lorenzo will ride across on their horses many years later). In this close, intimate world, an idyllic existence unfolds. Artemio seems to merge entirely with the world around him. His body is shaped in interaction with the natural elements: his chest made strong from swimming against the current, his hair combed by the river, his arms the color of green fruit (283/275). He and his uncle go about their daily tasks without speaking: "They weren't there to talk or smile but to eat and sleep together and together to go out every daybreak, always silent, always weighed down by the tropical humidity, and together to do the work necessary to go on passing the days" (281/273). The feeling of togetherness between Artemio and Lunero is so deep that speech is unnecessary. Their existence is ruled by elemental rhythms that obviate language. In this world there is no division between self and other, a division that language attempts to bridge, but of which it is also the record. Nor is there any division between the inner self and its externalization through its activities, for the narrator makes it clear that labor is not an extrinsic aspect of the life of Artemio and Lunero. Rather, the performance of their daily tasks is an integral part of the natural flow of time.

But Artemio's harmonious life by the river is not designed to last. Lunero learns that the new master of the land needs more laborers on his tobacco plantation, and that the master's agent will come to take hire away the next day. Artemio, hoping to avert the impending disaster, seizes a shotgun from the house, but in a moment of confusion he shoots and kills his uncle Pedro instead of the agent. Artemio's attempt to preserve the world of his childhood is doomed to fail: "And the shotgun weighed heavy, with a power that prolonged the boy's silent rage: rage because now he knew that life had enemies and that it was not any longer the uninterrupted flow of river and work: rage because now he would know separation" (305/296).

In returning to the hacienda at Cocuya many years later, Artemio evidently hopes to recreate his childhood world, and thereby to overcome the consciousness of separation that has haunted him ever since he was expelled from his childhood paradise. But it is significant that he hopes to accomplish this goal through his son Lorenzo: "For him alone will you have bought this land, rebuilt the hacienda, left him on it, the child-master, responsible for the harvests, open to the life of horses and hunting, swimming and fishing" (225/217). It is as if Artemio could only return to the past by means of the inheritance he grants his son. But the desire for permanence and continuity expressed in Artemio's dreams for his son is finally frustrated, in large part because Artemio's dreams are still so profoundly implicated in his family's turbulent and violent history.

Artemio's childhood world, apparently so peaceful and harmonious, is in reality already a divided realm. By the river, life unfolds in an uninterrupted flow. But immediately adjacent to this timeless enclosure stands the ruined mansion of the Menchaca family, symbol of historical decay and mutability, and, more in particular, of the abrupt, unpredictable cycles of nineteenth-century Mexican history. Clearly, Artemio's nostalgia is for the life he had with Lunero. The world Artemio tries to recreate with his son Lorenzo is in the first place one of intense proximity to nature. It is important to recall, moreover, that Artemio's mother was run off the Cocuya estate by Atanasio and that Artemio himself only barely escaped his father's murderous clutches: "Yes, Master Atanasio died at just the right time; he would have had the boy killed; Lunero saved him" (285/277). Artemio returns to Cocuya bearing his mother's name; on some level, he has come to reclaim his mother's rights to the land from which she was banished. In this way, it can be read as an act that is continuous with Artemio's killing of his uncle Pedro, an act of symbolical parricide with which Artemio revenges himself for the filicide his father was only just prevented from perpetrating. Cocuya represents, for the mature Artemio, a refuge from the male world of struggle and combat in which he has made a name for himself. Yet, in the end, he fails to free himself from the legacy of the Menchacas.

We may note that Artemio returns to Cocuya not in order to rebuild the hut in which he lived with his uncle Lunero, but in order to restore the mansion from which he had always been excluded. He may wish to avenge himself on his father, but he also wants to occupy his father's position. The rousing rides on horseback across the estate with his son Lorenzo represent a return to nature, but they also echo the conquering ways of Atanasio, who is repeatedly pictured on horseback, and so indirectly associated with the Spanish conquistadors. Furthermore, the bonding that takes place between Artemio and Lorenzo comes at the cost of excluding the boy's mother. In this way, it is almost as if Artemio were repeating his father's refusal to acknowledge the mother of his child.

The impossibility of returning to the undissociated realm of childhood illustrates how, for Artemio, such a world exists only in the realm of illusion. He can only live there by willfully ignoring the actual historical world. In this way, *Artemio Cruz* resembles Alejo Carpentier's *Los pasos perdidos* (1953) Carpentier's novel also recreates a place (Santa Mónica de los Venados) where the rift between nature and culture appears to have been healed. After witnessing the execution of a criminal (an episode structurally parallel to the episode in which Artemio shoots his uncle), the narrator, however, leaves Santa Mónica, and eventually must acknowledge that the utopia in which he had come to believe does not in fact exist. Yet *Artemio Cruz* cannot be read according to the same deconstructionist formula that has now become the standard reading of *Los pasos perdidos*.[70] The reconciliation of self and other, or of nature and culture, may remain out of reach for Artemio, but it is only so because of the nature of the choices he has made in his life, and, as we have now also seen, because of the burden of history which he bears. But the story of Lorenzo indicates that other choices can be made, while the references to Cuba suggest that the burden of history can be overcome. To place *Artemio Cruz* in the proper perspective, I turn now to *La campaña* (1990), a novel both more cheerful and less utopian than *Artemio Cruz*, a novel, furthermore, that illustrates the shift in Fuentes's work from a reliance on conceptions of identity to an interest in notions of alternativity. But first, I will show how this shift affected Fuentes's political commentaries in the 1980s.

NOTES

50. Carlos Fuentes, *La muerte de Artemio Cruz* (Mexico City: Fondo de Cultura Económica, 1962); English version, *The Death of Artemio Cruz*, trans. Alfred MacAdam (New York: Farrar, Straus & Giroux, 1991). Quotations from the novel will be followed by parenthetical page references to the Spanish original and English translation, respectively. I have made some changes in MacAdam's translation.

51. Raymond L. Williams uses *Artemio Cruz* to support his claim that Latin American

modernists "unlike many of their Anglo-American counterparts ... generally refused to lose a sense of history." See "Truth Claims, Postmodernism, and the Latin American Novel," *Profession* 92 (1992): 8.

52. Georg Lukács, *The Theory of the Novel*, trans. Anna Bostock (Cambridge: MIT Press, 1971), 121.

53. Gerald Martin, *Journeys through the Labyrinth: Latin American Fiction in the Twentieth Century* (London: Verso, 1989), 211–12.

54. In a fascinating account of the changes that have occurred over the years in his views of *Artemio Cruz*, Héctor Aguilar Camín recalls that in the early 1960s, when he first read the novel, he felt that Fuentes had not been severe enough in his condemnation of Artemio: "Fuentes had in my view made an unacceptable concession to Artemio Cruz in granting him the story of Regina.... Irascible young man that I was, I believed that a wretch like Cruz did not deserve this mouthful of fresh water in his life." But Aguilar Camín has now come to agree with a friend of his who back in the 1960s already argued that the story of Regina ought to be seen as "an act of generosity of the novelist toward his character" and as "a way of balancing the dark and critical perspective that governs almost the entire work." My reading of the novel will show in the first place that Fuentes makes more concessions to Artemio than Aguilar Camín recognizes: above all, the memory of his childhood and the moments of happiness shared with his son Lorenzo. In the second place, I will demonstrate that such concessions serve not only to make Artemio a more rounded character, but also to provide a more vivid sense of the extent and depth of Fuentes's condemnation of him, for the passages in question are to be seen as evocations of all that Artemio has lost as a result of what Aguilar Camín calls Artemio's "moral wretchedness." See "Algo sobre Carlos Fuentes y *La muerte de Artemio Cruz*," in Georgina García Gutiérrez, ed., *Carlos Fuentes: Relectura de su obra: "Los días enmascarados" y "Cantar de ciegos"*, 173.

55. Jonathan Tittler uses words such as "disintegration," "splintering," "dispersal," "destabilization," and "multiplication" to describe the state of Artemio Cruz's psyche. See *"The Death of Artemio Cruz*: Anatomy of a Self," in *Narrative Irony in the Contemporary Spanish-American Novel* (Ithaca, N.Y.: Cornell University Press, 1984), 31–57. Djelal Kadir speaks of Artemio Cruz's "shattered consciousness" and his "dismembered identity." He reads Fuentes's novel as an example of Gothic romance, a genre Kadir argues is centrally concerned with the "disintegration of the individual and his world." See *Questing Fictions: Latin American Family Romance* (Minneapolis: University of Minnesota Press, 1986), 79–80. Raymond L. Williams draws attention to the "subversion of individual identity" in *Artemio Cruz*, and, setting the novel in the context of the broader development of Fuentes's career, sees it as laying the groundwork for "a much more elaborate and complex fragmentation of the individual subject in *Terra Nostra*." See *The Writings of Carlos Fuentes* (Austin: University of Texas Press, 1996), 123.

56. Steven Boldy writes that "the deep impulse behind all the works of Fuentes is the millennium, an Arcadia in the past projected onto a utopia in the future." See "Fathers and Sons in Fuentes' *La muerte de Artemio Cruz*," *Bulletin of Hispanic Studies* 61 (1984): 32. At the end of this chapter, I will argue that Fuentes's more recent work puts forward a more qualified view of the possibility of utopia.

57. Carlos Fuentes, "La novela como reconocimiento: Jane Austen," "La novela como símbolo: Herman Melville," and "La novela como tragedia: William Faulkner," in *Casa con dos puertas* (Mexico City: Joaquin Mortiz, 1970), 13–78. Further references to these three essays will appear in parentheses in the text.

58. See Octavio Paz, *El arco y la lira*, 226–27. Roberto González Echevarría suggests

that Paz took his definition of the novel from Georg Lukács's *The Theory of the Novel*. See "*Terra Nostra*: Theory and Practice," in *The Voice of the Masters: Writing and Authority in Modern Latin American Literature* (Austin: University of Texas Press, 1985), 90.

59. In his translation of Paz, Lysander Kemp leaves the word "chingón" and its cognates in Spanish. See Octavio Paz, *The Labyrinth of Solitude*, trans. Lysander Kemp (New York: Grove, 1985). Alfred MacAdam translates "chingón" as "motherfucker" and "chingada" as "the fucked mother." I have decided to follow Kemp's example in quoting from *Artemio Cruz*.

60. See Paz, *El laberinto de la soledad*, 211–27.

61. Steven Boldy situates the relationship between Artemio and Lorenzo within "an archetypal structure of father, legitimate son and illegitimate son or symbolic heir which occurs three times in the novel. The first instance of this pattern is the relationship between Ireneo Menchaca and his two sons Atanasio and Pedro; the second is the relationship between Gamaliel Bernal, his son Gonzalo and his son-in-law Artemio; the third is the relationship between Artemio, Lorenzo and Jaime Ceballos." See "Fathers and Sons in Fuentes's *La muerte de Artemio Cruz*," 31.

62. Doris Sommer, "Irresistible Romance: The Foundational Fictions of Latin America," in Homi K. Bhabha, ed., *Nation and Narration* (London: Routledge, 1990), 91.

63. Doris Sommer, *Foundational Fictions: The National Romances of Latin America* (Berkeley: University of California Press, 1991), 29.

64. Roberto Fernández Retamar, "Carlos Fuentes y la otra novela de la revolución mexicana," *Casa de las Américas* 4 (October–November 1964): 126.

65. Gerald Martin, *Journeys Through the Labyrinth*, 212. María Stoopen voices a similar criticism, noting that the Lorenzo chapter "renews hope in the Revolution and faith in humanity," but then complaining that the episode, "in being displaced to a foreign setting, is devalued from the perspective of the actual history of the nation." Stoopen concludes that Fuentes has a one-dimensional view of Mexican history: "He sees no hope of salvation for our country." See "*La muerte de Artemio Cruz*": *Una novela de denuncia y traición* (Mexico City: UNAM, 1982), 131–32.

66. Fernando Moreno offers a striking description of the effect of Fuentes's use of repetition, as with the phrase "We crossed the river on horseback." It is, he says, "as if the ephemeral wished to make itself eternal." Moreno suggests that the river crossing allows Artemio and his son to accede to "another domain, in this case the domain of authenticity, of total communion." Moreno sees Artemio as a person defined by the experience of loss, by "an agonized consciousness of all that might have been." See *Carlos Fuentes. "La mort d'Artemio Cruz": entre le mythe et l'histoire* (Paris: Editions Caribéenes, 1989), 66, 133, 141.

67. Carlos Fuentes, "*El ángel exterminador*: nadie encontrará una respuesta dogmática," *Siempre!* (June 13, 1962): xix.

68. There have been many discussions of the significance of Artemio Cruz's name. Bernard Fouques wonders whether the name "Cruz" might not be "the 'x' which for Alfonso Reyes encoded the very enigma of Mexico?" See "El Espacio Órfico de la Novela en *La muerte de Artemio Cruz*," *Revista iberoamericana* 91 (April–June 1975): 237. Paul Dixon argues that Artemio's last name alludes to the novel's vision of Mexican culture as a "cross" of two races and two cultures. See "Simetría y centralidad en *La muerte de Artemio Cruz*," in Ana María Hernández de López, ed., *La obra de Carlos Fuentes: Una visión múltiple* (Madrid: Pliegos, 1988), 98. Robin Fiddian suggests that Artemio's surname refers to the "cara o cruz" of "a coin flipped to decide who wins and who loses a contest," and concludes that Artemio is "a faceless man who has fulfilled only half of his potential [and who] might also be described as 'cruz sin cara.'" See "Carlos Fuentes: *The Death of Artemio Cruz*," in

Philip Swanson, ed., *Landmarks of Modern Latin American Fiction* (London: Routledge, 1990), 103.

69. Fuentes, *The Buried Mirror*, 268.

70. See Roberto González Echevarría, *Alejo Carpentier: The Pilgrim at Home* (Austin: University of Texas Press, 1990), 155–89.

MARCO POLO HERNÁNDEZ CUEVAS

Modern National Discourse and
La muerte de Artemio Cruz:
The Illusory "Death" of African Mexican Lineage[1]

The ideal of *mestizaje*, so pejoratively translated as miscegenation, was
based in the reality of mixed races to which the positivists ascribed
different virtues and failings, and which had to amalgamate if anything
like national unity was to be produced. Unity, in positivist rhetoric, was
not so much a political or economic concept as it was biological. Since
growth meant modernization and Europeanization, the most extreme
ideologues (like Argentina's Domingo F. Sarmiento) advocated a
combined policy of white immigration and Indian or Black removal,
while others ... (as the Mexican ideologues) settled for redeeming the
"primitive" races through miscegenation and ideological whitening.

Doris Sommer

The modern Mexican nation emerged in the third decade of the 20th
century during "the cultural phase of the Mexican Revolution."[2] The *criollo*
(white) controlled government disseminated officially the myth that *mestizos*
were the offspring of Spaniards and Amerindians exclusively, in that order.[3]
Thereafter, this discourse was reproduced and reinforced through various
means of mass persuasion, including the novel, until 1968.[4]

The black African heritage of Mexican *mestizaje* was replaced in the
collective memory and national imagination with José Vasconcelos' "cosmic

From *Afro-Hispanic Review*, 23, no. 1 (Spring 2004): 10–16. © 2004 by *Afro-Hispanic Review*.

race" myth. This philosophy, a continuation of Spanish colonial beliefs, codified blacks as tame and their genes as recessive. By insisting that Spanish genes were dominant and that black African genes were recessive in the mestizo, criollos, as supposed heirs of the Spanish genes, "legitimated" a paternity claim; hence, a protagonist role in carving out the Mexican nation. This enabled them to transfer historical glory to their name. The history of *cimarronaje* was erased and African Mexican national heroes were whitened, thus African Mexican national achievements became *criollo* based.

According to Vasconcelos' creed, exposed in the first forty pages of his *La raza cósmica*, the black characteristics of the Mexican were receding through natural selection.[5] In his Christian-rooted vision, "beauty" was overpowering "ugliness" and the mestizo population was steadily and eagerly whitening. The modern nation builders adopted Vasconcelos' views as the unequivocal road toward modernization. *La muerte de Artemio Cruz* (1962) (*The Death of Artemio Cruz*),[6] by Carlos Fuentes, reintroduces and reinforces the myth of the Mexican populace's willing submission to whitening.

In this canonized post-modern novel, the central character, a post-revolution Mexican prototype, on a level, appears as a "mestizo" oblivious of his African family tree; but as he reels through memory from his death bed, the reader is informed that in the depth of his heart he despises his negritude. He is convinced that "the whiter the better." *La muerte* is read in this study as a link in the chain of canonized *criollo* works reflecting the cosmic race-discourse on nation whose iron-like determination, from the start, was the cleansing of blackness from the population, if at least psychologically.

Richard L. Jackson explains that defining "superior and inferior as well as the concept of beauty," on the basis of how "white" a person is perceived to be, is a "tradition dramatized in Hispanic literature from Lope de Rueda's *Eufemia* (1576) to the present" ("Black Phobia" 467). He has found in Latin American literature that the black image rendered by non-black authors, save a noticeable few, has unjustly represented black Africans and their descendants. Jackson reveals certain patterns wherever blacks are or have been (*Black Image* 1). He shows that these patterns have affected the manner in which writers and readers identify people of black African heritage in general (*Black Image* 37).

This study adopts Jackson's views as a critical approach and further subscribes to James Snead's angle on the coding of blacks. For Snead, the coding of blacks "in the wider society, involves a history of images and signs associating black skin color with servile behavior and marginal status" (142). He points out that, "while these depictions may have reflected prior economic oppression of blacks, they also tend to perpetuate it" (142).

La muerte continues the construction of a false national identity. The novel depicts and perpetuates stereotypes of blacks. It posits that for black characters to be rebellious, or to show intelligence, they have to be whitened. *La muerte* ignores that black Africans from the beginning of the *Maafa* or Black Holocaust have revolted. Alive in the late 16th and early 17th century, Yanga,[7] the maroon leader in Veracruz, the home state of the protagonist anti-hero of the novel, is a case in point.

   La muerte is read in light of pertinent portions of Octavio Paz' "*Los hijos de la Malinche*" (1950), *El perfil del hombre y la cultura en México* (1934) by Samuel Ramos, and *La raza cósmica* (1925) by José Vasconcelos to track down the codification of blackness under its various Mexican signifiers. The aim is to exhibit the intertextuality of these canonized *criollo* works, pillars of the modern nation, and disclose how they codify the African Mexican Experience.

   La muerte uses *chingar* as substance in constructing Cruz' character (143–147). It thereby makes him a prototype of the Mexican *pelado*, as pointed out by both Remigio Paez, the catholic priest, who brokers his marriage to the *criolla* Catalina (47), and Cruz himself (276). Regarding the Mexican *pelado*, Ana Maria Prieto Hernández reveals, "*zaragates, guachinangos, zaramullos, zánganos, ínfima plebe, chusma, peladaje* [plural pejorative of *pelado*] or "*léperos*" were the postcolonial names given to the various mestizos of African descent (17–19) (emphasis mine). These euphemisms replaced part of the "sixty-four" Spanish colonial categories used to refer to a person's degree of African heritage (Davis 37).

   "Los hijos de la Malinche," a parody of *los hijos de la chingada* (sons of the raped African Mexican woman), exposes that *chingar* is a "vulgar" word (Paz 67), and that the general population is master of its usage (Paz 67). It posits that *chingar* may be of Aztec origin (Paz 68). Thereby, it cleanses *léperos* or *pelados* from their African heritage. "Los hijos" claims the *mestizo*, *lépero* or *pelado* as the offspring of Spaniards and Amerindians, in that order.

   The Malinche,[8] a synonym of national treason, embodied in a pre-Hispanic born Amerindian woman who gives into Hernán Cortés, is inserted in the place of *la chingada*. Through its thesis, besides glorifying the *criollo* and marking the Amerindian genes of the mestizo as inherently "malinchista," it blocks the possibility of establishing the relations between *La chingada*, her Africaness and the African Kimbundu cradle of the verb *chingar* (Pérez 310).

   "Los hijos de la Malinche" replaces the maroon history of mestizaje in the national imaginary. It omits mestizaje's African heritage. "Los hijos" annuls the connection between Africans, African Mexicans, *alvaradeños, jarochos, chinacos, léperos*, or *pelados*. "Los hijos" is another vehicle of cultural misappropriation. It confuses ownership of the verb *chingar* and blurs the African origins and identity of the Mexican mezclas or mestizos.

"Los hijos" fuses all "social" classes through the word *chingar*. It presents Mexico and Mexicaness as one; this underlines the fallacy of Mexico as a racial paradise. By omitting its Africaness, it creates a "rightful" and preferential space for the *criollo* within a culture constructed by the Other. Ted Vincent exhibits the two separate worlds constructed in Mexico during the colonial period: the Spanish-*criollo* world marked by the minuet, wine and white bread; and the *mezcla* world marked by La bamba, tequila, and corn tortillas (5). For "Los hijos," Mexicaness, embodied in the *mestizo*, has Spanish and Amerindian roots alone, in that order.

"Los hijos" follows the "psychoanalytical profile" of the *pelado* in *El perfil*. After calling the *pelado* "fauna," *El perfil* characterizes the *pelado* as "a being without principles, generally mistrusting, full of bluster and cowardly" (Ramos 76). *El perfil* manifests that as a subject, the *pelado* "lacks all human values" and that in fact he is "incapable of acquiring" said values (Ramos 76). *El perfil's* evaluation of the *pelado* is linked to Vasconcelos and his philosophy on education (Muñoz 24). *El perfil* forwards the perspective that Mexican culture is a culture of cultures whose most valuable manifestation is the *criollo* culture. In *La muerte*, the protagonist recognizes Mexico as "a thousand countries under one name" (274) where *criollos* are the mark of civilization (50).

Cruz is narrated as a dying seventy-one-year-old (16) Mexican of African lineage who does not identify with his African heritage (276). He is the bastard son of a certain "Isabel Cruz, Cruz Isabel," a Mulatto woman whose true name is unknown (314). Cruz' father, Atanasio Menchaca, is a *criollo* who during the Porfiriato had been a powerful landowner. Cruz is six feet tall and weighs about 174 pounds (247). He has "pronounced features" (41), a wide nose (9) graying curly hair (16, 251) that once was black (314). He has dark skin (16), as the "very dark" skin color of his son (168). He has green eyes that project a cold, unwavering look (171), an energetic mouth, wide forehead, protruding cheekbones (149) and thick lips (115).

Cruz becomes Lieutenant Colonel during the armed phase of the Revolution. Through his cunning marriage to a *criolla*, the sister of a fellow soldier executed by a firing squad at the end of the armed conflict, he turns out to be first, a landowner and administrator, and later, a newspaper magnate and a millionaire by brokering government concessions to foreigners.

In *La muerte*, the images are patchy and colored in a cubist fashion. For instance, when Artemio tells himself:

> Although I don't want it to, something shines insistently next to my face; something that reproduces itself behind my closed eyelids: a fugue of black lights and blue circles. I contract the face muscles, I open the right eye and I see it reflected in the glass incrustations of a woman's purse (...) I am this old man with the features shattered by the irregular glass squares. (9)

The physical and ideological descriptions of the characters are introduced in scattered fragments and clues throughout the novel, as a puzzle that must be assembled. In the case of Cruz, this renders his heritage confusing. The analytical Afrocentric reader must amass the fragments to realize Cruz is an African Mexican. The level of difficulty of this decoding task is evidenced by the scattered page numbers where Cruz' characteristics and features are introduced bit by bit nonchalantly: 276, 324, 247, 41, 9, 16, 251, 314, 168, 171, 149, 115, and 316, among others.

The reader is forced to travel back and forth in time. The images evoked by Cruz flash in and out of focus. Time, space, physical and metaphysical barriers are shattered as the plot develops in Cruz' psyche. He brings the past to the present at will. One case in point is when he recalls his childhood, as in a close-up scene, and transports the reader to a different place in time (271).

The past and present dissolve into one plane when pain brings Cruz out of his lethargy and he becomes aware of the presence of others in the room (116). An uncertain future intermingles with the present when Cruz foresees what may happen (247). *La muerte* penetrates the memory of the reader lost in trying to put together the pieces and unexpectedly, subliminally lays an Eurocentrically idealized world in the place of historical facts. Thus, what never happened replaces maroon history. The novel shapes a national imaginary according to *criollo* beliefs.

Julio Ortega interprets *La muerte* as "the first product of Latin American post-modernity" and as "a disenchanted reading of compulsive modernity" (2). This is correct to a point. *La muerte* provides a "fresh" look at the Revolution and indicts the corrupted patriarchal system. Thereby, it passes within the guise of the long awaited voice of self—criticism of a decadent structure.

On a level, *La muerte* casts the illusion of condemning the existing political structure: the entrenched PRI[9] system that from the onset of the cultural phase of the Revolution sought total control and power over the people. *La muerte* condemns the Mexican post-revolution's social situation in part; nonetheless, at a subliminal level, it endorses the color divide imposed since the colonial period.

Through a close review, the Afrocentric reader is forced to question the authenticity of the character ascribed to Cruz as an African Mexican in modern Mexico, particularly in light of the prevalent *criollo* mentality that loathed even a drop of "visible" blackness in a person.

Had racism subsided in Mexico by 1920 as to allow a visibly black person to rise "freely" from rags to riches? How many visibly black Mexicans can be found as tycoons in the Mexico of the first half of the twentieth-century? If "it always has been an object of the novel to tell the other version of history, particularly starting after the 19th century" as Carlos Fuentes has declared (Güemes 2), would it not have been more true to life to have made the antihero a *criollo*?

Why make a "pelado" (Fuentes 47, 276) or mestizo of African descent the villain? Is the novel repeating and reinforcing the white myth of the "evil nature" of African blood? Is *La muerte* reintroducing and reinforcing the Eurocentric colonial stereotypes of *los hijos de la chingada* and the *pelados* found in *La raza cósmica*, *El perfil*, and "Los hijos"?

Snead clarifies that mass-produced images have political, ideological, and psychological effects upon an audience's beliefs and actions (132). Also, he states that "Stereotypes ultimately connect to form larger complexes of symbols and connotations. These codes then begin to form a kind of 'private conversation' among themselves without needing to refer back to the real world for their facticity" (141).

La muerte gets close to the origins of *chingar* and the *pelado*. It nearly makes the connections between the *mestizo*, his language, his worldview and his African heritage. This may have enabled a fuller explanation of the Mexican character[10] and his sense of humor[11] as early as 1962.

However, *La muerte* continues the same *criollo* aesthetic found in *La raza cósmica*, *El perfil*, and "Los hijos." Cruz is characterized as a mestizo who, notwithstanding, or because of, his visible African heritage, the knowledge of his birth, and his having been raised in an African Mexican environment until the age of fourteen, has virtually repressed his black legacy. It is a sign of indecency for Cruz "to live and die in [the] Negro shack" of his lineage and cultural heritage (276). *La muerte* whitens Cruz by making him particularly proud of his *criollo* identity. Cruz expresses that he has conquered "decency" for his children (276). He expects them to thank him for making them "respectable people," and keeping them out of the "Negro shack" (276).

According to Snead, a work "becomes 'propaganda' and no longer merely 'fiction' when its aim is to introduce or reinforce a set of political power relationships between social groups" (140). In *La muerte*, Mexicans whose African lineage is openly identified are characterized as rootless (302), backward, submissive, tame and servile (302, 303). They are caricatured as simple, as jungle beings (302) with an endless sexual appetite (279, 288, 289), as possessing an innate musicality (288), and as having a natural predisposition to relax (287).

This is remarkable when juxtaposed to *criollo* portrayal. *Criollos* are conceived as civilized (50), rooted to the land (48); as history makers (35), with an identity (50); as having feelings, ideals, and even as being chivalrous at the moment of defeat (50). This perception echoes *El perfil*'s notions about *criollo* supremacy. The Spaniards are capable of understanding, and of sacrificing body and soul for family and beliefs (Fuentes 50, 54, 103).

Snead explains, "'Codes' are not singular portrayals of one thing or another, but larger complex relationships" (142). He exposes how these relationships, under the will, imagination and ideological slant of the narrative maker, may "present fantasy or an ideal world that has nothing to do with the real world" as if it were the real world (134).

According to Lanin A. Gyurko, Cruz is developed as a "single character, powerful and complex enough to be convincing, not only as an individual but also as a national symbol" (30). In *La muerte*, this national character is imagined by his uncle as a black Moses (285). But paradoxically, and as if marked by his African blood, Cruz is constructed as an innate traitor, a despicable being: polygamous (122), immoral, greedy (15, 16), treacherous (24, 25), cowardly, and corrupted (16, 21, 50, 56).

Cruz is incapable of caring about high revolutionary ideals, or country (56). He is the opposite of José Maria Tecla Morelos y Pavón (Vargas) and Vicente "el negro" Guerrero, each a Black Moses. In Gyurko's words: "Cruz is literally an *hijo de la chingada*. Violation gave him life—rape of a slave woman by his father Atanasio Menchaca, violation pervades his life, and violation (mental and physical) characterizes his death" (35). For Gyurko, on the symbolic level, Cruz is a metaphor for the Frozen Revolution and a nation that "slavishly imitates the value systems of European and North American nations" (39).

Cruz is rich, powerful and married into a *criollo* family. However, it is made obvious that these "attributes," *per se*, cannot remove the color line that marginalizes him throughout the story. He enters a marriage where the color divide is kept and cultured within the relationship (103).[12] All the power Artemio Cruz has is not enough to free his conscience from the knowledge of being "the Other," even at home with his wife and daughter (31, 32).

This very power, impressive physique and ruthless character, given him so lavishly, mark Artemio Cruz and make him stand out as a whitened black (33). Cruz never gains control of his life, although a millionaire. This creates the illusion that the *criollos* he wishes to emulate are naturally superior to him and those he is the prototype of, nonwhite Mexicans (32, 33, 50). Snead identifies mythification, marking and omission as three particular tactics to forge and perpetuate black stereotypes (143). He points out that to make whites appear more civilized, powerful and important, they are shown in contrast to subservient blacks. *La muerte* does this.

Lunero, Cruz' Uncle, is a well-tamed and *criollo*-loyal young Mulatto who quietly accepts his fate (284). He is still in bondage at the beginning of the 20th century (295). He silently tolerates the sexual rape and physical abuse of his sister, Isabel, Cruz' mother, by the master, Cruz' father. Lunero helps Isabel during Cruz' birth (314). But he does nothing and stays quiet when the master, a known rapist of nonwhite women (229), beats Isabel with a stick and runs her off the property in his presence (286, 306). Lunero is unbelievably good and incapable of running away. He invents work to support his masters' household (285, 303) when they have become poor due to the war. He is very protective of Cruz and takes care of him for fourteen years even though, or perhaps due to Cruz' being a lighter black.

Jackson points out that discrimination, based on place of origin, color of skin, social class, and religious beliefs, has been instrumental in developing a narrative that depicts black people in "one dimension racist images," as purely sensuous, as merely musical savages waiting to be saved from their supposed incapacity to reason, and from their entirely emotional realm (*Black Image* 46).

Lunero is narrated as having the rhythm in him (Fuentes 287–288). Every afternoon he sings to young Cruz the songs brought by Lunero's father from Santiago de Cuba "when the war broke out and the families moved to Veracruz along with their servants" (286). He is a prisoner of fear and nostalgia. He fears the New World: the sierra, the Amerindians, and the plateau (302); and is nostalgic of the continent where "one like him would be able to get lost in the jungle and say that he had returned" (302).

Jackson exhibits that Latin American literature, guided by the white aesthetic, caricatures blacks, presents blacks as easily corruptible, with an endless sexual appetite, as possessing an innate musicality, as having a natural predisposition to relax, as inherently drunkard, as polygamous, as irresponsible parents and as devil-like (*Black Image* 49–59).

According to Snead:

> The history that whites have made (...) empties black skin of any historical or material reference, except as former slaves. The notion of the eternal black "character" is invented to justify the enforced economic disadvantage that we enjoy (or don't enjoy) (...). [B]lacks' behavior is portrayed as being unrelated to the history that whites have trapped them in. Let me repeat: that

behavior is being portrayed as something static, enduring, and unchangeable, unrelated to the history that whites have trapped them in. Blacks are seen as ahistorical. (139)

Isabel Cruz or Cruz Isabel, Artemio Cruz' mother, is a woman without a fixed name that appears in the narrative only as a vessel to bring another *hijo de la chingada* into the world (314). Although she appears fleetingly, she leaves the impression of being nothing more than a victim, a fearful presence incapable of making a sound despite the moment of delivery. Jackson has found that even in cases where blacks are defended, they are depicted, among other ways, as backward, submissive, tame, and servile ("Black Phobia" 467).

In *La muerte*, African Mexicans seem to inhabit Veracruz, and not to extend beyond the sierra. The hacienda of Cocuya is full of blacks (295), "Negroid" people (289), and "... clear eyed Mulattoes with skin the color of pine nuts" who were offspring of the "Indian and Mulatto women that went around bearing them" (289). One learns about blacks "brought to the tropical plantations with their hair straightened by the daring Indian women that offered their hairless sexual parts as a victory redoubt over the curly haired race" (279).

In contrast to *La muerte's* narrative, it is well documented that black Africans of the Diaspora were taken all over New Spain wherever there was mining, farming, ranching, factories, domestic work, or transportation of goods. History shows that African Mexicans, the infamous *mezclas*, became the majority of today's *mestizos* (Aguirre 276).

History confirms that the *mezclas* or mestizos of African descent fought valiantly under the name of "*chinacos*" and "*pintos*" during the War of Independence ([1810–1821] Riva Palacio, *Calvario*; Díaz, XVIII). It archives that later, they fought against the French and defeated them in Puebla (5 May 1862). History records that the *chinaco* and *pinto* liberals followed the French into the interior of the country and, against all odds, defeated and expelled them from Mexican national territory three years later.

"The omission of the black [heroes], then, has meant the presence of the stereotype" (Snead 147). *La muerte's* reintroduction and reinforcement of black stereotypes does not end there. Cruz' daughter, Teresa, who is a mestiza of African descent as well, is portrayed as oblivious of her African lineage. They are ideologically whitened. She appears as happily Americanized, going shopping, eating waffles and talking about North American movie stars (22–23, 25). *La muerte* suggests that post-revolution corruption in Mexico is tied to miscegenation and that *mestizaje*, of the type embodied by Cruz and his lineage, had a negative effect on the Mexican Revolution (50).

In conclusion, *La muerte* is a text where the modern Mexican nation is still being narrated in accordance to the "cosmic race" creed; a belief that the "improvement" of the nation rested on the cleansing, by mixing out, of all black African traces of the population. The novel perpetuates the myth of whitening that underlines the ideology of *mestizaje* in Mexico, as in other parts of the Americas. *La muerte* contributes to the erasure of the path that leads to the African family tree, of Mexican *mestizaje*. Just as *La raza cósmica*, *El perfil*, and "Los hijos," among other pillars of the imagined modern Mexican nation, *La muerte* reproduces and reinforces the confusion of the origins of the Mexican mestizo and his culture: "*a río revuelto ganancia de pescadores.*"

La muerte forges and perpetuates stereotypes of black people and their daughters and sons. It thereby codifies them as exhibited under Snead's perspective. The novel marks blacks, mythifies whites and omits mentioning, under a just light, Mexicans of African lineage who do not desire to be whitened and are not servile, tame, submissive, or backward. This renders the African Mexican ahistorical. Just as other Latin American writings studied by Jackson, *La muerte* replaces the historical image of prominent African Mexicans with caricatures.

NOTES

1. This work subscribes to the position that races and all of its nomenclatures are negative social constructs. Also, that racism, a direct negative consequence of such social constructs, and the damages it inflicts on people, are real. This work stands on the premise that all humans are equal and concurrently recognizes that racial terminology is heavily charged and promotes racism. Therefore, it must be emphasized that such language is used here subversively while alternatives are under construction. The aim is to help build a bridge out of Eurocentrism with the very stones that construct it.

2. I named thus the period 1920–1968 in my doctoral dissertation, "The Erasure of the Afro Element of Mestizaje in Modern Mexico: The Coding of Black Mestizos According to a White Aesthetic In and Through the Discourse on Nation During the Cultural Phase of the Mexican Revolution, 1920–1968." U of British Columbia, 2001. In that work, I opened the door for the present study. Part of my prior analysis of *La muerte* is incorporated here.

3. According to the 1956 Webster, a "mestizo" is "Esp. in Spanish America and the Philippines, a person of mixed blood; esp., the offspring of a European and an (East) Indian, Negro, or Malay." While according to 1995 Webster, a "mestizo" is "a person of mixed blood: *specif*: a person of mixed European and American Indian ancestry." This shows the fluidity of the essentialist Eurocentric discourse on the Other.

4. For an insight into the use of other cultural texts for whitening during the same period see my essays, "*Angelitos negros*, a Film from the 'Golden Epoch' of Mexican Cinema: The Coding of Visibly Black Mexicans In and Through a Far-Reaching Medium." *ALARA* (2001): 49–62. And, "*Memín Pinguín*: uno de los *cómics* mexicanos más populares como instrumento para codificar al negro." (*Memín Pinguín*: One of the Most

Popular Mexican Comics as an Instrument to Codify Blacks). *Afro-Hispanic Review*. Spring (2003): 52–59.

5. For more information on this topic, see my essay, "The 'Afro-Mexican' and the Revolution: Making Afro-Mexicans Invisible Through the Ideology of Mestizaje in *La raza cósmica.*" *PALARA* (2000): 559–83.

6. All translations in this paper are mine unless otherwise specified.

7. Yanga was "leader of a group of maroons, or run away slaves, in early seventeenth-century [Veracruz,] Mexico. [His group] became the only group of blacks in colonial Mexico to secure their freedom through rebellion and to have that freedom guaranteed by law ..." (Appiah 2034).

8. The myth of "La Malinche" is found in *Doña Marina* (1833) an historical novel by Ireneo Paz, Octavio Paz' grandfather.

9. PRI is the acronym for the *Partido Revolucionario Institucional* (Revolutionary Institutional Party) that usurped power immediately after the armed phase of the Mexican Revolution in 1920 and kept direct control of the country until November 2000.

10. In my essay, "The Afro Dimension of Mexican Carnival: Resisting the Rhetorical Labyrinth of the Discourse on Nation," to be edited and published by Ian I. Smart, I explain the Mexican Mestizo festive spirit in the light of his African heritage.

11. The African heritage of the Mexican picaresque sense of humor is explained in my unpublished essay, "*La vida inútil de Pito Pérez*: Tracking the Afro Contribution to the Mexican Picaresque Sense of Humor."

12. This type of marriage is described in Celestino Gorostiza's 1952 drama, *El color de nuestra piel (The Color of our Skin)*. See bibliography.

WORKS CITED

Aguirre Beltrán, Gonzalo. *La población negra de México. Estudio etnohistórico.* México, D.F.: Fondo, 1972 (1st ed. 1946).

Appiah, Kwame Anthony and Henry Louis Gates, Jr., Editors. *Africana.* New York: Basic Civitas Books, 1999.

Davis, James F. *Who is Black? One Nation's Definition.* University Park: The Pennsylvania State UP, 1998 (1st ed. 1991).

Díaz y de Ovando, Clementina. "Introducción." *Antología de Vicente Riva Palacio.* México, D.F.: UNAM, 1976.

Fuentes, Carlos. *La muerte de Artemio Cruz.* México: Fondo, 1990. (13th edition) (1st ed. 1962).

Gorostiza, Celestino. *El color de nuestra piel.* New York: The MacMillan Company, 1966.

Güemes, César. "Contar la otra version de la historia, tarea de la novela: Carlos Fuentes." *La jornada Online.* http://www jornada.unam.mx/1999/mar99/990313/cul-fuentes.html 16 March 2000.

Gyurko, Lanin A. "Structure and Theme in Fuentes' *La muerte de Artemio Cruz.*" *Symposium* 34, (1980): p. 29–41.

Jackson, Richard L. *The Black Image in Latin American Literature.* Albuquerque: U of New Mexico, 1976.

———. "Black Phobia and the White Aesthetic in Spanish American Literature." *Hispania* 58 (1975): 467–480.

Martínez Monticl, Luz María. *Negros en América.* México, D.F.: Mapfre, 1992.

Morin, Claude. "Age at Marriage and Female Employment in Colonial Mexico." Paper read at the International Conference "Women's Employment, Marriage-Age and Population Change," University of Delhi, Developing Countries Research Center, March 3–5, 1997. <http://www.fas.umontreal.ca/HST/u/morin/pubICIDHInd97.htm> 13 November 2000.

Muñoz Batista, Jorge. "Samuel Ramos y la educación mexicana". Universidad La Salle <http://hemerodigital. unam.mx/ANUIES/lasalle/logos/75/sec_6.htm>.

Ortega, Julio. "Diez novelas del XX". *La Jornada Semanal*, 24 de enero de 1999. Online 16 March 2000.

Paz, Octavio. "Los hijos de la Malinche". *El Laberinto de la soledad*. México: Fondo, 1989 (18th ed.).

Pérez Fernández, Rolando Antonio. "El verbo chingar: una palabra clave". *El rostro colectivo de la nación mexicana*. Morelia: Instituto de Investigaciones Históricas de la Universidad Michoacana de San Nicolás de Hidalgo, (1997): 305–324.

Prieto Hernández, Ana María. *Acerca de la pendenciera e indisciplinada vida de los léperos capitalinos*. México, D.F.: CONACULTA, 2001.

Ramos, Samuel. *El perfil del hombre y la cultura en México*, México, D.F.: UNAM, 1963 (1st ed. 1934).

Reynoso Medina, Araceli. "Esclavos y condenados: Trabajo y etnicidad en el obraje de Posadas". *El rostro colectivo de la nación mexicana*. Morelia: Instituto de Investigaciones Históricas de la Universidad Michoacana de San Nicolás de Hidalgo, (1997): 17–35.

Riva Palacio, Vicente. *Calvario y Tabor*. México D.F.: Porrúa, 2000. (1st ed. 1868).

Snead, James. *White Screens Black Images: Hollywood from the Dark Side*. Colin MacCabe & Cornel West eds. London: Routledge, 1994.

Sommer, Doris. "Irresistible Romance: The Foundational Fictions of Latin America." *Nation and Narration*. Homi K. Bhabha ed. Routledge: London (1990): 71–98. (Citation from page 81).

Vargas Martínez, Ubaldo. *Morelos: Siervo de la nación*. México, D.F.: Porrúa, 1966.

Vasconcelos, José. *La raza cósmica: misión de la raza iberoamericana*. Madrid: Agencia Mundial de Librería, 1925.

Vincent, Ted. "Racial Amnesia—African Puerto Rico and Mexico." *Ishmael Reed's Konch Magazine Online*. 16 July 1999.

Chronology

1928	Born in Panama City on November 11, son of Rafael Fuentes Boettiger and Berta Macías Rivas.
1929–1934	Lives in Panama City, Quito, Montevideo, and Rio de Janeiro, where his father occupies various diplomatic posts.
1934–1940	Lives in Washington D.C., where his father serves as Counselor for the Mexican Embassy.
1941–1943	Lives in Santiago and Buenos Aires with his family. Articles and short stories published in the *Boletín del Instituto Nacional de Chile*.
1946	Graduates from the Colegio Mexico (high school) in Mexico City.
1950	Attends the Institute for International Studies in Geneva.
1951	Serves as Press Secretary for the United Nations Information Center in Mexico City. Enters the law school of the National University of Mexico.
1954	Publishes his first book, *Los días enmascarados* (*The Masked Days*), stories. Serves as Assistant Press Secretary at the Ministry of Foreign Affairs.
1956	Co-founds (with Emmanuel Carballo) the *Revista Mexicana de Literatura*.
1957	Head of the Department of Cultural Relations at the Ministry of Foreign Affairs.

1958	Publishes his first novel, *Where the Air is Clear.*
1959	Publishes *The Good Conscience*, a novel. Marries the actress Rita Maceda. Travels to Cuba immediately following the success of the Cuban Revolution.
1960	Editor of *Siempre* and *Política.*
1962	Publishes *The Death of Artemio Cruz* and *Aura* (a novella).
1964	Publication of *Cantar de ciegos* (*Songs of the Blind*), stories.
1965–1966	Helps found the Siglo XXI publishing house. Lives in Paris.
1967	Publishes *A Change of Skin*, which is banned from publication in Spain. Publishes *Holy Place.*
1968	Lives in London and Paris. Publishes *París, la revolución de mayo* (*Paris, the May Revolution*; essay) and *Líneas para Adami* (*Lines for Adami*; essay).
1969	Moves back to Mexico. Publishes *Cumpleaños* (*Birthday*; novella), the *World of José Luis Cuevas* (essay), and *La nueva novela hispanoamericana* (*the New Hispanic American Novel*; essay). Divorced from Rita Macedo.
1970	Publishes *Casa con dos puertas* (*House with Two Doors*; essays), *El Tuerto es rey* (*The One-Eyed Man is King*; play), and *Todos los gatos son pardos* (*All Cats are Gray*; play).
1971	Publishes *Tiempo mexicano* (*Mexican Time*; essays). Father dies.
1972	Lives in Paris. Marries journalist Sylvia Lemus.
1974	Fellow at the Woodrow Wilson International Center for Scholars, Washington D.C. Birth of daughter Natascha.
1975	Publishes *Terra Nostra*. Serves as Mexican ambassador to France.
1976	Publication of *Cervantes o la crítica de la lectura* (*Cervantes or the Critique of Reading*; essay). Head of the Mexican delegation to the North-South Conference on International Economic Development.
1977	Lectures at the Colegio Nacional in Mexico City, at Barnard College, and at Cambridge University. Member of the Cannes Film Festival jury.
1978	Publishes *The Hydra Head*. Teaches at the University of Pennsylvania and Columbia University. Lectures at Princeton.
1980	Publishes *Distant Relations*. Receives the Alfonso Reyes Prize in Mexico City. Publishes *Burnt Water*, stories.

1985	Publishes the novel *El gringo viejo* (The Old Gringo).
1987	Publishes *Cristóbal Nonato*.
1990	Publishes *The Campaign*.
1992	Publishes *The Buried Mirror: Reflections on Spain and the New World*.
1993	Publishes *Geografía de la novela* (*Geography of the Novel*) and *Tres discursos para dos aldeas*.
1994	Publishes *The Orange Tree*.
1995	Publishes *Diana o la Cazadora Solitaria* (*Diana: the Goddess Who Hunts Alone*).
1996	Publishes *Frontera de cristal* (*The Crystal Frontier: A Novel of Nine Stories*) and *Nuevo tiempo mexicano* (*A New Time for Mexico*).
1999	Publishes *Los años con Laura Díaz* (*The Years with Laura Díaz*).
2001	Publishes *Inez*.
2002	Publishes *En esto creo* (*This I Believe: An A to Z Life*).
2004	Publishes *Contra Bush*.

Contributors

HAROLD BLOOM is Sterling Professor of the Humanities at Yale University. He is the author of 30 books, including *Shelley's Mythmaking* (1959), *The Visionary Company* (1961), *Blake's Apocalypse* (1963), *Yeats* (1970), *A Map of Misreading* (1975), *Kabbalah and Criticism* (1975), *Agon: Toward a Theory of Revisionism* (1982), *The American Religion* (1992), *The Western Canon* (1994), and *Omens of Millennium: The Gnosis of Angels, Dreams, and Resurrection* (1996). *The Anxiety of Influence* (1973) sets forth Professor Bloom's provocative theory of the literary relationships between the great writers and their predecessors. His most recent books include *Shakespeare: The Invention of the Human* (1998), a 1998 National Book Award finalist, *How to Read and Why* (2000), *Genius: A Mosaic of One Hundred Exemplary Creative Minds* (2002), *Hamlet: Poem Unlimited* (2003), *Where Shall Wisdom Be Found?* (2004), and *Jesus and Yahweh: The Names Divine* (2005). In 1999, Professor Bloom received the prestigious American Academy of Arts and Letters Gold Medal for Criticism. He has also received the International Prize of Catalonia, the Alfonso Reyes Prize of Mexico, and the Hans Christian Andersen Bicentennial Prize of Denmark.

LANIN A. GYURKO teaches in the Spanish and Portuguese department at the University of Arizona. Gyurko has published extensively on Argentine and Mexican Literature, and with Nancy Hall, edited the book *Studies in Honor of Enrique Anderson Imbert*. Gyurko is the author of two extensive monographs and more than sixty essays on the narrative and dramatic art of Carlos Fuentes.

WENDY B. FARIS teaches in the English Department University of Texas at Arlington. She is the author of *Carlos Fuentes; Labyrinths of Language: Symbolic Landscape and Narrative Design in Modern Fiction; Ordinary Enchantments: Magical Realism and the Remystification of Narrative;* and *Magical Realism: Theory, History, Community.*

STEVEN BOLDY is a University Senior Lecturer in the Department of Spanish and Portuguese at the University of Cambridge. He is the author of (among other works) *The Novels of Julio Cortázar, Memoria Mexicana,* and many articles on the authors Cortázar, Rulfo, Carpentier and Carlos Fuentes. His latest book is entitled *The Narrative of Carlos Fuentes.*

BRITT-MARIE SCHILLER is an Associate Professor of Philosophy at Webster University.

RICHARD J. WALTER is the author of *Politics and Urban Growth in Buenos Aires, 1910–1942; The Socialist Party of Argentina,1890–1930; The Province of Buenos Aires and Argentine Politics, 1912–1943;* and *Student Politics in Argentina: the University Reform and Its Effects, 1918–1964.*

SANTIAGO TEJERINA-CANAL is a Professor of Spanish at Hamilton College. He has written articles on Latin American literature and culture, and is also author of *La muerte de Artemio Cruz: Secreto generativo.*

ROBIN FIDDIAN is the author of *Postcolonial Perspectives on Latin American and Lusophone Cultures* and *The Novels of Fernando Del Paso.* He teaches Spanish at Oxford University in England.

CURRIE K. THOMPSON has published many articles on Latin American literature and film. He teaches Spanish at Gettysburg University.

CYNTHIA GIRGEN has taught at the University of Houston and has written on Chaucer, and Rick Bass among others.

MAARTEN VAN DELDEN is Associate Professor of Spanish at Rice University. He is the author of many articles on Latin American literature, and the book *Carlos Fuentes, Mexico, and Modernity.*

MARCO POLO HERNÁNDEZ CUEVAS is the author of *African Mexicans and the Discourse on Modern Nation* with the writer Richard Jackson.

Bibliography

Aizenberg, Edna. "The Untruths of the Nation. *Petals of Blood* and Fuentes' *The Death of Artemio Cruz*." *Research in African Literatures* 21, no. 4 (Winter 1990): 85–104.

Alonso, Carlos. "The Mourning After: García Márquez, Fuentes and the Meaning of Postmodernity." *MLN* 109 (March 1994): 252–67.

Baxandall, Lee. "An Interview with Carlos Fuentes." *Studies on the Left* 3, no 1 (1962): 48–56.

Boldy, Steven. "Carlos Fuentes." In *On Modern Latin American Fiction*, ed. John King. New York: Farrar, Straus & Giroux, 1989. 155–72.

———. "Fathers and Sons in Fuentes' *La muerte de Artemio Cruz*." *Bulletin of Hispanic Studies* 61 (1984): 31–40.

Brody, Robert and Charles Rossman, eds. *Carlos Fuentes: A Critical View*. Austin: University of Texas Press, 1982.

Castillo, Debra. "Travails with Time: An Interview with Carlos Fuentes." *The Review of Contemporary Fiction*, no. 2 (Summer 1988): 153–67.

Cuevas, Marco Polo Hernández. "Modern National Discourse and *La muerte de Artemio Cruz*: the Illusory "Death" of African Mexican Lineage." *Afro-Hispanic Review*, 23, no. 1 (Spring 2004): 10–16.

Durán, Glorian. *The Archetypes of Carlos Fuentes*. Hamden, Conn.: Archon Books, 1980.

Doezma, Herman P. "An Interview with Carlos Fuentes." *Modern Fiction Studies* 18, no. 4 (Winter 1972–73): 491–503.

Faris, Wendy B. *Carlos Fuentes*. New York: Frederick Ungar Publishing, 1983.

———. "Desire and Power, Love and Revolution: Carlos Fuentes and Milan Kundera." *The Review of Contemporary Fiction* 8, no. 2 (Summer 1988): 273–84.

Fiddian, Robin. "Carlos Fuentes: *The Death of Artemio Cruz*." In *Landmarks in Modern Latin American Fiction*, ed, Philip Swanson. London: Routledge, 1990. 96–117.

Guzmán, Daniel. *Carlos Fuentes*. New York: Twayne, 1972.

Gyurko, Lanin A. "Structure and Theme in Fuentes' *La Muerte de Artemio Cruz*." *Symposium* 34, no 1 (Spring 1980): 29–41.

"*La muerte de Artemio Cruz* and *Citizen Kane*: A Comparative Analysis" in *Carlos Fuentes: A Critical View*, ed. Robert Brody and Charles Rossman. Austin: University of Texas Press, 1982.

Hall, Linda B. "The Cipactli Monster: Woman as Destroyer in Carlos Fuentes." *Southwest Review* 60 (1975): 246–55.

Helmuth, Charlene. *The Postmodern Fuentes*. Lewisburg: Bucknell University Press, 1997.

Ibsen, Kristine. *Author, Text and Reader in the Novels of Carlos Fuentes*. New York: Peter Lang, 1993.

Kadir, Djelala. "Fuentes and the Profane Sublime." In *Other Writing: Postcolonial Essays in Latin America's Writing Culture*. West Lafayette, IN: Purdue University Press, 1993. 73–110.

Levitt, Morton P. "Joyce and Fuentes: Not Influence but Aura." *Comparative Literature Studies* 19 (1982): 254–71.

McShane, Frank. "A Talk with Carlos Fuentes." *New York Times Book Review*, 7 (Nov 1976), 50.

Moody, Michael. "Existentialism, Mexico and Artemio Cruz." *Romance Notes* 19 (1968): 19–32.

Shaw, Donald. "Narrative Arrangement in *La muerte de Artemio Cruz*." In *Contemporary Latin American Fiction*, ed. Salvador Bacarisse. Edinburgh: Scottish Academic Press, 1980. 34–47.

Sommers, Joseph. "The Field of Choice: Carlos Fuentes." *After the Storm: Landmarks in the Modern Mexican Novel*. Albuquerque: University of New Mexico Press, 1968. 133–64.

Tittler, Jonathan. "*The Death of Artemio Cruz*: Anatomy of a Self." In *Narrative Irony in the Contemporary Spanish-American Novel*. Ithaca, NY: Cornell University Press, 1984. 31–57.

Thompson, Currie. "The House and the Garden: The Architecture of

Knowledge and *La muerte de Artemio Cruz.*" *Hispania* 77, no 2 (May 1994): 197–206.

van Delden, Maarten. *Carlos Fuentes, Mexico, and Modernity.* Vanderbilt: Vanderbilt University Press, 1998.

Walter, Richard. "Literature and History in Contemporary Latin America." *Latin American Literary Review* 15, no. 29 (January–June, 1987): 173–182.

Williams, Raymond Leslie. *The Writings of Carlos Fuentes.* Austin: University of Texas Press, 1996.

Acknowledgments

"Structure and Theme in Fuentes' *La Muerte de Artemio Cruz*" by Lanin A. Gyurko. From *Symposium* 34, no 1 (Spring 1980): 29–41. © 1980 by the Helen Dwight Reid Educational Foundation. Reprinted by permission.

"*La muerte de Artemio Cruz* and *Citizen Cane*: A Comparative Analysis" by Lanin A. Gyurko. *Carlos Fuentes: A Critical View*. © 1982 by the University of Texas Press. Reprinted by permission.

"Fragmenting Forces in the Revolution and the Self: *The Death of Artemio Cruz*" by Wendy B. Faris. *Carlos Fuentes*. © 1983 by Frederick Ungar Publishing Co. Reprinted by permission.

"Fathers and Sons in Fuentes' *La muerte de Artemio Cruz*" by Steven Boldy. From *Bulletin of Hispanic Studies* 61 (1984): 31–40. © 1984 by Liverpool University Press. Reprinted by permission.

"Memory and Time in *The Death of Artemio Cruz*" by Britt-Marie Schiller. From *Latin American Literary Review* 15, no. 29 (January–June 1987): 93–103. © 1987 by *Latin American Literary Review*. Reprinted by permission.

"Literature and History in Contemporary Latin America" by Richard Walter. From *Latin American Literary Review* 15, no. 29 (January–June, 1987): 173–182. © 1987 by *Latin American Literary Review*. Reprinted by permission.

"Point of View in *The Death of Artemio Cruz*: Singularity or Multiplicity?" by Santiago Tejerina-Canal. From *The Review of Contemporary Fiction* 8, no. 2 (Summer 1988): 199–210. © 1988 by *The Review of Contemporary Fiction*. Reprinted by permission.

"Carlos Fuentes: La Muerte de Artemio Cruz" by Robin Fiddian. *Landmarks in Modern Latin American Fiction.* © 1990 by Routledge. Reprinted by permission.

"The House and the Garden: The Architecture of Knowledge and *La muerte de Artemio Cruz*" by Currie Thompson. From *Hispania* 77, no 2 (May 1994): 197–206. ©1994 by American Association of Teachers of Spanish and Portuguese. Reprinted by permission.

"The Magic Word in Carlos Fuentes' *The Death of Artemio Cruz*" by Cynthia Girgen. From *Hispanic Journal* 16, no. 1 (Spring 1995): 123–134. © 1995 by Indiana University of Pennsylvania. Reprinted by permission.

"Modes of Redemption" by Maarten van Delden. *Carlos Fuentes, Mexico, and Modernity.* © 1998 by Vanderbilt University Press. Reprinted by permission.

"Modern National Discourse and *La muerte de Artemio Cruz*: The Illusory "Death" of African Mexican Lineage" by Marco Polo Hernández Cuevas. From *Afro-Hispanic Review*, 23, no. 1 (Spring 2004): 10 –16. © 2004 by Afro-Hispanic Review. Reprinted by permission.

Every effort has been made to contact the owners of copyrighted material and secure copyright permission. Articles appearing in this volume generally appear much as they did in their original publication with few or no editorial changes. Those interested in locating the original source will find bibliographic information in the bibliography and acknowledgments sections of this volume.

Index

Characters in literary works are indexed by first name (if any), followed by the name of the work in parentheses